FINDING & FIXING
THE OLDER HOME

FINDING & FIXING
THE OLDER HOME

Joseph F. Schram

Structures Publishing Company
Farmington, Michigan   1976

Manufactured in the United States of America

Edited by Shirley M. Horowitz

Cover design by C. H. Ashby

Book design by Patrick Mullaly

Current Printing (last digit)
10 9 8 7 6 5 4 3 2 1

Structures Publishing Co.
Box 423, Farmington, Mich. 48024

Schram, Joseph F
    Finding & fixing the older home
    Included index.
1. House buying. 2. Dwellings — Remodeling.

I. Title.

TH4817.5.S37
ISBN 0-912336-31-5   643   76-25112
ISBN 0-912336-32-3 pbk.

TABLE OF CONTENTS

SECTION ONE: FINDING

OLDER HOME VALUES

As you drive through a quiet, mature residential neighborhood, or walk down tree-lined streets of older homes, many of the values of the existing home become apparent:

— There is a variety of style apart from the customary ranch home which has overwhelmed the new construction market for the past 15 to 20 years.

— The distinctive architectural lines have weathered to a mellow patina. Tudor design may blend with the Early American or Provincial next to it. Or the street may be all of one style like the handsome Victorians in San Francisco, the brownstones of Washington, D.C., or the Federalists in rural Indiana.

— Construction of these homes was accomplished, for the most part, with top-quality materials by craftsmen in no real hurry to complete the job and who gave their best efforts to it.

— Room sizes are usually very generous. Two or three-story design is prevalent. And most of the homes include basements with still more working and living space.

Once inside most older homes you are immediately attracted by the highly polished and attractive decorative moldings and trim often found in every room. Built-in closets, shelves, or cabinets may have leaded-glass doors for showcasing china or other treasured possessions.

The fireplace is frequently the center of attraction, flanked by convenient bookshelves or cases. And the mantel brings additional attractive woodwork into play.

If you lift up the rug or remove the wall-to-wall carpeting you will probably find a hardwood surface that could look like new with a few hours of polishing. Then again, it may require a sanding job and refinishing — with a highly appealing end result.

Most older homes come with dining rooms, although many homes built in the late 50's and 60's lack this nicety. And the nearby kitchen is probably considerably larger than those found in newer homes. It may require some remodeling to suit your specific needs, but the space is there, with a well laid-out, functional arrangement. Perhaps there is even space enough for a new lavatory or powder room.

The basements and attics common to older homes can provide a considerable amount of bonus living space for your family. The attic may be nothing but a shell depository for family antiques and long-forgotten furniture, but with a "completion" project you may be able to secure another bedroom, a playroom, office-hide-away, etc. The basement, too, may be unfinished even to the point of requiring a bit of excavating (by hand, of course) but its future use is nearly unlimited.

Existing homes offer buyers an established neighborhood, mature trees, developed community services and many more attributes. This two-story home has attached garage, fireplaces in the living room and master bedroom and a well maintained exterior.

Brick and wood siding were combined in the original construction of these three and four-bedroom split-level homes, which also have full basements and are air conditioned. (Photo: Chrysler Corp.).

Decorative touches play a big role in the appearance of a house. Here shutters in contrasting color, and wall-hung flower boxes, help to balance the window areas. The double-door entry is flanked by carriage lamps (Photo: U.S. Plywood Corp.).

A well-maintained older home can provide all the conveniences of a newer home. This asphalt-shingled house features a bow window in the living room, enclosed breezeway between attached garage and second-floor bedrooms (Photo: Bird & Son).

Colonial styling with two-story columns adds to the appearance of this home surfaced with vinyl siding. Note the two-car garage located under the bedroom area. Wrought iron rails are used for both sections of steps (Photo: Bird & Son).

In buying the older house you should keep in mind its resale potential, and always look upon the house in terms of not what the house is today, but what it can be tomorrow through improvement and remodeling.

In an old neighborhood, it may make sense to purchase a house in poor condition if the house's skeleton is sound and the house is surrounded by homes in good condition. Occasionally an older home can be acquired where no sprucing up is required. But this is the exception, and you should plan on basic, necessary improvements as well as the major cosmetic changes you feel desirable.

Most older homes offer the added benefits of streets, sidewalks, sewers and street lighting "in and paid for." Be sure to check this point, as the home may still be in a period of "assessment" added annually to your local real estate taxes.

If you really love a house, hold off buying it until you check that it's in a location you'll enjoy, with good quality schools, a convenient and well-equipped shopping center, and access to recreational, medical and library facilities.

If this house has most of the above things, a drawback or two may be insignificant. For example, a 20 to 30 minute drive to work will be outweighed by the hours of enjoyment the house gives.

You know how much room you need now, but are you also seeking the room you will need in the future when your children are older and require more space and privacy? You may be planning to stay in this home for only four or five years, or then again, you may be planning to stay until the family is grown, or until you wish to retire to a more modest home or apartment.

The specific interests of a family help greatly to determine the type and size home required. A camera buff may need darkroom space; a green-thumber will want ample gardening area; a motor-car enthusiast will desire a large garage with ample area for puttering; teen-agers will almost require a family room, recreation room or area away from the more quiet living area.

No single floor plan is best for all homes. Later chapters of this book will deal with "good basics," but it will be up to you in the end to select the plan that best meets the needs and tastes of your family.

A well-designed home today usually has separate entrances for family and guest traffic. Family traffic should enter the kitchen or family activity area and be able to move from there to the bedrooms without having to pass through living areas.

A well-planned living room avoids cross-traffic from other rooms and preferably is dead-end space with all traffic into the space being handled at one end. During social activities, people congregate in fairly small groups so the ideal "conversation circle" is approximately 10 feet in diameter.

YOUR FINANCIAL SITUATION

The advantages of buying the older house are many — possible assumption of the seller's mortgage; lower price than for comparable space in a new home; many existing features that you would otherwise have to buy and add to a new home (landscaping, hardware, blinds, etc.) and an established neighborhood (which hopefully you have checked out already).

In today's economy, the right time to buy a house is today. The reason for this is simply that everything is going up in price, and the house you don't buy now will cost more next year. The housing crunch is on nationally, and those wage earners who can afford to buy should do so now.

Typical of the local situations which bring one to this conclusion is the Santa Clara County area of California, which includes San Jose. Since 1972 there has been an 8.9 percent increase in the county population and a 45 percent decrease in available housing, coupled with a 60 percent decrease in the number of building permits issued as of the time this book is written. And while 9.2 percent of the 1972 housing was in the above - $30,000 class, today more than 67 percent of the homes are in the $40,000 and above class. Almost 15 percent are in the $60,000 and over range.

To determine your financial limits in buying a home, take your annual gross income, before taxes, and multiply first by 2 and then by 2½. The answers form the price range of homes you can afford. But keep in mind that while this calculation is useful, it doesn't take into account such variables as family size, assets, or expenditures. Thus, you'll have to plug in monthly expenses versus income. The 2 to 2½ formula is your highest figure, and conservatism is usually a wise move if you have a growing family.

Using this calculation, if you have an annual income of $15,000, you could afford a house in the $30,000 to $37,500 bracket, or less. With a 20 percent downpayment and approximately $2000 worth of closing costs and prepaid items, you'll need about $9500 downpayment to swing the deal. If your loan is for $30,000 over a period of 25 years at, say 9 percent interest, your monthly payment will be $252 plus taxes and insurance.

It's well to prepare a monthly expense worksheet listing such items as food, car payment, car insurance, clothing, entertainment, gasoline or transportation, telephone, life insurance, health insurance and other expenses. With this total you will be able to compare it with net monthly income and more closely determine the amount you have available for housing payments.

In mortgage lending there is probably nothing that requires more analysis of people and their living habits than credit approval for a house purchase. One family may be willing to spend more for housing, use a cheaper car, and give up other things which another family with the same income would insist on having. Probably one of the best guides to a family's ability to carry the mortgage debt is what it is accustomed to spending for housing. One family pattern may show that 20 percent of the income is the maximum which the family can reasonably spend for housing. While another family might be approved with a housing expense of 35 percent of its income.

Generally speaking, the Department of Housing and Urban Development (HUD) which governs FHA-approved home financing, considers income adequate if the total housing expense does not exceed 35 percent of net effective income, and the combined total of housing expense and other recurring charges does not exceed 50 percent of net effective income. This is true unless the family has already demonstrated an inability to manage its affairs adequately when housing expense and/or total obligations were at or below those figures.

HUD-FHA and conventional financing add on the wife's salaried income when there is confirmation of employment with a good possibility for its continuation. This confirmation may be based on the length of employment, or on special training or skills in a particular position.

Established patterns of employment in the unskilled labor market may also show a stable pattern and are recognized by HUD-FHA as essential for wives in low-income groups. The allowable income of the wife is treated the same as that of the husband.

Some housing experts recommend that you buy at the absolute maximum price you can afford having taken into account your particular family expenses, because it's a pretty sure bet that five years from now your mortgage will be less of a strain than it is now. Working people's incomes usually increase and, historically, the value of homes has also increased (and so, unfortunately, do property taxes).

If the house you are buying will require major improvements or if you are planning major additions, it may be well to arrange for the lowest possible down payment so you will have cash to put into these improvements. Or you may wish to check into the possibility of an "open-end" mortgage which will make funds available for such improvements, if this type of financing is legal in your state. Your mortgage lender can be helpful in supplying answers to specific questions.

CONDUCTING A HOUSE HUNT

NEWSPAPER ADS

The local "House For Sale" advertisement in the daily or weekly newspaper more often than not is the first "look" a homebuyer gets of his future residence. This is especially so in many areas where local ordinances prevent the use of "For Sale" signs on the property. Newspaper real estate ads in most areas are grouped by city location to help you pinpoint what's being offered in a specific neighborhood that may be of interest to you. These ads will appear as either part of a real estate broker's listing, or as a private individual advertisement placed by the homeowner.

Depending upon the advertising space rate, you may or may not find a photograph of the house you are seeking via the real estate advertising section. In most instances, there will be no photograph and the ad writer (often an advertising sales person) will do his or her best to whet your appetite by pointing out the basics and special charms of the home being sold.

Price, of course, is a major factor and it is here that the local classified real estate ads can save some wear and tear on your car and nerves. You generally can determine the going rate for homes in a given area by studying the real estate ads and plotting them on a city map available from your service station or local Chamber of Commerce. There is no sense in aggravating yourself by looking at $100,000 homes if your cost potential is in the $40,000 range.

Because the cost of the real estate ad is "by the inch" of space used in the paper, a shorthand system is often employed to keep cost at a minimum. It's well to understand this shorthand, and chances are you'll pick it up quickly and fast become an expert! Here are a few of the usual abbreviations you can expect to encounter in a budget-conscious advertising of real estate:

BR	Bedroom
Ba	Bath
Lr	Living room
2-S	Two-story
A.E.K.	All-electric kitchen
FR	Family room
WBFP	Wood-burning fireplace
Sep DR	Separate dining room
w/w cpt	Wall-to-wall carpeting
drps	Drapes
2/D gar	Two-door garage
W/D incl	Washer-dryer included
Lg cor lot	Large corner lot
Nr S&S	Near schools and shopping

A/C	Air conditioned
W BB ct	With basketball court

Shopping the real estate ads you are certain to encounter some of the most descriptive and attractive words found in the dictionary. "Sumptuous hillside view ... gorgeous ... delightful ... amazing" etc. And it's up to you to judge their validity first-hand while inspecting the home.

With your "houses to see" circled and related to a local map, it's time to begin your physical house-hunting. The first step, usually, is to drop the kids at the neighborhood movie or hire a sitter so that you can concentrate your efforts on the job at hand and not be concerned about little fingers getting into places they shouldn't. Shopping the older home market will mean viewing furnished homes, whereas a new home often is displayed without furnishings or with bolted-down items.

Carry as part of your home-hunting package: notebook, pencil, checklist of basics you are seeking in a new home (number of bedrooms, baths, garage, etc), tape measure, flashlight and compass. You may also wish to use an "instant" camera to photograph "prime" houses you want to reconsider. Be sure to put the address on the reverse side of the photos taken so you won't confuse locations.

When you are looking for a house to purchase, don't keep it a secret from your friends and relatives. Many choice houses never see a newspaper advertisement or a broker listing — they are grabbed up the minute the owner wishes to sell, thanks to the interest of a friend of a friend.

By telling your friends the type, size, and style and location of the home you are seeking, you often can get help in finding the specific house you want. Of course, this also can be done adequately by a local real estate agent or broker who has access to literally hundreds of home listings via his own contacts, and the now familiar multiple listing services used in most areas.

In major cities, it may pay to make a telephone call or personal visit to the personnel division of a major corporation — one that moves its people from city to city and division to division. Often such firms will buy homes from their employees and then sell them to facilitate the personnel move.

Your local Chamber of Commerce and Building Department are two more places worthy of a telephone call. They may know of specific areas where homes will be coming on the market.

USING A REAL ESTATE BROKER

Figures compiled by the National Association of Realtors show that 95 percent of all residential homeowners sell their property with the help of a real estate firm. This being so, there is an excellent chance that you will encounter a licensed real estate broker when buying an older home, and furthermore, he will primarily be representing the seller.

Acting as the agent for the seller, the real estate broker screens prospective buyers, conducts house inspections with potential buyers, helps secure financing and handles a great deal of the necessary paperwork in the transaction.

Real estate brokers devote considerable time and effort to learning their trade before taking an extensive test which they must pass in order to be licensed by the state in which they plan to work. These salesmen then generally work for a firm which in turn may be required to obtain a local city and/or county license.

Over 500,000 real estate brokers in the United States belong to the National Association of Realtors and are therefore entitled to use the term "Realtor" in their public dealings. These Realtors belong to local and state chapters and form the basis for the multiple-listing services which greatly expand home sale transactions.

In dealing with a Realtor, you can have the benefit of not only his training, experience and knowledge, but also his access to literally hundreds or thousands of "for sale" listings which can be narrowed down to the specific area, size and house and price range you are seeking. Generally speaking, this will cost you nothing, as the seller pays the 5 percent to 6 percent real-estate commission.

Some cities across the country are now equipped to handle multiple listings via computer, which can save you valuable house hunting time. Likewise, franchise real estate firms are coming into vogue as persons moving from distant areas can send ahead their requirements and be met at the airport by a real estate broker who is ready to show them potential new residences.

Local real estate brokers in most instances are fully acquainted with their area of operation in regards to community facilities, zoning, restrictions, schools, transportation and other factors you will make a part of your home-buying decision.

Real estate brokers can also be helpful in arranging financing with firms they deal with on a regular basis, and help to speed the completion of necessary forms that will protect your purchase. In the absence of a real estate broker, it is important that you secure the services of an attorney so that your new investment is properly transacted and recorded.

Platform frame construction.

Balloon frame construction.

Drawings by National Forest Products Assn.

UNDERSTANDING HOUSE CONSTRUCTION

Fully ninety percent of the homes in this country are of wood frame construction, regardless of age. Many of them are covered with wood siding, brick veneer or stucco.

A well-built woodframe house is one of the most durable of structures. Some of the oldest existing buildings in the United States are woodframe, as well as most of the newer homes. In both instances, woodframed housing usually costs less than other framing types, provides better insulation, and provides more house for the money.

Basically, there are two types of wood framing used for house construction: platform frame and balloon frame.

The platform frame is the easier of the two to erect because it provides a flat surface, at each floor level, on which to work. The subfloor extends to the outside edges of the building and provides the platform upon which exterior walls and interior partitions are erected. This construction is generally used for one-story houses. It is also used alone or in combination with balloon construction for two-story structures.

Platform construction has been in favor in recent years due to its easy adaptability to various methods of prefabrication. With this system, it is common practice to assemble wall framing on the floor and then tilt the entire unit into place. Prefabricated mechanical cores (containing plumbing walls for kitchen and bath) also are used.

In balloon frame construction both studs and first floor joists rest on the anchored sill (see drawing). The second-floor joists bear on a 1x4-inch ribbon strip which has been let into the inside edges of the studs. Balloon type framing is preferred for two-story buildings where exterior covering is of brick or stone veneer or stucco, as there is less likelihood of movement between the wood framing and the masonry veneer.

Where exterior walls are of solid masonry, it is also desirable to use balloon framing for interior bearing partitions. It eliminates variations in settlement which may occur between exterior walls and interior supports.

Most existing homes were put together with nails using one- and two-inch framing lumber. Building codes and accepted construction practices have designated the size nail to be used for various fastenings and the most practical and beneficial way of driving the nail. For example, you'll find the basic wall studs attached to the sill are toe-nailed; that is, the nail is driven at an approximate 30 degree angle to the grain.

Still another popular version of wood framing is plank-and-beam construction used for floors and roofs in many homes. Whereas conventional platform and balloon framing methods utilize joists, (rafters and studs spaced 12 to 24 inches on center), the plank-and-beam method requires fewer and larger sized pieces, spaced farther apart.

While the most successful plank-and-beam houses are those which are designed so from the beginning, the system nevertheless can be easily used for remodeling and add-ons.

Plank subfloors or roofs are usually of 2-inch nominal thickness, supported on beams spaced up to 8 feet apart. The ends of the beams are supported on posts or piers. Wall spaces between posts are provided with supplementary framing to the extent required for attachment of exterior and interior finish. This supplementary framing and its covering also serve to provide lateral bracing for the building.

FOUNDATIONS

Footings of plain concrete or reinforced concrete support the house framing system. Local building codes determine the size of the footing, which should extend to a depth below the frost line and be of a depth equal to the thickness of the foundation wall it supports. The projection of the footing should be equal to one-half the thickness of the foundation wall.

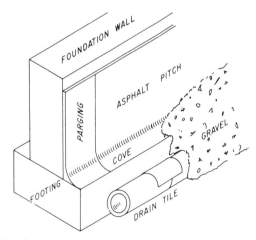

Continuous foundation wall and footing. Drawing: National Forest Products Assn.

The foundation wall itself may be of poured concrete or of masonry units. If masonry units were used, check to see that a ½-inch coat of portland cement mortar was applied to the exterior wall and then covered with two coats of asphalt. Drain tiles should be located around the exterior of the footings and connected to a positive outfall to assure a dry basement.

In California, and elsewhere, many homes have no basement and are supported on foundations consisting of free-standing piers, piers with curtain walls between them, or piers supporting grade beams. Size is related to the weight to be carried and spacing depends upon arrangement of the floor framing and location of load-bearing walls and partitions. Usually, the distance is 8 to 12 feet apart.

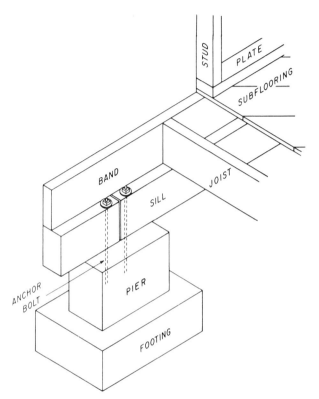

Pier foundation at exterior wall.

Floor Framing

Typical floor framing consists of sills, girders, joists and subflooring, with all members tied together in such a way as to support the loads expected on the floor and to give lateral support to the exterior walls.

Bolts embedded in concrete or masonry are used to secure sills on foundation walls or piers. Beams and girders usually consist of solid timbers or built-up members which bear a minimum of 4 inches on supports. Span tables provide maximum allowable spans for joists fabricated from various lumber species and grades.

Subflooring

Wood subflooring usually consists of square-edged or tongue-and-grooved boards or plywood panels. Joints in subflooring are made over the joists unless end-matched boards are used. The subfloor is used as the base of finished wood flooring, carpeting, or resilient flooring.

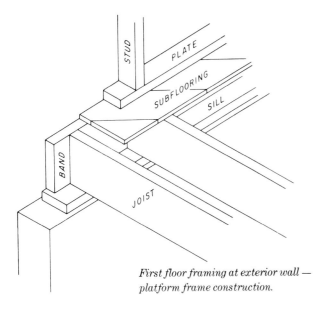

*First floor framing at exterior wall —
platform frame construction.*

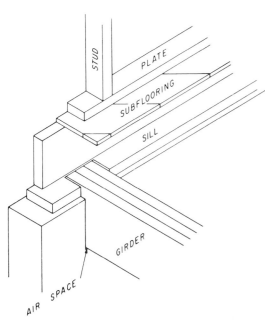

*First floor framing at girder and exterior wall
using platform frame construction.*

Concrete Slabs

Homes built on concrete slabs are widely used in some parts of the United States. In colder climates insulation along the edge of the slab, to prevent the movement of heat into the cold ground, is vital. If the home you are considering does not have this insulation, don't let that keep you from purchasing it. Insulation can be added later, as shown in the "Fixing" section of this book.

Inspect the concrete floor for evidence of excessive settlement or heaving. The presence of either may pose serious problems, unless the damage indicated is the full extent of it and no further deterioration is likely to occur. If the slab

incorporates hot-water radiant heating, look for leaks. Be sure the piping is copper, otherwise you may have expensive problems in the future.

Some concrete slab homes have hot-air heat. Hot air is pumped through pipes to the registers, usually around the perimeter of the home. With this type of home, remove the register to check for any evidence of moisture in the pipes. If moisture is present, you may have grounds to reject the home.

One essential for all homes on concrete slabs, in all parts of the country, is a vapor barrier. If none has been installed there is nothing that can be done. Inspect wherever there is a break in the slab to find evidence of this important material. It is usually two mil polyethylene film. If necessary, drill a hole through the slab to satisfy yourself of its presence (if the owner will let you!). Under the vapor barrier, there should be a granular substance, such as gravel, to insure proper drainage.

Exterior Wall Framing

Framing for the exterior wall should provide a strong and stiff support for lateral loads from the floors and roof as well as resist the lateral loads resulting from winds and, in some areas, earthquakes. Studs generally are at least nominal 2x4's in one and two-story buildings, with 2x6's used for the lower floor in three-story homes.

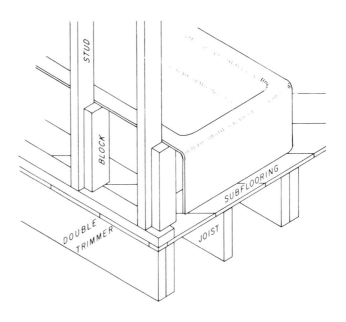

Support of bathtub against wall framing.

Drawings by National Forest Products Assn.

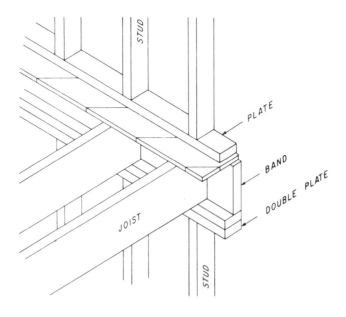

Second floor framing at exterior wall using platform frame construction.

Depending upon the age of the home you are buying, you'll find the studs located on 16 or 24-inch centers. The wider spacing has been much used in one-story homes built in recent years. In multi-story homes, the 16-inch measurement is required.

Wall Sheathing

Sheathing is used to brace exterior walls with additional stiffness, often provided by a 1x4-inch member let into the outside face of the studs at a 45 degree angle, nailed to top and bottom plates and studs. Wood sheathing boards applied diagonally eliminate the need for the let-in braces. Sheathing is usually wood, plywood or fiberboard. Wood sheathing is often covered with asphalt-saturated felt or other impregnated paper having water-repellent qualities.

Interior Partitions

Two types of interior partitions are found in house construction — bearing partitions which support floors, ceiling or roofs, and non-bearing partitions which carry only the weight of the materials in the partition.

Bearing partitions are constructed with nominal 2x4's set with the wide dimension perpendicular to the partition and capped with two pieces of nominal 2-inch lumber, or by continuous headers which are lapped or tied into exterior walls at points of intersections. Studs supporting floors are spaced 16 inches on center; studs supporting ceilings and roofs may be set 24 inches on center.

Non-bearing partitions usually are nominal 2x3's or 2x4's with wide faces set perpendicular or parallel to the partition. Spacing may be 16 or 24 inches.

Exterior Siding

Among the many types of siding used to cover wall framing are wood, wood shingles, asbestos, metal, vinyl and masonry veneer. All nailable types should always be installed with corrosion-resistant nails, usually galvanized or aluminum.

More information on specific types of siding and residing materials are given later in a separate chapter.

Roof Framing

The two basic types of roof framing used in residential construction are the on-site piece-by-piece type and prefabricated lightweight trusses made in special table jigs for fast placement at the job-site. Both styles should be strong and able to withstand anticipated snow and wind loads.

Roof framing methods vary according to the types of materials to be used as finish roofing, as well as to meet specific codes and requirements for various pitches. Here again, this subject is dealt with in more detail in an upcoming chapter, as are finish materials such as flooring, windows, doors, etc.

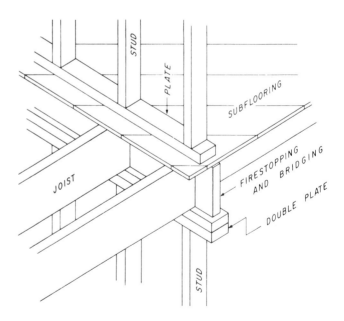

Second floor framing over bearing partition, using platform frame construction.

Drawings by National Forest Products Assn.

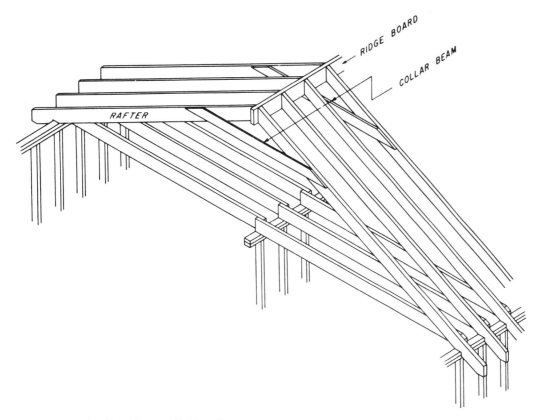

RIDGE BOARD

COLLAR BEAM

RAFTER

Roof framing with ceiling joists parallel to rafters.

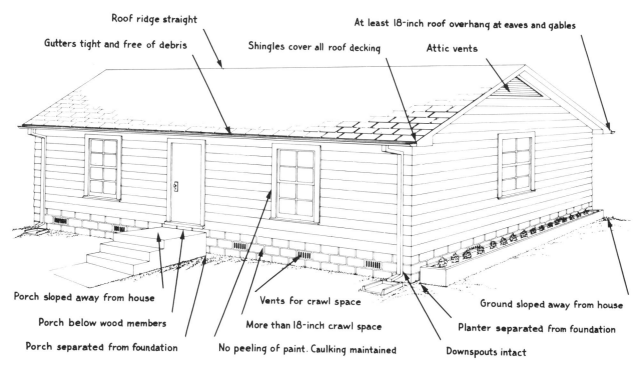

Roof ridge straight

Gutters tight and free of debris

Shingles cover all roof decking

At least 18-inch roof overhang at eaves and gables

Attic vents

Porch sloped away from house

Porch below wood members

Porch separated from foundation

Vents for crawl space

More than 18-inch crawl space

No peeling of paint. Caulking maintained

Ground sloped away from house

Planter separated from foundation

Downspouts intact

WHAT TO LOOK FOR WHEN INSPECTING A HOME

- *Is all the wood in the house above the level of the soil?*
- *Does water drain away from the house?*
- *Does the crawl space have adequate clearance and ventilation?*
- *Are there signs of dampness in the basement?*
- *Have earthfilled porches and other structures separated from the house?*
- *Is the roof overhang sufficient (18 to 30. inches)?*
- *Has caulking around doors, windows and joints been maintained?*
- *Are gutters and downspouts intact?*
- *Is attic ventilated?*
- *Is roof decking completely covered, especially at the roof edge?*
- *Does roof sag, indicating possible rafter decay?*
- *Is paint peeling or blistering?*
- *Are decorative and other items attached to the house likely to admit or trap moisture?*
- *Is plumbing, including drains, free of leaks?*

- *Do doors or windows stick? Are frames decayed?*
- *Is caulking around tubs, sinks and showers intact?*
- *Are floors level? Do areas feel spongy when walked on?*
- *Do ceilings have water damage?*
- *If the house is in a zone of high termite hazard, is there a structural pest control contract on it? Does the contract include a guarantee?*
- *Was the soil under the house treated with insecticide during construction? Afterward?*
- *Has the soil under additions been treated?*
- *Are any termite shelter tubes visible on foundations? On pipes?*
- *Does the crawl space contain stumps or wood debris?*
- *Are there small holes in unfinished wood in the crawl spaces or elsewhere with powder under them?*
- *Will an expert inspect the house for termites or other structural pests before the sale?*

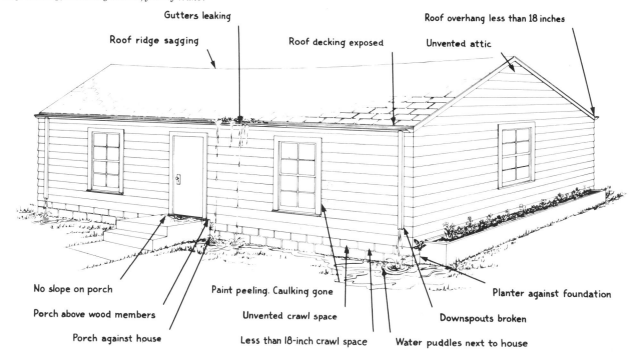

Gutters leaking

Roof ridge sagging

Roof decking exposed

Roof overhang less than 18 inches

Unvented attic

No slope on porch

Porch above wood members

Porch against house

Paint peeling. Caulking gone

Unvented crawl space

Less than 18-inch crawl space

Water puddles next to house

Planter against foundation

Downspouts broken

Drawings: U.S. Department of Agriculture-Forest Service.

APPRAISING HOUSE CONSTRUCTION

STRUCTURAL DAMAGE

In determining whether to purchase a house which otherwise meets your needs, careful attention should be paid to structural features. Many telltale signs can help you spot trouble areas which could result in expensive repairs.

If the home is so situated on the lot that drainage is graded away from the house, you probably won't encounter conditions which could cause wood decay. Likewise, if termite shields were used around foundation members during construction this should be no problem. In many areas, a termite inspection by a qualified termite company is required before title can be passed from one owner to another. Damage found at this time must be repaired by the owner before sale.

Signs of Interior Damage

Dry rot. In checking interior (basement and elsewhere) framing for dry rot, use an ice pick to push into the framing member to determine if it's structurally sound. If wood toughness has been attacked by decay, the wood may break across the grain and lift out with little resistance.

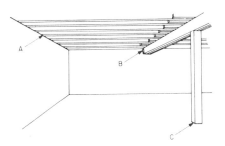

Check wood for decay at points of contact with concrete, such as: A, floor joists supported on concrete walls; B, framing supported in a pocket in a concrete wall; and C, wood post supported on a concrete floor.

Settling. Opening and closing of all the doors, and checking windows, will quickly indicate any unusual "settling" problems. Settling may distort windows and door frames, and loosen interior finishes. Sloped floors are another indication of this problem and may call for the installation of adjustable steel columns which, over a period of time, would be adjusted to remedy the situation. A little settling is normal; a lot indicates a new foundation would be required, and the house is probably not worth rehabilitation.

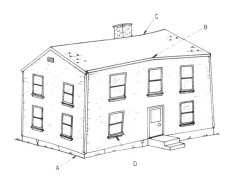

Uneven foundation settlement: A, may result in a house badly out of square. Evidences may include B, eaveline distortion; C, sagging roof ridge; or D, loose-fitting frames or even binding windows.

Basements. Basements should be checked for severe cracks, bulges, dampness, signs of flooding, or a musty smell. Can the area be aired out? Are there any traces of "sawdust" caused by termites or carpenter ants? Are the stairs of sound construction? The basement will be dry if the walls were properly built and waterproofed. Damp basements can be traced to many sources — clogged drain tile, clogged or broken downspouts, cracks in walls, lack of slope of the finished grade away from the house foundations, or a high water table. It is best to examine a basement a few hours after a heavy rain.

Floors. In a house with a basement, the floor is supported by wood or steel posts. Examine the posts. Wood posts should be on pedestals rather than embedded in the concrete floor. Examine the base of wood posts for decay, even if they are above the floor slab. Steel posts are usually supported on metal plates. The girders that rest on top of these posts should be checked for sag. Sag is a permanent deflection downward that can be noticed, especially near the middle of a structural member. It is seldom a problem with a steel beam, but may be with a wood beam. Some sag is common, especially in beams supporting a bathtub, a heavy appliance. Unless sag has obviously distorted parts of the house, it is rarely important.

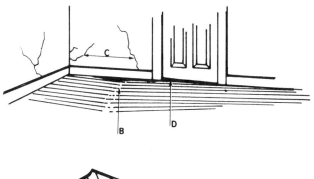

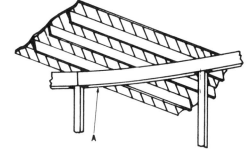

Badly sagging horizontal member A, has resulted in: B, uneven floor; C, cracked plaster; and D, poorly fitting door (defects accentuated to illustrate problems).

Floor sag is also readily apparent, and common. It is usually not a serious problem unless the foundation system has settled unevenly, causing excessive deflection in parts of the floor system.

Windows. Windows are another easily evaluated feature. They can present serious problems in old woodframe houses. If they are loose-fitting and not weatherstripped, they let in uncomfortable drafts and let heat out. Check the tightness of fit, and examine the sash and the sill for decay. Also check to see if the windows open and close without binding. When considering replacing windows, measure window dimensions. If the window is not a standard size or if a different size is desired, the opening will have to be reframed or a new sash must be made, both of which are expensive. Where openings are quite large double-weight glass may be required.

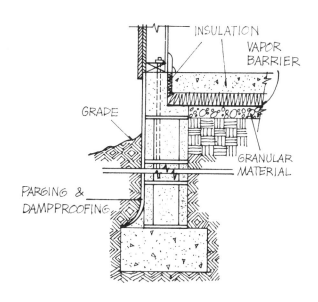

Slab on ground for habitable space above finish grade. Horizontal insulation extends minimum of 2 foot-0 inches around perimeter.

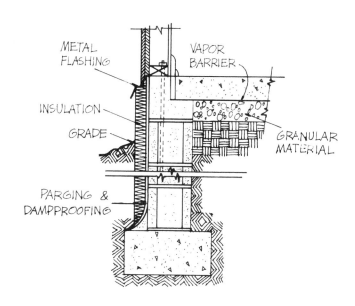

Adding insulation to a slab on ground after construction. Insulation may be fiberglass with a water proof covering, foamglass, or vermiculite (Zonolite) concrete.

Walls. Lack of insulation in walls and in the ceiling-roof structure will add to your heating and/or air conditioning costs and could be a serious problem in some parts of the country. Batt or blanket-type insulation is generally applied between studs and in ceiling joists or rafter spaces during construction. If it has not been put in, the problem often can be solved at a later date with blown-in insulation to fill the cavities.

Heating and Cooling. The heating and cooling systems should be of adequate size for the house. Ask when it was last serviced and check the monthly utility bills for the past year. This should prove helpful in establishing a monthly house expense budget as well as reveal any out-of-line costs.

Depending upon quality, water heaters last 7 to 15 years. Check the age of the unit, its capacity and test the faucet outlet used for periodic draining. Generally, a 40-gallon gas water heater will handle the average family's needs; an electric water heater should have a 50 gallon capacity or higher.

Plumbing. Be sure to turn on the sink faucets and flush the toilets to determine pressure. Check the gauge on the pressure tank; it should read at least 20 pounds, preferably 40 to 50. Hot water should become clear and hot in a few seconds, and remain hot.

Plumbing fixtures that are very old may be rust-stained and require replacement, or you may wish to put new ones in just for the sake of appearance. Rust or white or greenish crusting of pipe or joints usually indicates leaks in the water supply system.

Ventilation. The two major areas where good ventilation is required are between the ceiling and the roof, and the crawl space. General adequacy of ventilation can be observed just from the degree of dampness.

Moisture passes from the house into the attic; it condenses as the moist air cools down or contacts the cold roof members. For good circulation of air through all the attic area, both inlet and outlet vents must be located properly. These vents not only help keep the attic dry in winter, but keep hot air moving from the attic during summer and help to cool the house.

Observe the size and location of crawl space vents. For optimum cross ventilation and minimum dead air space, at least four vents should be located near building corners.

Wiring. Most homes used to be wired for 60-amp, 120-volt electric service. Today adequate wiring involves a minimum of 100 amps. If the house is large or if air conditioning is added, the service should be 200 amps. If the main distribution panel has room for the circuits, additional circuitry can be added to supply power where there is a shortage. Otherwise another distribution panel may be added. Examine electrical wiring wherever possible. Some wiring is usually exposed in the attic or basement. Wiring should also be checked at several wall receptacles or fixtures. If any armored cable or conduit is badly rusted, or if wiring or cable has deteriorated or is damaged or crumbly, the house wiring probably has overloaded or just fallen apart from age. It should be replaced.

Make sure there are convenience outlets where you need them. At least one electrical outlet on each wall of a room and two or more on long walls is desirable. The kitchen usually requires more outlets than elsewhere; if you plan to add an electric range, make sure you have a 3-phase line.

Signs of Exterior Damage

Termites. There are two types of termites: subterranean termites, which must have access to the ground or other water source, and nonsubterranean termites, which do not need direct access to water.

Subterranean termites often build earthen tubes on the surface of foundation walls as runways from the soil to the wood above. When the subterranean termites eat their way through the wood, they often follow the grain of wood, leaving galleries surrounded by an outer shell of sound wood.

Nonsubterranean termites live in wood without such connections with the ground. In their paths through the wood, they cut freely across the grain, rather than following the grain as the subterranean termites do. These nonsubterranean termites exist only in warm climates and particularly along warm coastal areas. Combating these insects usually involves the services of professional exterminators.

Roofing. Damaged roofing will have to be replaced quickly to prevent more extensive damage to the house. Flashing (sheet metal) at valleys, gutters, and around flues should be inspected to make certain no water is getting through the framing. Examine the roof for sagging of the ridge, the rafters, and the sheathing. This is easily done by visual observation. If the ridge line is not straight or the roof is wavy, some repair may be necessary. The ridge will sag due to improper support, inadequate ties at the plate level, or even from sagging of the rafters. Rafters will sag due to inadequate stiffness or because they were not well seasoned. If the sheathing sags, it may indicate the rafters are too far apart, strip sheathing is too thin, or plywood is too thin or has delaminated.

Watch for sag at A, ridge; B, rafters; or C, sheathing. Rafters are frequently tied, as at ceiling joist, D, to prevent from spreading outward. Flashing, E, is used at intersections of two roofs or between roof and vertical planes.

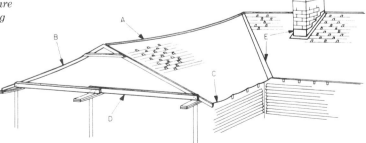

Walls and Siding. Moisture is the major cause of siding and wall damage. When you encounter siding that has mildew on the surface or that obviously is not holding paint properly, there is a good chance that moisture from within the house is going through the wall and is not being stopped by a vapor barrier. Or moisture can enter from the outside if there is no roof overhang, or if the flashing or roofing need repair. The problem of moisture condensation is eliminated in most homes through the use of screened louvers at the roof peak, through-the-roof-top vents, or horizontal sheetmetal ventilator screens along overhanging eaves.

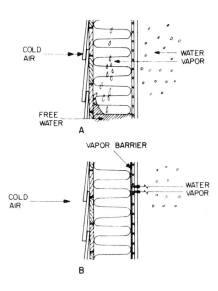

Vapor barriers reduce moisture problems in walls. A, without a vapor barrier water vapor from the room moves through the wall, is cooled, condenses, and wets the insulation. B, vapor barrier has greatly retarded moisture movement in to the walls.

Check to see that all wood siding, trim, and other exterior wood work are at least 6 inches above the ground and that the exposed masonry foundation has no evident cracks or breaks that have not been repaired. If the cracks and crumbling of mortar are confined to a small area, repair is possible.

Look for space between horizontal siding boards by standing very close and sighting along the wall. Some cracks can be caulked, but a general gapping or looseness may indicate new siding is required. If the boards are not badly warped, renailing may solve the problem. Check siding for decay where two boards are butted end to end, at corners, and around windows and door frames.

Good shingle siding appears as a perfect mosaic, whereas worn shinges have a ragged appearance and close examination will show individual shingles to be broken, warped, and upturned. New siding will be required if shingles are badly weathered or worn.

Cracking paint on window frames and other surfaces of the home often is a reliable clue to water leakage, just as a pronounced stain found beneath a faucet indicates it cannot be shut off properly.

Sewage System. Check whether the house is served by a sewer system or septic tank. If the latter is used, is it large enough, when was it last inspected, and by whom? The average 3-bedroom house will require a 900-gallon tank; a 4-bedroom house requires 1125 -gallon capacity. Add another 270 gallons for each additional bedroom.

NEIGHBORHOOD VALUE

How much a house is worth at any given time depends upon a number of factors including the condition of the house itself, its location, and the real estate market in general. The house should check out structurally, be in a neighborhood of comparably priced housing (or higher priced) and have no "hidden" encroachments.

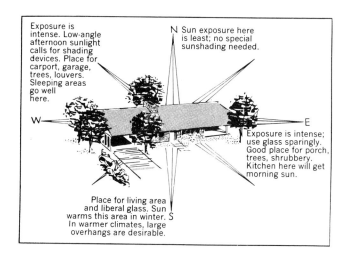

How your house is oriented toward the sun can have an important bearing on how much you enjoy it. As this drawing illustrates, good orientation combined with various methods of minimizing solar heat gain gives the most comfort whether or not the home is air conditioned. Ideally, large glass areas should have a southern exposure, with minimum glass on the east and west walls which face the nearly horizontal rays of the rising and setting sun. Where this isn't the case, screening devices such as awnings, fences, landscaping, blinds, and curtains, together with structural modifications such as trellises, porches, carports, etc. can keep instantaneous heat gain to a minimum.

Be sure to consider the location of railroads, airport, busy highways, brightly illuminated signs, open creeks and heavy industry with its accompanying noise, fumes and traffic problems. These will detract from house value.

Your neighborhood should be zoned for residential use and protected from future business use. The location of the house on the lot should conform with the building code and the house itself should conform with neighborhood restrictions.

Streets look better when the setback of homes on the lots is wide and varied. And a variety of home styles should be present on adjacent lots. Heights of homes should vary, but not markedly.

Landscaping can be extremely important. Creative landscaping can screen out a funny-looking window, make a short house look tall and emphasize any architectural assets of a home. It's possible to get a good-looking lawn in a year, but not much exciting happens to a tree in a year.

In appraising a house that greatly appeals to you it is wise to make a room by room list of features and deficien-

cies. Also a list of possible changes and improvements and their potential cost. Doing so BEFORE buying will enable you to better see what you are going to be living with in the months and years ahead. Such lists are also helpful in comparing one house with another in making your final selection.

Many homebuyers seek professional help in selecting a home. A building-inspection serviceman can provide you with a written report on the condition of the house you plan to buy. His services are generally listed in the telephone book Yellow Pages.

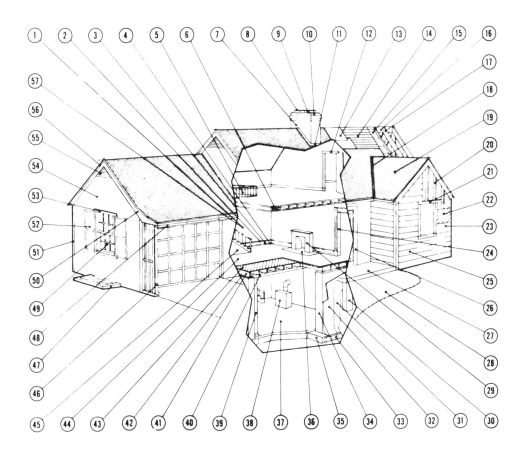

1. Interior Wall Finish	16. Ridge Board	30. Stoop	44. Finish Floor
2. Base Mold	17. Rafters	31. Fill, Gravel	45. Stairway
3. Base	18. Roof Valley	32. Waterproofing	46. Downspout
4. Base Shoe	19. Shingles	33. Tile, Drain	47. Sash Areaway, Cellar
5. Balusters	20. Studs	34. Foundation Wall	48. Gutter
6. Cross Bridging	21. Headers	35. Footing	49. Window
7. Chimney, Brick	22. Sheathing, Diagonal	36. Hearth	50. Frieze
8. Flue Linings	23. Building Paper	37. Cement Floor	51. Corner Board
9. Chimney Pots	24. Opening, Cased	38. Heating Plant	52. Shutters
10. Chimney Cap	25. Siding	39. Girder Post	53. Frame, Window
11. Flashing	26. Exterior Trim	40. Girder	54. Gable End
12. Doors and Trim, Interior	27. Stoop, Cement	41. Joists	55. Louvers
13. Roofing Felt	28. Grade	42. Mud Sill	56. Cornice
14. Roof Boards, Laid Close	29. Fireplace	43. Sub Floor, Diagonal	57. Plaster
15. Insulation			

In appraising an older house it's well to have a talking knowledge of basic terms most often encountered in discussing a house with a real estate broker, owner or lending institution. Here are some of the most often used terms (Drawing: Kaiser Industries).

FINANCING A HOME

MORTGAGES

Money to finance home loans in the United States historically has come primarily from banks, thrift institutions and insurance companies. In more recent years, the savings-and-loan (or building-and-loan) associations have played a dominant role.

Although banks, thrift institutions and life insurance companies are similar in some respects, banks and life insurance companies are more diversified in their operations than thrift institutions and have more investment opportunities available to them. Thrift institutions — particularly the savings-and-loan associations — tend to be specialized institutions. They are more limited in where they can invest their funds. In the case of the savings-and-loans, they are so specialized that they are largely confined to the mortgage market — the financing of homes, apartment houses, shopping centers and various other kinds of real estate developments.

A related type of business which fills a key role in the home finance industry in the United States is the mortgage company or the mortgage banker. He brings together those who have money and those who need money. Among other things, this helps satisfy the requirements of capital-surplus areas of the country for investment opportunities, and the needs of the capital-deficient areas for investment funds.

A mortgage banker will characteristically have business contacts with several different institutions in various places around the country which have funds to invest in mortgages.

All of these enterprises dealing in mortgage money have one thing in common — they are subject to periodic fluctuations in the cost of money. This in turn causes variations in the amount of money available for investment in mortgages. Although it is not always the case, as a general rule when interest rates are high and money is tight, the supply of money for mortgages dwindles. When interest rates are lower and more money is available, the supply of money for mortgages increases.

In the case of the diversified institutions — the banks and insurance companies — a period of higher interest rates generally means they can make more money by putting their funds into investments other than mortgages.

In the case of the specilized institutions such as the savings-and-loans, a period of higher interest rates generally means that savers put their money elsewhere as savings-and-loans are limited by regulation as to the rate of interest that can be paid on savings. This means the flow of money into savings decreases and this important source of funds for home loans is unable to meet the demand.

All firms extending mortgages to home buyers look upon the mortgage as an investment. Whoever puts up the money for the mortgage expects to get a return, a profit, on his investment. He expects to get back not only the original amount of money he put up, but also some interest.

As is well known, interest rates go up and down. Some interest rates change more than others. Mortgage interest rates generally change more slowly and they change relatively less than the interest rates on, for instance, the bonds offered for sale by a major utility corporation.

If you are in the same boat as the huge majority of American families buying homes, you undoubtedly will need financing beyond the downpayment you can make at purchase time. It's well to keep several factors in mind in seeking this financing: naturally, try to get the lowest interest rate possible, keep the length of life of the mortgage as short as comfortably possible, and make the largest possible downpayment without strapping yourself.

In each discussion with a possible loan source, ask for a written list of "closing" costs so that you can accurately determine what immediate cash you will need beyond the actual downpayment itself. These closing costs will be discussed in more detail, later in this chapter, but generally they include title insurance, transfer fees, loan set-up charges, pro-rated real estate taxes, etc.

It should be evident that the lower the amount you borrow and the lower the interest rate involved, the less your monthly payment will be. (See table on interest costs.) However, the more you can reasonably pay each month, the shorter period of time you will have to pay and the less total interest it will cost you.

Most mortgages are long-term, commonly 20 or 25 years. Some run as short as 15 years and others run as long as 30 years. If the borrower defaults on the loan, the lender may take over and sell the property to recover his investment.

The downpayment may range from 5 percent upward, and generally is 10 to 20 percent of the purchase price. Generally speaking, mutual savings banks and savings-and-loan associations permit lower downpayment than the more conservative commercial banks that tend to require two-thirds of the appraised value of the house as a downpayment.

Since 1930, the fully "amortized" mortgage has been the commonplace mortgage loan for most Americans. Before then, most mortgages were short term (five years) and required a "balloon" payment at the end of the term. Most persons who used such loans generally applied for still another loan at the end of the first term as they were unable to meet the balloon payment.

With the fully amortized loan, the total amount of principal and interest due is divided into equal periodic payments, usually monthly. This payment remains constant throughout the life of the mortgage. During the early years, more of the payment goes for interest and less for principal. Gradually this changes and the interest portion decreases with more of the payment going toward the principal or equity which you are building through ownership.

Another type of home mortgage loan sometimes available is that which carries a "variable or flexible" interest rate. A predetermined indicator is applied to this type of loan based on the lender's cost of money. When interest rates go up, so does the monthly payment. If interest rates decline, the mortgage payment decreases.

According to the American Bankers Association, this type loan is generally reviewed every six months and is allowed to fluctuate only a quarter or half percentage point at a time, and no more than 2½ percent above or below the original rate.

The much-used FHA and VA loans are made by private lenders (banks, savings and loans, etc) with a government-backed guarantee. If you default on the loan, the government will make good on the mortgage to the lender. FHA-insured loans are designed to help persons of moderate means afford housing, while VA mortgages help veterans to purchase homes. Generally, a government-backed loan requires a lower downpayment than conventional loans, but this often is compensated for by a "point" charge at settlement. The "point or points" make up the difference between the lender's current interest rate on conventional mortgages and the lower rate on FHA and VA mortgages.

On FHA and VA loans, the seller pays the points, although VA buyers may be asked to pay up to one point in some cases. In practice, many sellers anticipate paying points and raise their asking price accordingly. This is a factor when negotiating price with the seller. If you plan to use a "conventional loan" the seller may be willing to lower the asking price since he won't have to pay points.

VA mortgage qualifications are greatly misunderstood with tens of thousands of eligible veterans denying themselves their earned rights. Many veterans assume their eligibility has run out when in truth it is still there for the asking. Many changes have been made in the VA home financing program over the years and current eligibility can be based on service in World War II or Korea as well as current members of the armed services on duty after only 181 days of service. And even if part of a veteran's allowance

has been used, he might still qualify in terms of today's benefits. Another fallacy concerning VA financing is that it is restricted to "lower" priced homes. VA financing today is being used for homes in the $60,000 bracket and above.

Government-insured loans have an important feature — they do not contain a prepayment clause. No penalty will be assessed should you sell your home and pay off the mortgage in a few years. It's always wise to check this prepayment situation before signing a mortgage.

With mortgage interest rates having risen considerably in recent years many home purchasers have attempted to assume existing mortgages when purchasing an older home. This sometimes is permitted by the holder of the first loan (bank or savings-and-loan) with the new buyer paying a fee for such privilege. Sometimes, however, such requests are refused as the lender desires to establish a totally new loan at the prevalent higher interest rate.

In some states, land contract sales (also called "contract of sale" or "contract for a deed") are used to maintain a lower interest rate for the new buyer and, often, as a sales feature for the seller. In such transactions, the seller retains his equity interest in the property and the buyer makes payments to the seller until the home is completely paid for or until he can obtain a mortgage for the remaining balance.

The advantage to the seller (which he sometimes passes on to the buyer) is that his original mortgage may be at 6 percent or some other low rate, and his loan to the buyer could be at a higher percentage rate, allowing him to profit from the difference. And, just as it does for the buyer, it permits him to move his home in a mortgage market that might effectively prevent a sale. The advantage to the buyer is that he may be able to finance his purchase through the seller in a period of otherwise "tight" mortgage money. The buyer, of course, does not receive the deed until the seller has received all the amount agreed upon.

Land contract requirements and laws vary from state to state and should be thoroughly checked with an attorney. In California, a landmark decision was handed down by the State Supreme Court in October, 1974, which held that the acceleration clause common to most mortgages (the so-called "due on sale") may not be automatically exercised where the borrower sells the property to a buyer under a contract of sale payable in installments.

This California ruling made it possible for individuals to sell their property to another while retaining their original loan. The original lender, however, does have the right to make certain that the new buyer has sufficient credit so that he will not risk the lender's interest in the property.

One drawback in using such arrangements, at least in California, is that since the seller maintains his equity and liability for the original mortgage, the new buyer may not borrow additional funds for remodeling the property without the seller granting approval and actually signing for the improvement loan.

Several repayment plans have been used with installment contracts of sale. In one, the new buyer pays directly to the original mortgage holder. In another, the buyer pays directly to the seller who in turn keeps the mortgage current. And in still another, the buyer pays a neutral third party (usually a title company) who makes payments to the lender.

Home mortgage loans consist of two basic documents — a promissory note spelling out the specifics of the loan (the amount, schedule of payments and term) and a mortgage or deed of trust which pledges the home as security for the borrowed money. The lending agency will hold the note and mortgage until the loan is repaid in full. In some states, the deed of trust is recorded and given to you; in other states it may be held in trust (by an escrow agent) until the loan is repaid. In all instances, you should obtain a certificate of title that gives you assurance that the property is in your name. You should also have copies of the note, mortgage and deed.

Two additional factors closely related to your new mortgage are taxes and insurance. Some mortgages include charges for these items on a prorated monthly basis, collecting from you and then paying the bills for you. (See chapter covering insurance.) Some mortgage holders will permit you to make direct payments for taxes and insurance, but will require a copy of the insurance policy with a mortgagee clause attached.

Paperwork

When applying for a mortgage loan the lender will provide you with a printed application requesting the following information:

- How much money you wish to borrow

- How long you wish to borrow the money

- An identification of the property being purchased. The bank or lender will make an independent appraisal of the property to determine how much they will loan against the property value.

- Information about you including age, marital status, dependents, employment and salary, other income, your present residence and how long you have lived there, driver's license number, current obligations (including payments for car loan, Master Charge, etc.), active credit cards held, possible future obligations, location of checking and savings accounts, social security numbers for you and your spouse, assets, credit references and other specific data.

Based upon this application, obtaining a credit check and the property appraisal, the lender will or won't commit himself to granting your loan. A letter of commitment often is issued by the lender before the loan is formally granted. This permits you to proceed with the purchase.

Once the loan has been approved, title records are examined and you are ready for the "closing" at which time you will be expected to make your downpayment and pay closing costs. You will be expected at this time to sign the promissory note, mortgage and receipts relating to these two documents. Read these documents carefully before signing and ask questions you may have or check with your attorney.

HOMEBUYING BORROWING COSTS

Year	Rate	Year	Rate
1956	NA	1966	6.77
1957	5.61	1967	6.81
1958	5.60	1968	7.50
1959	6.23	1969	8.62
1960	6.04	1970	8.40
1961	5.69	1971	7.59
1962	5.53	1972	7.56
1963	5.45	1973	8.78
1964	5.45	1974	9.51
1965	5.62	1975	9.74

Source: U.S. Commerce Department

Monthly Mortgage Payments

The following table will let you quickly calculate "principal and interest" payments based on the amount of money borrowed (in $1000 increments) and the length of the loan period. Assume you purchased a $50,000 house and made a 20 percent downpayment, leaving a mortgage loan of $40,000 to be paid at 9 percent interest for 25 years. Simply take the $8.40 figure (in the 25 year column at 9 percent interest) and multiply it by 40 (representing the $40,000 mortgage) and you'll come up with a monthly payment of $336.00.

INTEREST RATE	LENGTH IN YEARS				
percent	10	15	20	25	30
8	12.14	9.56	8.37	7.72	7.34
8¼	12.27	9.70	8.52	7.88	7.51
8½	12.40	9.85	8.68	8.06	7.69
8¾	12.54	10.00	8.84	8.23	7.87
9	12.67	10.15	9.00	8.40	8.05
9¼	12.81	10.30	9.16	8.57	8.23
9½	12.94	10.45	9.33	8.74	8.41
9¾	13.08	10.60	9.49	8.92	8.60
10	13.22	10.75	9.66	9.09	8.78

Some lenders also require that you pay monthly one-twelfth of the annual real estate taxes and insurance. If these were $1200 per year, this amount would be $100 per month. Thus the total monthly would be $436. This $100 per month is accumulated in an escrow account so that sufficient funds are available when the taxes or insurance premiums are due.

Buyers of older homes start out with rather clear objectives as to what they need in their home, but then sometimes lose sight of these and make their decision on unrelated aspects which have an emotional appeal to them. A rating chart like the one below may be helpful in providing self-discipline. List all of the characteristics of your proposed purchase and assign to each a relative value from one to ten. You can then rate each home offered to you, proportionally in value. For instance, if you believe that schools are of utmost importance in your decision, then assign them a value of 10. The home offered to you where the schools are only so-so would then be rated at 5 or 6. Some characteristics may be so important to you that you may wish to assign a "knockout factor" to them. In the case of schools, you may decide that schools with a relative value of 8 is your minimum acceptable quality. Therefore, you will automatically reject any home in a school district not meeting your quality standards.

In the chart below, the first three lines are examples. You may assign any of the element values that you wish. In the "KO" column mark an X and the minimum value you are prepared to accept. The totals do not necessarily indicate one home being more desirable than another, but at least it is a guide.

HOME RATING CHART

Location_____

Realtor_____

Item	Relative Value	KO	Assigned Value
Schools (Example)	10	8X	6
Bedrooms(3)(Example)	8		7
Landscaping(Example)	5		4
Location			
Floor Plan			
Bedrooms Number			
Bathrooms Number			
Remodeling Required			
Interior Decorating			
Exterior Finish			
Structural			
Electrical			
Heating			
Kitchen			
Appliances			
Windows			
Roof			
Concrete			
Garage			
Water Supply			
Taxes			
Available Financing			
Schools			
Shopping			
Security—Police Protection			
Totals			

CLOSING COSTS

As stated earlier, when finalizing the purchase of a house you'll encounter "closing costs" represented in all the charges and fees incurred in transferring ownership of your new home to you. These costs, according to a HUD survey, average $558 and can run much higher, particularly for expensive properties.

Depending upon where you live, these are some of the charges you may find on your settlement statement:

Title Search. A title or abstract company or a lawyer will search through records of previous ownership and sale to establish the right of the seller to sell the property to you.

Title Insurance. A policy which protects the *lender's* interest in the property against any title defects not disclosed by the title search. Whether the buyer or seller pays for this varies with local custom. Only one premium payment is required, and it is due when the insurance policy is issued. If the buyer wants protection for himself, he must request an additional policy and pay the premium.

Attorney's fees. Even if you do not hire your own attorney, the lending institution may require you to pay a fee for its lawyer to handle the closing or advise concerning the title.

Survey. The lender may require a survey to determine the precise location of the house and the property.

Preparation of Documents. The deed, mortgage, and other necessary papers for transacting the sale must be prepared by a lawyer, the lender or some other party.

Closing Fee. A charge may be made for handling the settlement transaction.

Credit Report. The buyer's history is requested by the lender.

Termite Inspection. Many lenders request that the property be checked for harmful pests before granting a loan.

Initial Service Fee or Origination Fee. This is the lender's fee for originating the loan and is usually a small percentage of the face value of the mortgage. In FHA and VA transactions involving existing structures, the origination fee can be no more than 1 percent of the mortgage amount. On transactions where the lending institution makes inspections and partial disbursements during construction of a structure, both FHA and VA permit an origination fee in excess of 1 percent.

Mortgage Discount "Points". As detailed earlier, this one-time charge assessed at closing by the lender increases the yield on the mortgage loan to a competitive position with the yield on other types of investments. Each "point" is one percent of the original mortgage amount. In FHA and VA transactions, the home buyer is not permitted to pay points. No limit, however, is placed on the number of points which may be paid by the seller.

Appraisal Fee. The lender will request an appraisal of the property. In the case of a HUD-insured or VA-guaranteed mortgage loan, the fee is established by government regulations.

Recording Fee. The local authority's charge for recording documents pertaining to the sale.

State and Local Transfer Taxes. In some localities, these taxes are levied when property changes hands or when a real estate loan is made.

Mortgage Insurance Premiums. A fee to a company or government agency which guarantees the lender against loss if you fail to make your payments. This insurance is often required if the loan will exceed 80 percent of the property's value or if it is insured by the FHA. This kind of policy should not be confused with mortgage life or disability insurance policies designed to pay off your mortgage in your behalf in the event of your physical disability or death. Such policies are available should you desire to purchase them, but are not usually required by lenders.

Escrow Fees. When funds to adjust taxes, insurance or interest are needed, or when documents must be held prior to recording by a third party (escrow agent), escrow fees may appear on the statement. In some areas an escrow agent handles the entire settlement.

Miscellaneous. Notary fees, inspection fees, charges for photographs of the property, a schedule of mortgage payments, and other incidental expenses payable by either buyer or seller may appear on the statement.

Prepaid Adjustments. Some items, such as the entire year's taxes on a house, may have been prepaid by the seller. He is entitled to a refund for the portion of the year that the buyer will own the house. This also is true of special assessments, such as those for street and sewer improvements, and for property insurance if an existing policy is being transferred to the new owner.

The Real Estate Settlement Procedures Act of 1974 (RESPA) requires that a standard form containing actual costs for all of the above items be prepared and presented to the buyer and the seller in advance of "closing" of all transactions involving federally related loans. Along with this listing, the lender must give the buyer a government prepared, prescribed and approved booklet "Settlement Costs and You" explaining each numbered item on the disclosure forms.

In buying a home and encountering closing costs, it is well to ask each step of the way "if this cost can be bypassed in one way or another?" For example, the seller may have his old survey which may be acceptable to the lender. Or the title company may give a "reissue rate" on the search if they wrote the previous one and it is of recent vintage.

TITLE INSURANCE

Because of its great value, your home is protected by many special laws. As a result, you — and your family and heirs — have strong rights in the real estate. But the enduring nature of the land also makes it possible for others to claim rights on your property. When they do, it can limit your use of the real estate, cause you financial loss, and even result in the loss of your home.

Typical claims against your property can include an easement across the real estate (such as used for power and telephone utilities), a tax judgment against the property, and many others. Naturally, you need protection against this type challenge to your ownership, and you obtain it through an abstract and title insurance.

Members of the land title industry provide home buyers, mortgage lenders and other real estate investors with assurance they can use and enjoy property free from claim and loss related to title hazards. They offer their services throughout the nation, usually operating independently at the local level.

These firms perform three basic functions of great importance to you. First, they search many, separately located public records for matters affecting real estate ownership. Then, they review the findings of the search to determine the soundness of a land title before the real estate transaction is completed. Finally they issue title insurance, based on a search, that protects against title hazards including those even the most thorough search cannot reveal.

Examples of hidden hazards included a forged deed that conveys no title to real estate, a mistake in the records, an undetected mechanics lien, and others.

Depending upon local law and custom, a title search may be performed by an abstracter, a title insurance agent, an attorney, or a title insurer. In a search, public records may be checked in offices including those of recorders or registers of deeds, clerks of courts, and municipal and other county officials. These records include all the recorded documents and also judgments, other liens, general taxes, street assessments, sewer system assessments, and other special taxes and levies.

Through the title search, land title problems such as recorded workmen's liens against the property, unsatisfied mortgages, and many others are exposed to the home buyer, mortgage lender and investors who can then take appropriate action before the transaction is completed.

Following the title search and a review of the evidence it discloses, title insurance normally is issued to provide protection for the real estate investors. Title insurance is available for a one-time charge paid at closing of the transaction.

Coverage of title insurance includes payment for a legal defense against an attack on a title as insured and payment of valid claims. There are two basic kinds of title insurance — lender's and owner's. Lender's title insurance protects only the mortgage lender. As a homebuyer, you need owner's coverage.

The American Land Title Association points out that title insurance is quite different from casualty insurance (such as "Homeowners" house coverage) in that great emphasis is placed on risk elimination *before* insuring against problems that originated before your ownership, and they charge just a one-time premium. The firms spend a substantial part of their operating income maintaining this capability to expertly eliminate risk.

Even if the seller of a home you want to buy seems honest, and even if he recently has obtained a title search and title insurance to safeguard himself, you as a purchaser still need up-to-date protection. The seller's search and title insurance do not protect the buyer. Title problems that can cause you problems and cost you money may have occurred near the end of the seller's ownership. And, problems that date before your ownership may not be disclosed in a search, so that you need all-inclusive protection. According to the American Land Title Insurance Association, title insurance company files contain many cases demonstrating the need for land title protection. In one instance, a family made a downpayment and moved into a home, receiving a deed from a woman who then disappeared. Some time later, another couple appeared with a deed to the same real estate. It was then learned that the woman who disappeared had provided a forged deed, which conveyed no title to the home. The family with the forged deed thus did not own the property and faced serious financial loss. Fortunately, the family was protected by title insurance. In another instance, a young couple interested in buying a home was told by the seller that it wasn't necessary to obtain an up-to-date title search and the new title insurance. The seller offered to give the couple his owner's title insurance policy, dating back to when he purchased the real estate. Also, the seller pointed out, there was an FHA-insured loan on the property, and he said the federal government would never insure a mortgage on a home with a bad title. A title search was made, and it was found that three federal tax liens had been filed against the seller and that he had not paid a paving assessment. The couple did not go through with the purchase, thereby avoiding possible loss.

An abstracter, under the terms of the certificate he affixes to a completed abstract of title, has a legal and financial responsibility for the accuracy of his work. In those rare instances where clerical errors or mistakes of judgment do occur, losses are paid promptly.

The cost of title insurance varies according to local condi-

tions. In some instances, the cost rate is prescribed by the state agency responsible for the proper operation of title insurance companies. However, the pure basic premium rate for owner's title insurance varies within the narrow range of $3.50 to $5.00 per $100 of coverage. This is for the insurance alone, without the cost of the required title search. In most instances, the search and insurance costs will be combined and presented to the buyer as a package.

INSURING YOUR HOME

Mortgage lenders will require that you insure your newly bought home for fire and lightning, and some lenders will demand additional coverage depending upon location and other circumstances.

Home insurance begins with an initial layer of fire and lightning and is then built up with succeeding layers of (1) extended coverage, (2) vandalism and malicious mischief and (3) all-risk or special form coverage. The commonly known "Homeowners" policy combines all the risks encountered by the home and the personal belongings (furniture, clothes, etc.) plus liability and living expenses incurred by a fire or disaster.

Depending upon the location of your home, you may also be required to secure flood coverage, which for the most part is limited to a maximum of $35,000 coverage. Earthquake coverage generally carries a 5 percent or $5000 deductible, whichever is greater. And almost all policies carry a $100 or greater deductible on all claims.

A special insurance now being offered nationally by the Continental Insurance Companies combines full coverage on you, your home, and your auto. Called "Personal Comprehensive Protection" or "PCP" the package covers:

- property losses — to your home, second home, automobile, personal property at home and away, additional living expenses made necessary by fire, wind or other insured peril;

- legal liability — liability claims arising from your residence premises, your personal activities, operation of your car;

- medical payments — for you and your passengers in an auto accident, for the public if an accident occurs on your premises, or in your personal activities;

- optional — personal injury protection, disability income, hospital indemnity, mortgage life and excess liability.

A special feature of this coverage is "no depreciation, replacement cost" basis used in settling losses on residence building, or on household furnishings if the loss exceeds $2,000, plus renewal guarantee at five annual renewals, at the rates in effect at each time of renewal.

Home insurance rates don't fluctuate as greatly as car

insurance rates and are determined in a large part by the location of the house and its proximity to water and fire services. Independent rating bureaus determine a coverage number for each area ranked from zero to 9 percent and the higher the number the higher the cost of coverage.

The amount of coverage you carry on your home will probably be specified by your lender based on replacement costs in the area. You may find that this replacement cost has very little relation to the sales value of the home.

Your home should be insured from 80 percent to full value if the insurance company is to replace it at "replacement" cost. For example, if you have but $40,000 coverage on a $60,000 insurance value and incur a $6000 fire damage, the company will pay 4/6ths (coverage-over-insurance value of the loss) or $4000, leaving you with a net loss of $2000. This, in effect, is the penalty you pay for underinsuring a home.

Most insurance firms are now selling policies on only an annual basis and are adding an inflation guard endorsement which automatically increases the coverage as the U.S. Commerce Department's Construction Cost Index rises.

The minimum home insurance policy offered by most firms is $15,000 for fire or homeowner. If the home to be covered is over 30 years old, proof of "wiring up to code" may be required.

It is well to check with your local building department in purchasing a new home to see that it can be rebuilt should you suffer a fire loss. "Grandfather" protection exists for many homes that are not up to current local standards, but once the structure has been changed (by fire, etc.) the "Grandfather Clause" no longer exists and the structure may have to be totally demolished. This is especially true where there are two homes on a single lot, or where there may be additional living quarters above a garage or carriage house, or a separate rental unit on the property.

Home insurance can be purchased from licensed agents, brokers or solicitors. It may be paid for on an annual, semiannual or quarterly basis, but you would do well to consider the annual method which protects you from rate increases during this period.

Keep in mind that home improvements increase a dwelling's value. When you remodel a kitchen, add on a room, replace the heating system, install built-in sound systems and the like, you are adding considerably to the "replacement" value of the home. This should be accounted for in the insurance coverage.

As for furnishings, most insurance people recommend a minimum of 50 percent coverage. That is, if you value your furnishings and equipment at $20,000, you should have a $10,000 policy. Over 9 out of 10 insurance companies depreciate furnishings when covering a loss as opposed to paying replacement costs.

How To Determine Insurance Needs

A quick and highly accurate method enabling homeowners to determine how much to increase their property insurance to cover inflated rebuilding costs has been developed by McGraw-Hill Information Systems Company. The new insurance service, called Dodge Home Valuator, involves a simple three-step calculation that lets homeowners decide for themselves how high inflation has driven up the replacement value of their homes.

Instructions for estimating these insurance needs are printed in the form of a brochure available from insurance agents of the Hartford Insurance Group, Home Insurance Company, the Security Insurance Group, and the Travelers Insurance Companies.

The first step in the Dodge estimating method involves a "construction unit" approach to the value of a house. A homeowner uses a table to assign a whole or half unit rating to each major component of his home.

For example, a kitchen, full bathroom, finished attic, attached two-car garage, central air conditioning and aluminum siding are each worth one unit. A half bathroom, attic with restricted headroom, attached one-car garage, and brick or stone exterior walls are a half unit each.

After adding up the units in his house, the homeowner selects a cost figure from a table showing costs for average, good and custom-built construction of houses with different unit totals. The brochure defines the three qualities of construction to aid the homeowner in making a realistic selection.

Finally, the homeowner multiplies the cost figure by an adjustment percentage figure called a location multiplier. He selects the appropriate multiplier from a table listing one for each state and 114 cities. His final figure is the minimum amount for which he should insure his house.

The replacement value reflects the cost of equivalent living space, since in many cases the homeowner would be unable to duplicate his present house. Some homes are in nonconforming use because of changes in local zoning laws, and other homes include building materials no longer available, such as tile roofs and Victorian gingerbread decorations.

An alternative method, also in the form of a brochure, uses square feet instead of construction units to arrive at the estimated rebuilding cost for a house. This square footage approach is also available from the same insurance companies.

Warranty Insurance

Consumer protection movements have stimulated the use of warranty programs on existing homes in many parts of the United States and this coverage seems certain to increase in popularity with home buyers. Such programs protect buyers of existing homes against any problems with the most important components of the home and prevent substantial cash layouts for unseen problems that may be found once they move into the structure.

The National Association of Realtors has been among those organizations seeking such protection for home buyers and estimates that some 200,000 homes will be so covered by the end of 1976; 500,000 the next year and nearly 1 million homes in 1978.

Existing home warranties provide the buyer with a certified condition report on the condition of the home's plumbing, heating, air conditioning, electrical system, walls, roofs and foundation. The warranty usually covers from 12 to 18 months, during which time if anything goes wrong the repairs will be made by a local contractor and the cost covered by the insurance firm backing the warranty.

Similar programs have been in effect for several years on new construction built by some members of the National Association of Home Builders. Some of these warranties are for periods up to 10 years, guarding primarily against structural defects.

Some of the existing home insurance warranties require a house inspection by an independent agent, while another warranty firm offers coverage on all properties sold by a given real estate firm without inspection. Annual cost for such policies runs from $200 to $250, with the homeowner paying a $20 to $25 service fee for each service call.

Remodeling can often accomplish what would appear to be a miracle. Shown in these before-and-after photographs is a home built in 1816 as a homestead at Newville, Pennsylvania. Weatherbeaten, devoid of paint and in a state of disrepair, the house was built of logs and later covered with sheeting.

The remodeling contractors who undertook the job of renovating the dwelling tore off the outer work and returned to the basic structure. Three metal jacks and one stout beam were used to square the floor. One sill under the house was replaced. New windows and doors replaced old. Porch overhangs were replaced.

Aluminum siding was applied to the exterior and wood paneling to the interior. An 8x40 foot concrete patio was added along one side of the house.

Additional construction (accomplished following this "after" photograph) included a detached garage. And landscaping finished the project.

Few remodeling projects today would involve such dated and dilapidated houses, but this certainly proves what can be done! (Photos: Crown Aluminum).

SECTION TWO: FIXING

IMPROVING YOUR HOME

If you are handy with tools and have the experience, you can save money by doing many jobs yourself. But unless, you are skilled in wiring, plumbing, installing heating systems, and cutting through walls, it may be best to rely on professionals for such work.

USING A CONTRACTOR

Having a home improvement contractor do your work for you will cost more but will save you much time and energy. The contractor will take responsibility for the complete job, but will expect you to select the materials and tell him, before work is started, exactly what you want done. To do this, you may need the assistance of a designer, architect or architectural draftsman to come up with the plans. However, often times you, the homeowner, can sketch your designs and the contractor can take it from there.

If you decide to use a contractor, obtain several cost estimates and make certain they are all based on the same specifications, such as labor and materials. Be very specific about the quality of the materials you want used, and if at all possible, specify the actual brand and pattern or model numbers.

The best way to assure that the estimate covers only that work you want done is to write down exactly what you want done and have all the contractors bid on only those specifications, with any additional work or changes to the original request as a separate bid.

In selecting a contractor, take care to choose one with a reputation for honesty and good workmanship. Don't select on the basis of cost alone. Consider how long the contractor has been in business, and his reputation for giving satisfactory service.

You can "check out" a contractor by consulting your local Chamber of Commerce, Better Business Bureau, building products distributors and dealers, and local lending institutions. Talk with people for whom he has done work and check his place of business to see that he is not a fly-by-night operator. Always ask for references and check them carefully.

Many contractors offer package plans that include the whole transaction. Under such a plan the contractor provides all the materials used, takes care of all work involved, and arranges for your loan. You must repay the loan, so it is important that you see the work done correctly and verify that all subcontractor and materials bills have been paid by the contractor.

The contract that both you and the contractor sign should state clearly the type and extent of improvements to be made and the materials to be used. Before you sign, get the contractor to spell out for you in exact terms:

- How much the entire job will cost you.

- How much interest you will have to pay on the loan.

- How much you will pay in service charges.

- How many payments you must make to pay off the loan and how much each of these payments will be.

- Dates of the contract, names of persons and firms involved, commencement date, time schedule for work, and approximate completion date.

- Material specifications, including brand names of products to be used, quantity, quality and styles. These should be referenced to floor plans or architectural drawings.

- Statement that all elements of the remodeling will conform to state, county, and local building codes and zoning laws.

- Warranties covering work and materials and the extent of each.

Additional items that you should consider including in the contract include: possible change of orders that can be made during construction, made in written form, with extra costs subject to approval of both parties; that the contractor will provide a performance bond guaranteeing completion of the project; proof that the contractor carries adequate insurance; and guarantee that he will pay all bills and provide a full waiver of liens before he is paid.

The contractor's estimate should include the cost of all materials and labor, plus sales tax, material delivery charges and profit. Most estimates can be broken down thus: Materials: 25 to 30 percent of total estimate; Labor: 40 to 60 percent; Markup to cover expenses and profit: 15 to 20 percent. A legitimate downpayment on a remodeling project is 10 to 20 percent of the total cost estimate and rarely should you extend more than one-third this cost at the outset.

It's good practice to never make oral agreements with contractors — get it in writing, and if the job is a major one, let an attorney specializing in construction take a look at any contract before you sign it. And once you do sign the contract, make certain to obtain a copy for your own use.

Federal Trade Commission regulations give you a three-day "right of recision" or "cooling-off period" during which time you may cancel the contract by giving the contractor a written notice. Provisions for this should be clearly stated in any contract before you sign it and it should read, according to the FTC, "You, the buyer, may cancel this transaction at any time prior to midnight of the third business day after the date of this transaction."

After the entire job is finished in the manner set forth in your contract, you sign a completion certificate. By signing this paper you certify that you approve the work and materials and you authorize the lender to pay the contractor the money you borrowed.

Most dealers and contractors conscientiously try to give their customers full value for their money. Unfortunately, home improvement rackets do exist. Here are a few commonsense rules offered by the U.S. Department of Housing and Urban Development:

- Read and understand every word of any contract or other paper before you sign it.

- Never sign a contract with anyone who makes fantastic promises. Reputable dealers are not running give-away businesses.

- Never consolidate existing loans through a home-improvement contractor.

- Do not let any salesman high-pressure you into signing up to buy his materials or services.

- Be wary of salesmen who try to scare you into signing for repairs that they say are urgent. Seek the advice of an expert as to how urgent such repairs are. High-pressure and scare tactics are often the mark of a phony deal.

- Avoid salesmen who offer you trial purchases or some form of bonus, such as cash, for allowing them to use your house as a model for any purpose. Such offers are well-known gimmicks of swindlers.

- Never sign a completion certificate until all the work called for in the contract has been completed to your satisfaction. Be careful not to sign a completion certificate along with a sales order.

- Proceed cautiously when the lender or contractor demands a lien on your property. FHA requires a lien in the case of a Title I loan over $7500, though a few Title I lenders do add this precaution on their own initiative to loans below $7500.

When work is about to begin, don't handicap the contractor with furniture, boxes and other items that he will have to remove from the area. Do this ahead of time and present him with clear sailing when the workmen arrive. Try to keep youngsters out of the area and if possible set up a secured area such as the garage where materials may be stored until needed.

DO-IT-YOURSELF

Never before have homeowners been offered such a wide selection of high-quality materials for finishing walls, ceilings and floors, and for making other improvements. Many of these products and materials have been engineered or designed specifically for the home handyman who likes to work around the house and save money at the same time.

Free instructions for the do-it-yourselfer are practically unlimited. You can obtain guide books at the library on almost every type of specific home repair and improvement; building material dealers can supply you with colorful and instructive manufacture literature that will take you from step one to completion; and many dealers, associations and stores conduct regular home improvement courses making skilled craftsmen readily available to the homeowner for free counseling.

In serving as your own general contractor you may wish to subcontract part of the work; for example, hire a plumber to install new bathroom fixtures. You may be well qualified to wallpaper or paint the room and install new flooring and cabinet hardware; be cautious in undertaking difficult tasks if you have little or no practical experience.

Home workshop

A home workshop is the first home improvement project undertaken by many home buyers as it then becomes the focal point for home repair activities. Many setups are elaborate, while others are strictly basic to handle day-to-day needs.

Tool makers offer easy-to-build plans for work benches which for practical purposes usually are 42, 50 or 60 inches long, 22 to 24 inches deep and 32 inches high. Most are equipped with a vise which can be woodworking style or a general-purpose type with drop-in jaws to handle pipe stock.

It is well to keep in mind when buying tools that they should be of good quality and expertly designed. It is better to pay a little more, and have tools that will give better performance and last many more years.

In moving into an older home you'll find yourself tackling many household repairs and improvements. Some may be as simple as hanging a picture, tightening a door knob, oiling a hinge, replacing a broken window pane, or replacing a washer in a leaking faucet. In each instance, the task is impossible without the proper tools.

Here's a suggested list of everyday hand tools for getting those and other jobs done efficiently:

- 16-oz. nail hammer

- 4, 6, and 8 inch-long flat-tipped screwdrivers

- No. 1 and No. 2 Phillips screwdrivers

- Hand or push drill (if you don't get a power drill)

- 6-inch pliers with "combination" jaws

- 8-inch adjustable wrench

- 10-foot steel measuring tape with ¼-inch blade

- Bell or ball-shaped "plumber's helper"

- Nested saw with changeable keyhole, compass and metalcutting blades

- 16-oz. half hatchet

- Utility knife and extra blades

- Putty knife 2½ to 3 inches wide

- 6-inch-wide "C" clamps

Power tools

Portable power tools are one of the best "buys" offered today's homeowner. Advanced design and manufacturing techniques plus increased competition have brought price tags down to a reasonable level.

Most persons starting a home workshop begin their power tool collection with an electric drill — ¼, ⅜ or ½ inch capacity — with single-speed, two-speed or variable-speed action. More versatile units even provide a reverse action for removing screws.

As you undertake more and more repair and improvement tasks you'll find yourself becoming a regular purchaser at the local hardware or building material tool counters. This is the best way of building a complete work shop, as you will tend to be more selective in buying each tool and will have a specific use in mind for each before you make the purchase.

Most retail dealers can supply you with catalogs illustrating basic hand tools used for woodworking, metalcrafting, plumbing and other projects. They can also acquaint you with the wide range of fastening devices from common nails and screws to toggle bolts, molly screws, plastic anchor screws and the like.

The power drill is extremely valuable to home repair and

It's handy to have a portable work center that can be moved about the house. This Workmate by Black & Decker will hold projects of all sizes firmly and at comfortable heights so that your hands are free to maneuver tools. The unit folds for compact storage.

remodeling projects. Equipped with a gear-type chuck, the drill can be fitted with expansion bits that drill holes several inches in diameter, and with attachments that do several other jobs including grinding, honing, polishing, shaping, sanding, wire brushing, paint stirring, and driving screws. Some drill models are sold with vertical stands which hold the drill so that the user can conveniently control and position work against revolving accessories.

A circular power saw permits you to cut wood materials easily and quickly. When fitted with appropriate blades or wheels, this tool will also cut stone, ceramics, fiberglass and metal. Home-use models have blades ranging in diameter from 6½ to 8¼ inches. The smaller blade size will give a 2 inch vertical cut and approximately 1¾ inches at a 45° angle. Larger blades usually cut deeper, but it is well to check maximum cut dimensions on the manufacturer's literature before investing in a power saw. Likewise, check to see that a rip guide is included and that the saw has a three-prong plug for grounding safety.

The other member of the home workshop "Big Three" is a belt sander which quickly sands large surfaces such as floors, walls, and planks. It can remove old paint, erase scratches or smooth uneven workmanship. With the proper abrasive belt, the sander can work on wood, metal, glass, ceramics, plastic and stone.

Rated work capacities of sanders are noted on the tool or in the tool literature. Units generally use 3- or 4 inch-wide belts and operate in a range of 900 to 1600 square feet per minute. Some units can be equipped with dust bags or have a flexible hose that connects to a vacuum cleaner.

The more sophisticated home handyman will want more advanced power tools. These include: a bench saw, either tilt table or arbor, which cuts rips, mitres, dadoes and handles most any type of cutting job; a radial saw (also stationary) which does all the jobs of a bench saw, and also accepts attachments for sanding, grinding, shaping, drilling, molding, and planing; a lathe, which holds and revolves material for shaping; a jig saw to cut irregular figures; a jointer — a large plane for smoothing board edges; and a professional belt-type sander which uses an adhesive belt to do heavy sanding jobs quickly.

FINANCING REMODELING

The best way to finance home improvements is to pay cash, if at all possible. But since most persons are unable to use this method for such major undertakings as replacing a furnace, adding a room, converting a garage, etc., the home-improvement loan becomes the best avenue for borrowers.

Like buying anything else, you should shop for the best possible home-improvement loan you can obtain. Begin by contacting your local bank where you have a checking account or savings account. They will be able to provide you with a folder detailing their various types of loans and current interest rates. Then try a savings-and-loan or a company credit union and ask for similar information.

Today there are a number of good plans for financing home improvements on reasonable terms. The kind of loan that is best for you will depend upon the amount of money you need to borrow, how long you will need it and the cost of getting the loan (interest).

These are six most-used types of home-improvement financing.

(1). Commercial loans from commercial banks, usually for 3 months to a year in term, with the amount largely determined by the borrower's income and credit standing.

(2) Commercial home-improvement loan from commercial banks, usually for 5 to 15 years, with the maximum amount being up to 75 percent of the home equity.

(3) Savings & Loan home-improvement loan, usually for 10 years but sometimes for as long as 15 years, generally limited to 75 percent of equity with maximum of $10,000.

(4) Title I, HUD-insured home-improvement loan from a lending institution participating in this government program, for a maximum 12-year term, covering up to $10,000 on individual homes. Maximum financing charges on this loan: 12 percent per annum.

(5) Credit union home-improvement loan, usually for 5 to 10 year term, with amount varying according to individual credit union policy.

(6) Still another possibility is to arrange for the original mortgage loan to cover projected improvements. The lender can pay out the additional amount once the improvements are completed. This will save money in interest costs. Some lenders have "open end" mortgages that permit you to borrow additional money for home improvements on the original mortgage after some of it has been paid off.

HUD-insured (FHA) Title I loans may be used for any improvements that will make your home basically more livable and useful. You can use them for dishwashers, refrigerators, freezers, and even ovens if they are of the built-in style and not free-standing units. You cannot use this type of loan for certain luxury items such as swimming pools and outdoor fireplaces, or for work already done.

Among the advantages of the FHA-loan insurance plan are:

• You seldom need any security for loans under $7500 other than your signature on the note, and you need no co-signer.

- You do not have to disturb any mortgage or deed of trust you may have on your home.

- You have to meet only three requirements: own your property or have a long-term lease on it; have a satisfactory credit rating; have enough income to repay the loan over its term.

- Only three simple forms are involved: an application, a note and a completion certificate (if work or materials are furnished by a dealer or contractor). Usually only the lender has to approve your loan and can give you an answer in a few days.

- You receive some protection from the wrong kind of dealer or contractor, because HUD-FHA requires that any dealer who arranges a loan for you must first be approved by the lender.

It is extremely important to guard against unnecessary high interest costs and other questionable financing practices that often accompany home-improvement schemes of various kinds. FHA Title I regulations and procedures provide some protection for the consumer. Remember that home-improvement loans or loans to finance the purchase of major appliances are often figured on "discount" interest. This means that in order to finance $1000 for one year at 6 percent interest, you sign a note for $1060. But, since you are going to be making monthly payments, you will actually only have use of an average of $500 during the year, so your interest rate is 12 percent.

In obtaining a loan, make sure the interest rate quoted to you conforms with the new Federal Truth-In-Lending statues. If the rate does not equal or better the equivalent FHA Title I maximum rates, check to see why. Negotiate the best possible rate, or check other lending institutions for a better deal. If you can't find terms equal to or lower than FHA Title I, contact your local FHA office or Home Builders Association.

UNDERSTANDING THE BASICS OF YOUR HOME

PLUMBING

When moving into a new home you should have a basic understanding of the overall plumbing system (although you should have appraised it during your house selection) and how it operates. Stated simply, the system provides hot and cold water for a range of purposes and disposes of waste via a drainage system.

Your plumbing system begins with a main supply connection, usually at the street edge of your property, where incoming water is metered as you draw upon the source. In most cities, local plumbing codes determine the size of the source pipe and the material from which it is fabricated.

It's good practice to know the exact location of the turn-off control at the main source, in the event that you have to use it in a hurry. Sometimes it will be located at the street-lot line connection and other times it may be closer to the house foundation where the supply lines first enter the house.

Copper and galvanized steel are the most used piping materials for supply lines of older houses. Cast iron drainage lines are usual although plastic drainage and vent systems have made substantial breakthroughs in the past decade. Plastic pipe is used in many communities for cold water supply lines, but most types of this piping are not suitable to carry water above 120°F. And in some communities polyvinyl chloride or polyethylene plastic pipe is used for mains and service lines.

It is estimated that about 10 percent of the homes in the United States are located beyond municipal water systems and are served by private water systems. These systems usually require a pump to move water from the source to the faucet. If this is the case with your house, make certain the pump is in good working order and of sufficient size to handle your peak needs without trouble.

Water supplied via municipal lines usually is delivered under about 40 pounds per square inch pressure. Turning on all the faucets in the house simultaneously will indicate quickly if you have a serious supply problem due to lack of adequate pressure.

The impact of rushing water sometimes results in the banging sound of "water hammer" in a piping system. This occurs when the plumbing system is not properly adapted to absorb the impact of the rushing water when the faucet is abruptly turned off. The reverberation can cause real damage to the piping and fittings, as well as annoyance to

everyone's ears. The most usual way, but not the best, to prevent water hammer is to install air chambers at all points where the faucets and valves are connected to pipes. An air chamber is a vertical length of pipe with a natural air pocket that cushions the force of the water. Eventually, however, the air in the piping chambers is absorbed by the water and you hear the constant sound of water hammer while your plumbing suffers. The entire plumbing system must then be drained to recharge the air chambers.

Plumbing experts believe better protection is installation by a plumbing contractor of a special shock absorber device. Larger than a pipe air chamber, these units absorb water shock with a rubber-type tube that expands inside a rigid shell containing a pliable insulation material. Because it does not depend on the air pocket to cushion the water, this unit never needs any kind of recharging to continue protecting the plumbing system from damage and your ears from needless noise.

Copper has long been the most desirable material for supply lines installed in the walls of houses. With its non-rusting, smooth surfaces, copper piping and tubing do not build up scale which can clog the line and thereby reduce the amount of flow to the faucet. Rust which sometimes occurs in galvanized steel piping will also discolor water, sinks and fabrics washed in water containing it.

Characteristic of water is its ability to dissolve other substances. Given half a chance, it can irreparably damage the faucet in a sink or lavatory, and waste your money. Figures from the Plumbing-Heating-Cooling Information Bureau shows that a ⅛ inch drip from a faucet can send 12,-000 gallons of water down the drain in a month. This means paying for water you don't use.

This flow of water from the faucet also dissolves the seat, against which the washer should seal. This erosive action can ruin a faucet, making it necessary to replace it years sooner than would be the case if proper maintenance were given when needed.

Washer replacement is a relatively simple homeowner chore and once accomplished you should never give an extra twist to a faucet handle to shut the water off. This, too, can ruin the faucet seat.

Modern household water demands usually require a water heater with 60-gallon or larger capacity, depending upon the use of an automatic dishwasher and the frequency and amount of laundry washing, plus the number of persons in the family who may be bathing simultaneously.

Water heaters on the market today come factory-assembled with glass-lined tanks, fully-automatic controls with 100 percent safety shut-off, gas pressure regulators, glass fiber insulation, temperature and pressure relief valves, thermostat controls and fast-connect hook-up feature. Units carry various guarantees and warranties which should be carefully read before completing the purchase. The normal setting for a water heater is about 140°F but some models can be set as high as 180° for periodic faster recovery. Do not leave units set at the higher temperature for extended periods of time.

In-the-wall drain, waste and vent (DWV) systems in older homes are most commonly of cast iron pipe construction. In recent years, thousands of new homes have been constructed with plastic DWV pipe and fittings made from polyethylene (PE), polyvinyl-chloride (PVC) and acrylonitrile-butadiene-styrene (ABS).

One of the most common problems encountered by homeowners is that of blocked or clogged drainage piping inside the house, caused by flushing down wrong types of waste and by rough pipe interiors. Improper waste includes melted grease and fat which cool and congeal — often combining with solid kitchen waste particles which completely block drainage. Grease and fat should be placed in containers for disposal with garbage.

If household drainage chemicals can't unclog a blocked drainage line, try using a suction plunger. Should this fail, remove the drain trap and run an auger, or plumber's snake, through the blocked pipe. After rotating it several times, reconnect the trap and flush the line with a good household chemical and hot water.

Waste dispensed from your house travels through a main drain directly to a sewer line, septic tank or cesspool disposal system. With city sewerage all drain lines, including both rainwater and sanitary lines, remove the waste entirely from your property. With a septic tank, sanitary waste is piped from the house to an underground steel or cast concrete chamber located on the immediate property. Such disposal systems are regulated and inspected by local authorities to meet health standards and must be periodically cleaned to operate at full efficiency. In general practice, when the total depth of solids and scum in a septic tank are in excess of one-third the liquid depth of the tank, the solids must be removed. Cleaning usually takes place in the spring of the year. The cesspool system, prohibited by many local communities, consists of a covered pit with an open-joined lining that receives waste as it is discharged. Such installations usually are constructed of stone or hollow concrete block. Plumbing fixtures are dealt with in the kitchen and bathroom chapters of this book and thus are not detailed here.

In many areas the basic water source to a home will be "hard" and require the installation of a quality water softener. Hard water costs consumers $6.3 billion annually, according to the Water Quality Research Council. It wastes $1.8 billion in soaps, detergents, shampoos and other cleaning materials. It deteriorates plumbing at an estimated $2.7 billion annual rate. It does $1 billion in damage to sheets, linens, towels and washable clothing. In addition, by depositing insulating scale in water heaters, it adds $800 million to the nation's already oversized fuel bills. Almost 80 percent of the United States and Canada has hard water. Yet it has been only over the past decade or two that the soft water industry has begun to grow at the pace expected.

Those homeowners enjoying the benefits of water softeners report lower water bills, less soap and detergent usage, and the elimination of unnecessary staining and spotting of plumbing fixtures, china and glassware.

However, keep in mind that the water-softener salesman wants to sell you a softener, so get an independent test of your water by a county or state agency before purchasing a water-softener system.

HEATING

All central heating systems used today in homes can be divided into two broad categories — nonducted systems and

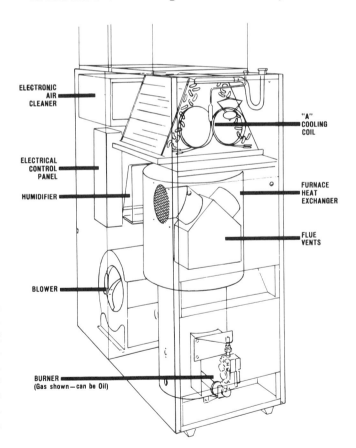

ELECTRONIC AIR CLEANER

ELECTRICAL CONTROL PANEL

HUMIDIFIER

BLOWER

BURNER (Gas shown—can be Oil)

"A" COOLING COIL

FURNACE HEAT EXCHANGER

FLUE VENTS

Forced warm-air furnaces used in many older homes are either gas or oil fired. Newer furnaces include electronic air cleaners and can be supplied with cooling coils for summer cooling. The same ducts can be used for both systems. Drawing: U.S. Dept. of Agriculture No. 2235.

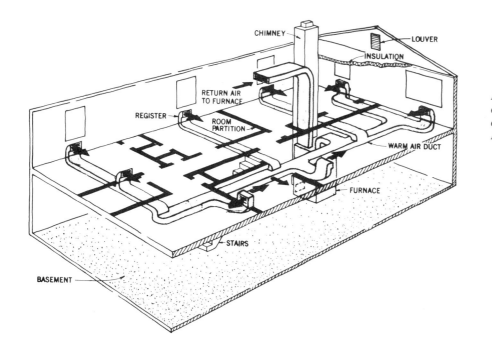

Popular forced warm-air systems usually have a cold air return in each room (except kitchen and bath) as well as heat supply register. Drawing: U.S. Dept. of Agriculture No. 2235.

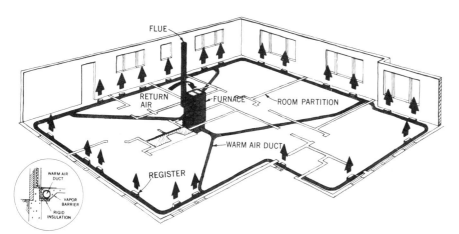

Perimeter loop heating systems are used in many basementless homes constructed with a concrete slab. The inset shows how the warm air duct is placed in the concrete slab. Drawing: U.S. Dept. of Agriculture No. 2235.

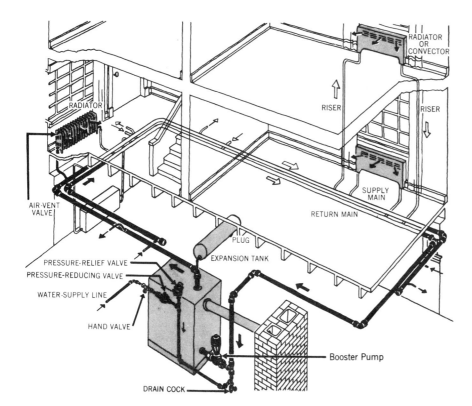

Two-pipe forced hot water systems have two supply pipes or mains. One supplies the hot water to the room heating units, and the other returns the cooled water to the boiler. Drawing: U.S. Dept. of Agriculture No. 2235.

ducted central systems. The nonducted system puts a heating element of some type into every individual room. Heat transfers from this unit to the air, furniture and walls of the room, and produces the desired temperature. In the ducted central system, one heating element is used for an entire house or for all the rooms in one zone of a house. A centrally located blower or blowers will move air over the heating element (or elements) and this warmed and conditioned air is then moved into the various rooms through ducts.

Each system has its own advantages and disadvantages and each can be used with any type of fuel — gas, oil or electricity — for homes of any size or type.

Baseboard radiation is the most common type of nonducted system, using either hot water for its source of heat or an electric heating element. Units are compact and are installed on perimeter walls, usually under window areas. Room air that comes in contact with the heated surfaces of walls, floor and ceiling becomes warmed. The age-old cast iron radiator for many years (and in some areas, still today) provided this type of heating for homes and apartments. The old-fashioned units accepted air at the bottom, heated it as it contacted a heating element, and permitted it to rise by natural circulation to drift out grilles at the top.

Two other types of nonducted systems are ceiling radiant and floor radiant, where elements are embedded in either surface. In both cases control of room humidity is difficult because of the lack of moving air.

Hydronics, the science of heating and cooling with liquids, is still another form of nonducted comfort control. Water is heated in an appliance-styled boiler and circulated by means of a small pump through finger-sized tubing to room heating units, usually baseboard units, convectors, or modern recessed radiators. Water-carrying tubing may also be embedded in concrete floors to provide this type of heating.

The ducted central system method of heating places the heating element in a remote location from the room or rooms being heated. Ducts remove the air from the room, bringing it back to a centrally located blower. Here the air is filtered and conditioned and moved back over the heating element and then taken through ducts back to the room.

This type of system can be a direct-fired warm air furnace, hot water coil or electric heating element. The direct-fire furnace gets its name from the fact that oil or gas fire is contained in a gas-tight steel enclosure. The fire heats the steel and the steel in turn heats the air directly. Hot water heat used in a central ducted system is considered indirect. Here the fire occurs in a steel or cast iron boiler with the heat transferring from the fire to metal and from metal to water. Water is then conducted to a heat transfer coil in the ducted central system where air moves over the coil and picks up warmth from it. There is one extra heat transfer involved here, water, hence the term "indirect".

With modern, highly sensitive, low-voltage room thermostats, it is possible to get even and satisfactory temperature comfort with either a nonducted or ducted system. These quality thermostats command short and very frequent on-cycles for the heat source, whether gas, oil or electric.

In any room where you have large glass areas like floor-to-ceiling window walls or sliding glass doors, a ducted system is your best answer to comfort control. Heating elements of nonducted systems will not create sufficient air velocity to counteract the cold air which cascades off these surfaces, where upward-moving air of ducted units will do the job. In rooms with a modest amount of window area, either ducted or nonducted heating systems will produce equal temperature control.

If you plan to replace the existing heating system in your home, give serious consideration to installing a system that provides separate zone control. This is especially important in a two-story or split-level house where large areas may not be in use at the same time.

Ducted heating systems offer other potential benefits to the homeowner. These units will help to "change" the air throughout the house giving it a freshness not possible with nonducted units. With the ducted unit you can add a humidifier, an electronic air cleaner or activated charcoal purifier, as well as obtain full-house air conditioning.

Still another newer type of heating and cooling unit is the electric heat pump which acts as a reversible refrigeration unit. This system relies entirely on electricity and nature's heat to take the place of a central air conditioner and forced-air furnace in new or existing homes. The heat pump cools in the summer, like a central cooling system, by collecting the heat inside your home and transferring it outside. In winter, it heats by reversing this process.

The efficiency of the heat pump depends upon climate and installation, but generally will supply as much as 2½ times heat output as straight electric resistance heat for the same amount of electrical energy input. For example, one heat pump on the market operating when the outside temperature is 45° can deliver 60,000 BTUs of heat into the home while using only 23,600 BTUs of electricity.

The initial cost of a heat pump is a little more than that of a central heating system plus a central cooling system in new construction. Installation in an existing home may require additional insulation, or ductwork depending upon the home construction and heating system.

All-electric heat pumps offer the advantage of not polluting the air in your home. Furnishings may stay cleaner longer since there is no smoke, grime or soot from burning fossil fuels.

AIR CONDITIONING

Quiet, efficient central air conditioning systems can be added directly to most forced-air heating systems. The cooling coil fits into an existing furnace ductwork and is connected to a weather-resistant condensing unit located outdoors. The furnace fan provides air circulation.

This type of system is known as the split-system air conditioner and is offered in many capacities to fit most homes. One manufacturer, for example, offers 18 different models in capacities from 13,000 BTUs up to 70,000 BTUs.

In these days of mounting energy sources and costs, efficient home cooling performance is frequently referred to by Energy Efficiency Ratings (EER). The EER is a measure of the amount of cooling an air conditioner can do as related to the amount of electricity it uses. The higher the air conditioner's operating efficiency, or EER, the lower the operating cost per unit of cooling capacity.

EER might be compared with automobile gas mileage. The number of miles driven is divided by the number of gallons of gas consumed to arrive at the miles per gallon (mpg). The higher the gas mileage, the less gas is used by the car per mile.

The same is true in the air conditioner. To determine EER, divide the number of BTUs of cooling by the number of watts used. BTU cooling capacity and watts consumed are stated on the air conditioner nameplate.

The number of BTUs required to cool a room varies, depending upon the number of windows, outside walls, height of the ceiling, type of floor, number of people, lights and electrical equipment in use, and the doors and arches continuously open to unconditioned space. Manufacturers offer load calculators designed to help you determine your home cooling needs and it is wise to consult with a heating-cooling specialist before selecting a system.

Should you not wish to air condition your entire home, you may find a permanent or portable room air conditioner the answer to a specific room cooling problem. These units are offered in many capacities, sizes, and styles for use in sections of a window or through-the-wall in specially-designed metal sleeves.

Some room air conditioners are equipped with automatic controls that turn the air conditioner up or down, even off and on, as the room temperature changes. A few models are so designed that an electric air cleaner can be installed to capture dirt, dust, pollen, smoke and other pollutants from the circulated air. The cleaner fits behind the louvers of the air conditioner where it electronically charges air impurities and locks them like a magnet to the grid elements. It holds them until the element is removed for cleaning.

The profile of room air conditioners as well as central heating and cooling systems has changed substantially in recent years. Less space is required for units and their sleek design is coupled with quiet, efficient and trouble-free operation.

Central furnace units can be installed in many locations: a basement or closet, utility room or garage, crawl space or attic. These variations make possible up-flow and down-flow systems, or side-flow in right or left direction.

General Electric's intermediate and large-capacity air conditioners are now being equipped with a power-saver switch that helps reduce electrical consumption without sacrificing cooling. Savings up to 12 percent are possible when the unit is operated in the "save" position, which automatically shuts off the compressor and fan motor when the thermostat senses the room has reached the desired temperature.

A few square feet of space are all that is required for a year-round all-electric heat pump. This General Electric Weathertron pulls warm air out of the house during the summer and reverses the process in the winter.

Through-the-wall room air conditioners come in a variety of capacities and offer decorator styling. This Whirlpool unit has an American oak wood-grain front which complements the surrounding wood paneling.

New heating and cooling equipment generally is sold with a full one-year warranty covering all parts, except filters, found defective in materials or workmanship. You'll usually be responsible for any labor charges.

Some firms also offer service contracts to protect you against the cost of unexpected breakdowns. These contracts are available at the time of unit purchase and can include both parts and labor.

Design and installation of all types of heating and cooling systems should involve the services of a qualified heating contractor who can provide you with cost data related to your local fuel costs, equipment availability and installation practices.

SOLAR HEATING

Solar energy is expected to fulfill a significant percentage of residential energy needs over the next decade. Many believe that solar energy can handle all the heating and cooling needs of single-family residences in addition to heating the family swimming pool.

Considerable research is underway on developing methods of using solar energy and systems are in actual use in many areas of the country. At least two states — Indiana and Arizona — have passed incentive legislation to facilitate the installation of solar energy equipment for home use.

Solar energy offers the advantage of having almost no environmental pollution and no depletion of natural resources. While it costs more to install today (than oil, gas, electric systems), it is expected that rising fuel costs will make the system highly competitive in the near future.

PPG Industries, Inc., makers of glass for construction and other purposes, first introduced aluminum flat-plate solar collectors in 1974 and now has a new copper flat-plate collector for heating homes and their hot water supplies. The corrosion-resistant copper construction permits selection from a wide range of heating fluids, including water.

PPG's standard copper collector consists of a black-coated copper energy absorber plate and two clear heat-treated glass panels separated by an air space. Each unit — about 6 feet long and 3 feet wide — is encased in stainless steel and insulated with fiberglass backing. Energy absorbed by the copper plate is transmitted to copper tubes soldered onto the collector's back. A fluid circulating through the tubes is heated and piped to a thermal storage unit, which furnishes heat for a building's interior and hot water. Two models of this unit are available, one for the moderately sunny but colder northern climates, and a single-glazed, insulated collector for warmer locations.

A typical solar hot water system with from two to four standard copper collectors can meet a substantial portion of the hot water needs of a family of four. Such a system consists of the collectors — arrayed on a rooftop or separate structure and angled for maximum sun exposure — plus piping, pump and thermal storage unit.

HUMIDITY CONTROL

In most areas of the country, humidity control is desirable. Humidification is needed in the winter and dehumidification is wanted in the summer. The extent to which equipment can provide effective humidity control is largely determined by house design characteristics such as insulation, weatherstripping, double-glazing, etc.

Most warm-air heating plants have available accessory humidifiers for installation within the heating unit and are controlled electrically by means of a humidistat located in the living quarters.

Portable electrically operated humidifiers are available, incorporating a water reservoir, spray device and fan. These are the plug-in variety designed to operate from the standard 115 volt convenience outlet. Portable electrically operated dehumidifiers are also available for use in damp areas, particularly basements and utility rooms. These units usually incorporate a ⅛ or 1/6-HP refrigerating machine and are designed to plug into standard convenience outlets.

Depending upon size, typical units will remove from 13 to 27 pints of moisture per 24 hours. Automatic units can be set to the humidity level desired and will switch on or off accordingly. Automatic water level control automatically shuts the unit off when the moisture container is nearly full. Likewise, some units can be equipped with a drain hose which directs the water into a floor drain.

Dehumidification charts offered by equipment manufacturers will help you to determine the proper size unit for your specific situation. For example, during warm and humid outdoor conditions, a 1500 square-foot house with wet walls or floor sweat will require the removal of 26 pints of water per 24 hour period. If the area is just moderately damp with a musty odor only in humid weather, this same house will call for the removal of 18 pints per 24 hours.

WIRING

To realize the tremendous evolution of electrical living in the United States one has to only know that less than 2 percent of American homes were wired for electricity at the beginning of this century. Today we have upwards of 100 appliances at our disposal (there were only 19 in 1931) and most are readily taken for granted as standard necessities.

Years ago, most homes were wired for lighting and for a few appliances — washing machine, toaster, radio, ironer. The wiring installation was made according to code safety standards. But with continual growth in appliance usage these wiring systems have lost their convenience and flexibility.

In buying an older home it is well to understand some of the basics of home wiring so that you can determine if it is adequate to meet your family needs or if it will have to be improved to prevent possible safety hazards and gross inconvenience.

To begin with, your home must be wired according to the National Electrical Code, which is a basic minimum standard to safeguard persons and property from the hazards of electricity. Next, your home must meet local electrical codes which cover design standards for branch circuits, feeders, protective devices, service entrance arrangements, outlets, switches, wires, cables and other elements.

The discussion of each of these elements is not intended as an instruction manual for untrained persons. Be sure to engage the services of a qualified electrical service company in making any necessary changes in your home.

Electrical power supplied to your home is "dropped" from a utility company pole (or run underground) to a "service entrance" or panelboard located on either the outside or inside of a convenient exterior wall. These devices have been greatly improved in recent years and now offer almost unlimited circuitry to meet your electrical needs.

Up to six circuits can be served directly from the service entrance conductor. This means that multiple mains can be conveniently arranged to serve heavy-duty appliance circuits — for range, water heater, dryer — and feeders to branch circuit distribution panels and power centers. The rating of the service entrance will enable you to determine, for example, if you have enough power to add air conditioning or an electric water heater, or change to electric home heating.

Several types of circuits are essential in home wiring. Actually, six types are found in modern homes, three each related to 115-volt and 230-volt service. The first type in the 115-volt catagory serves two or more plug outlets for small appliances such as coffee makers, toasters, food mixers, etc. This circuit should be protected by a 20-ampere fuse or circuit breaker, and adequate for loads up to 2300 watts. In newer homes, you may find two of these circuits serving the kitchen area.

A second type of 115-volt circuit (similar to the first) handles small appliances plus lighting. It will have a 2300 watt capacity. The third type of 115-volt circuit may be similar to the first but with a single outlet or single-use special circuit designed to serve 115-volt appliances such as dishwasher, food waste disposal unit, or small room air conditioner.

In the 230-volt classification, all three circuit types are single-outlet, special-purpose circuits for serving such items as ranges, clothes dryer, large air conditioners, etc. Capacities, depending upon size of wire, are 11,500, 6900 and 4600 watts.

Keeping in mind that the 2300 watt capacity of a circuit is able to simultaneously operate a 1000-watt hand iron and a 1200-watt dishwasher, it's easy to see that the addition of a 1200-watt toaster would boost the load on the circuit beyond its rated capacity. Here is where you encounter overload and possible danger. With a circuit protected by a properly matched fuse or circuit breaker, power would cease everywhere and you would have to replace the fuse or reset the breaker (after turning off one of the appliances, of course) and you would be back in business. If the wires and safety devices were not properly matched (as possible in older homes) overheating could build up in walls where the wires are buried, and cause a fire hazard.

In working with the electrical designer in making system improvements for your home, it is good practice to calculate a 20 percent spare capacity into each circuit over and above its maximum probable use. On a general-purpose circuit, the normal load of lights and portable appliances usually will not exceed 50 percent of the rated circuit capacity. This provides sufficient extra capacity for temporary portable appliances.

Use of a dimmer control can reduce voltage and wattage substantially and increase bulb life by 4 to 40 times. A 10 percent reduction in voltage saves 15 percent on wattage. And a 25 percent reduction in voltage will save 36 percent on wattage. Shown here are a variety of energy savers by Leviton including: (61000) incandescent rotary dimmer for lighting control; (6602) Trimatron compact dimmer for quick installation; (6151) replacement socket for converting any lamp into an infinitely variable light source; (6156) a table-top dimmer for controlling table, pole or swag lights; (6250) a lamp cord dimmer that converts any table or portable incandescent lamp into a mood-setting dimmer lamp.

Few homes have a sufficient number of convenience outlets in which to plug lamps, television, electric blankets, etc. Good general practice calls for duplex outlet placement so that no point along the floor line of an unbroken wall space is more than six feet from an outlet. This covers living rooms, dining rooms, bedrooms, family rooms and general living areas. A convenience outlet should be located every 12 feet in hallways.

In kitchens and workshops, spacing of outlets should be reduced to four feet behind all working counters and benches. Lavatory bowl and medicine cabinet placement dictates convenience outlet location in bathrooms and powder rooms.

Exterior convenience outlets should be weatherproof and located for each 15 feet of usable wall space on porches, terraces and patios. Many outdoor lamp posts come equipped with convenience outlets which prove handy when using electric shrub trimmers, lawn clippers and power mowers.

Numerous types of switches on the market today make it possible to correctly and safely control all residential electrical equipment. Beyond the common wall switch, you can choose from units which turn lights on and off as the door opens and closes, to the more romantic dimmer controls which permit you to dial just the amount of illumination desired at the moment.

Certain switching practices are "musts" for every home including:

- light control at every entryway to a given area or room;

- switches at the top and bottom of stairways;

- timer controls on heating lamps to prevent accidental overuse;

- interior control switches for exterior lighting at entrances, garage front and on patios;

- switch-and-pilot light combination to show at a glance that power is being supplied to a freezer or that the basement lights are "off" when the area is closed off by a door.

Some homeowners building or remodeling find a bedside master control switch a great convenience. It permits them to control nightlights, outdoor floodlighting, bathroom electric heater, coffeemaker start-up, and all interior lighting without moving from room to room.

Multi-point and distant control of lighting (from such areas as the bedside) has been perfected in recent years through the use of low-voltage wiring whereby a relay unit isolates all switches from 115-volt circuits and permits long runs of inexpensive wiring. Low-voltage control is ideal for house modernization jobs where existing control is operated at line voltage, which is the case in most American homes.

Electrical Demand Factors and Load Calculation

Ckt. No.	Location	Lighting Outlets	Conven. Outlets	Estimated Watts	Amperes	Conductor No. & Size	Watts Load
1-G	Dining, Laundry, Living	4	3	1250	15		
2-G	Entry, Kitchen, Bath No. 2	5	1	1250	15	3-#14	
3-G	Hall, Den, Bedroom No. 1	3	4	1100	15		
4-G	Bedroom No. 2, Bath No. 1	3	4	900	15	2-#14, 1-#12*	
	NOTE: General lighting circuits total 4500 watts or 3.00 watts/sq. ft.						
5-A	Kitchen, Dining		4	1000	20	2-#12	
6-A	Kitchen, Laundry		4	1000	20	2-#12**	
7-A	Dining, Laundry		3	750	20	2-#12	
8-A	Garage-Workshop		3	1250	20	2-#12	
				8500			
			First	3000	@ 100%		3000
			Balance:	5500	@ 35% (approx)		2000
9-I	Range: 12kw model, max demand 8kw		1			2-#8, 1-#10	8000
10-I	Water Heater		1	4000	20	2-#10	
11-I	Bathroom Heater		1	1500	20	2-#12	
12-I	Furnace (1/4 & 1/200 HP motors)		1	600	20	2-#12	
13-I	Automatic Washer (1/6 HP motor)		1	450	20	2-#12	
14-I	Dishwasher		1	1000	20	2-#12	
				7550	@ 75% (approx)		5700
							18,700

Calculated load for service size: Watts (18,700) divided by Volts (230) = Amperes (81.3) = 100-ampere service

Watts (18,700) divided by Volts (230) = Amperes (81.3) = 100-ampere service

* This #12 conductor is neutral common to circuit No. 11-I

** One of these #12 conductors is neutral common to circuit No. 13-I

Home Circuit Listing and Load Estimate for a 1,750 square foot one-story home to assist in making your own load calculation. Circuit numbers are grouped into general purpose, appliance and individual circuits. Estimating practice may vary somewhat in different areas; inquire about local practices from electric utility company.

Allowable Wiring in Electrical Boxes

Box Size (inches)	Maximum Number Of Conductors			
	No. 14	No. 12	No. 10	No. 8
1-¼ × 3-¼ octagonal	5	5	4	0
1-½ × 4 octagonal	8	7	6	5
1-½ × 4 square	11	9	7	5
1-½ × 4-11/16 square	16	12	10	8
2-1/8 × 4-11/16 square	20	16	12	10
1-3/4 × 2-3/4 × 2	5	4	4	4
1-3/4 × 2-3/4 × 2-½	6	6	5	4
1-3/4 × 2-3/4 × 3	7	7	6	4

Box Capacities for Wiring depend upon conductor sizes. Chart indicates the maximum number of conductors allowed by box size.

Grounded and Grounding

In electrical terminology, there is a distinct difference between "grounded" and "grounding." The current-carrying conductor that has a white or neutral grey color (or in sizes above No. 6 have white marks at terminals) is a neutral conductor. It runs through the circuitry back through the distribution panel and perhaps to the service entrance, to be attached to a single system ground. This may be provided by a clamp on the cold-water main-supply line coming up from underground. In other cases, it may be connected to an outdoor ground pipe driven adjacent to the meter location. Such an electrical system is a "grounded" system. In addition, it is now required practice to provide what amounts to emergency "grounding" of all electrical system enclosures, boxes, switches, receptacles, lighting-fixture metal parts. This is done by grounding wires screwed or clipped to outlet boxes. Remember colors. White or grey for neutral conductors with a system ground connection at only one point. Green for enclosure, fixture and box grounding wires.

The exception to this rule for conductor insulation colors occurs with cable runs to switch legs. A switch is an interrupting device in a hot line to a fixture or device.

Certain runs can be of 3-wire cable (or conduit containing two hot conductors and one neutral to serve two circuits). As the NEC explains, such 3-wire circuits can supply a load that would need four conductors if 2-wire circuits were used. And the percentage of voltage drop is only half as great in 3-wire circuitry as in 2-wire. However, in using 3-wire conductors or cable for two circuits, each "side" should be suitably balanced by an approximately equal number of outlets or probable load. Voltage drop or loss is greater for longer conductor runs. Minimize lowered voltage wherever possible, by keeping runs as short as possible.

Note the difference, too, between this type of 3-wire circuitry which has 115 volts per side with no outlets providing service to 230-volt devices or equipment, and the 3-wire circuits using heavier conductor sizes to provide 230-volt service on individual circuits.

Ground Fault Interrupters

A 1975 series of revisions in the National Electrical Code resulted in some new requirements for residential electrical systems and their use of grounding-type outlet receptacles.

While the grounding system as evidenced by the use of 3-hole receptacles for 3-prong plugs gave protection to circuits and appliances in case of serious short or overload, it was possible for electric current to leak to the grounding channel in small amounts insufficient to trip protective breakers, but more than adequate to cause serious shocks to people. The grounding system, in other words, doesn't protect people against shocks from touching parts of outlet boxes, tools or equipment with grounding leakage.

The device developed to meet this hazard is called a "ground fault interrupter." It constantly monitors the grounding circuit and when it detects any small flow of current in the range between 5 and 15 milli-amperes, it interrupts the circuit, shutting it off. Thus, a person who touches such a faulty grounding part or cover may induce a more direct flow of such small current to ground through his body. He'll receive an initial shock but the interrupter operates within 1/40 of a second and so the victim can then free himself and thereby avoid serious shock injury.

GFI protection is now required by NEC on all 15-amp and 20-amp receptacle outlets installed in bathrooms, or outdoors or within 15 feet of swimming pools. Also for any outlets used to connect submersible pumps or fountains. GFI-protective devices come in two forms — a circuit breaker that installs in a distribution panel and protects an entire circuit, and a standard GFI outlet receptacle that gives protection only to the devices plugged into that particular outlet. GFI protection is also NEC-required for outlets for temporary wiring at construction sites. Both types of GFI protective devices contain a reset button to bring the device back into readiness again after the fault has been corrected, and a test button to determine whether the device is operable and in working order. The test button should be pushed regularly to verify that the GFI protection is in effect.

Signal Circuits

Commonly called bell or intercom circuits, these signal circuits according to the NEC supply energy "to an appliance that gives a recognizable signal." Such a signal might be the doorbell, buzzer, chime, code-calling system, signal light, intercom-music system, speaker wiring, or various alarm or detection device connections.

For doorbell, door-chime and radio-intercom-music systems, light-duty insulated wire conductors can be strong and stapled into place without need for any sheathing, conduit or other special protection. For door-chime purposes, the common conductor remains the same as it has been for years, AWG No. 18 size wire. But whereas it used to come with a waxed spiral wrapping today's bell wire is usually plastic-wrapped.

For intercom-music equipment designed to incorporate branch stations in various rooms and at entry doors, check the manufacturer's specifications and instructions. The wiring runs between stations and to the main control unit will usually involve multi-wire cable with a specific number of color-coded conductors of a specific size.

Another type of low-voltage wiring installed in many new homes is that used for telephone service at several locations within the home. Prior to installing, check with your local telephone company to find out what their practice is with new homes. In some cases wiring is strung and stapled into

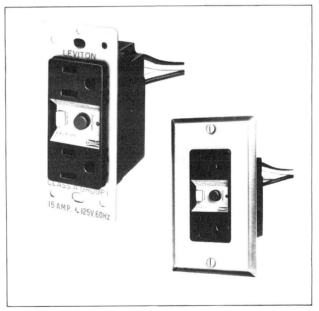

Ground Fault Interrupter is combined with a duplex convenience outlet in this Leviton-made device which should be used for outdoor outlets and in other hazardous locations where the entire circuit is not protected by a GFT-type breaker at the circuit distribution panel. The interrupter is sensitive to leaking current protecting against the possibility of serious shocks. It includes a test button to verify proper operating condition.

place much like other signal circuits. In other cases, the phone company may want to have short runs of conduit from a telephone outlet location to an accessible space such as an attic or crawl space.

Except for telephone wiring, the signal circuits at some point or other will require connection to line voltage of 115 volts. In the case of intercom-music equipment, that is usually done at the main control panel which comes with a rough-in enclosure or mounting bracket to which an outlet box is attached. This is then wired in with the house circuitry just like a general-purpose outlet. The same may apply for fire- and burglar-alarm devices.

The signal system for door-chimes or bells-buzzers usually operates on 24 volts. A transformer is needed to provide this low voltage. Door-chime suppliers can furnish small transformers for this purpose. They may mount by screws adjacent to an outlet box or junction box, or may be equipped with an integral connector that fits a box knock-out hole. Bell wire runs then are made from the transformer's output terminals to the front and rear entry doors, with the leads being brought down to small drilled holes adjacent to the door jambs on the knob side.

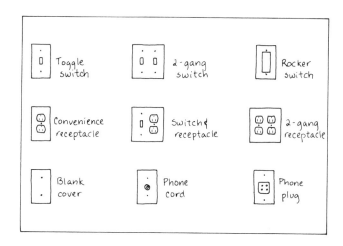

Types of Wall Plates for Devices come in a wide range of styles, finishes and colors. Shown: standard-sized plates and common two-gang or combination devices.

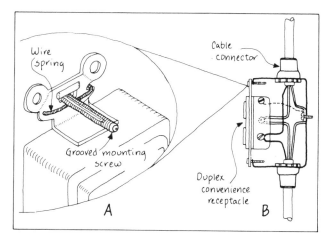

Receptacle Grounding Detail indicates two methods of providing adequate electrical bonding of the switch or outlet receptacle to the electrical box to maintain grounding continuity. In sketch (A), a built-in wire spring is provided in some devices so proper box contact is made when the device is screwed to the box. In sketch (B), an alternative method. The dashed line represents a bonding jumper wire from the bonding screw terminal to the box ground screw. The National Electrical Code requires bonding of all electrical system enclosures such as raceways, cable armor, cable sheath, frames, fittings and noncurrent-carrying metal parts.

LIGHTING

Structural lighting or "built-in" lighting can be a basic part of every room in the home. Among the many built-in possibilities are lighted cornices, luminous ceilings, lighted wall brackets, valances, and concealed or recessed spot or flood bulbs.

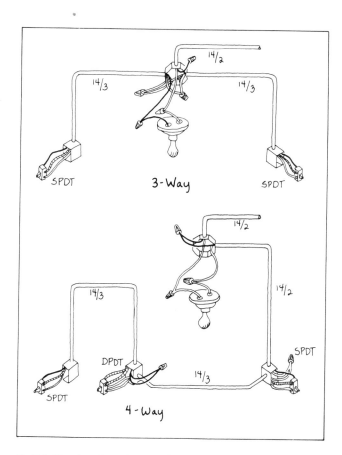

Switch Circuits where the same lighting outlet is to be controlled from more than one location such as the top and bottom of stairs. In the sketch, the striped conductor represents the hot red-insulated conductor in a cable, black is for the black-insulated and the white for white or grey insulation of the neutral conductor. In these cases, as required by the National Electrical Code, the neutral is serving as the return conductor from switch to outlet and should have its white or grey insulation painted blue at the switch and outlets.

Structural lighting as opposed to portable lamps, can be incorporated into niches, alcoves, panels, room dividers as well as entire walls and ceilings. Both incandescent and fluorescent fixtures are widely used for these purposes.

Because structural lighting is built right into the walls and ceilings, it can be designed to blend with any period decorative motif or color scheme. It can blend or contrast with its background. And since it has very little styling, structural lighting does not become dated in appearance.

With structural lighting, colors of wall coverings and draperies become more vivid and windows have daytime charm, even after dark. Because the major source of light in the room is the entire wall surface instead of a small fixture or lamp, the resulting room lighting is soft and relatively shadow-free. This "horizontal" lighting molds forms and features in a more flattering way than light from above or below.

The three basic structural lighting techniques for walls are: (1) valance, used with a window; (2) wall bracket, fluorescent used like a valance only away from the window; and (3) cornice, which is mounted at the junction of wall and ceiling either at the window or away from the window. Accompanying lighting data sheets show construction for each of these methods.

The lighted valance usually directs light both upward over the ceiling and downward over the wall and drapery.

Face boards can either be simple and unobtrusive or stylishly decorated.

Fluorescent wall brackets can be used in any room, high on the wall for general lighting, or lower on the wall for specific task lighting, such as above a bed headboard.

Installation of fluorescent brackets for lighting valances is relatively simple with prewired channels holding all the necessary equipment — a ballast, starter and two lamp holders or sockets. Holes in the channel simplify attachment to the wall with screws. (Photo: General Electric).

Suggested Home Lighting Levels

Room Size	A. Surface and Pendent Fixtures*		B. Recessed Fixtures*	C. Wall Lighting**
	Minimum Size of Shield	Minimum Bulb(s) or Watts per sq. ft.	Minimum Wattage or Watts per sq. ft.	Length of light source; or Wattage and spacing of fixtures
VERY SMALL (Up to 125 sq. ft.)	12" to 15"	One 100-watt or Three 40-watt	150-watt fixture for each 75 sq. ft. floor area or fraction thereof	6' or 75-watt fixtures on 3' centers
AVERAGE (125 to 225 sq. ft.)	15" to 17"	One 150-watt or Four 40-watt	150-watt fixture for each 75 sq. ft. floor area or fraction thereof	8' to 12' or 75-watt fixtures on 3' centers
LARGE (Over 225 sq. ft.)	17" to 22"	100 watts for each 100 sq. ft. *footnote	150-watt fixture for each 75 sq. ft. floor area or fraction thereof	16' to 20' or 75-watt fixtures on 3' centers

*More than one fixture is usually needed on ceilings and/or walls for minimum general lighting. Dining area fixture should provide predominant downlight on table.
**Fixture recommendation applies to lighting one long wall. For most effective design, consult electric utility, lighting fixture distributor, or manufacturers' booklets.

Guidelines for Lighting Intensities are given in this chart prepared by the American Home Lighting Institute. The chart was issued prior to the focussing of attention on energy conservation and the wattage intensities given may accept a bit of trimming in the interests of lower utility bills.

STRUCTURAL LIGHTING DATA SHEET • LIGHTED BRACKET

HIGH BRACKET

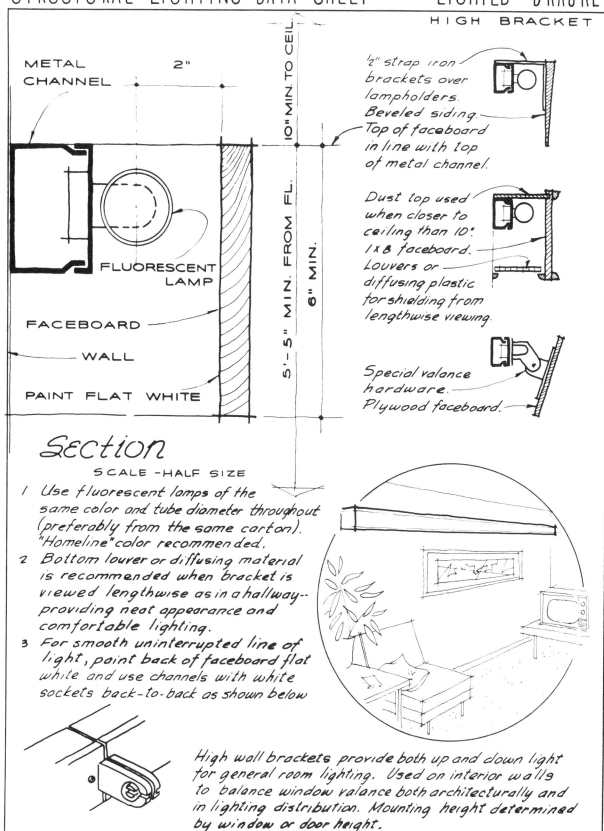

METAL
CHANNEL

2"

FLUORESCENT
LAMP

FACEBOARD

WALL

PAINT FLAT WHITE

10" MIN. TO CEIL.

5'-5" MIN. FROM FL.

6" MIN.

½" strap iron
brackets over
lampholders.
Beveled siding.
Top of faceboard
in line with top
of metal channel.

Dust top used
when closer to
ceiling than 10".
1 x 8 faceboard.
Louvers or
diffusing plastic
for shielding from
lengthwise viewing.

Special valance
hardware.
Plywood faceboard.

Section

SCALE –HALF SIZE

1 Use fluorescent lamps of the
same color and tube diameter throughout
(preferably from the same carton).
"Homeline" color recommended.

2 Bottom louver or diffusing material
is recommended when bracket is
viewed lengthwise as in a hallway--
providing neat appearance and
comfortable lighting.

3 For smooth uninterrupted line of
light, paint back of faceboard flat
white and use channels with white
sockets back-to-back as shown below

High wall brackets provide both up and down light
for general room lighting. Used on interior walls
to balance window valance both architecturally and
in lighting distribution. Mounting height determined
by window or door height.

STRUCTURAL LIGHTING DATA SHEET • LIGHTED BRACKET

LOW BRACKET

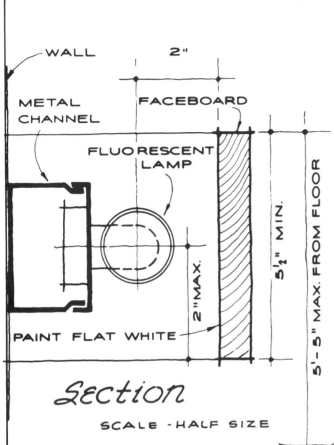

WALL

METAL CHANNEL

2"

FACEBOARD

FLUORESCENT LAMP

5½" MIN.

2" MAX.

5'-5" MAX. FROM FLOOR

PAINT FLAT WHITE

Section

SCALE - HALF SIZE

½" strap iron brackets under lampholders. 1 x 6 faceboard.

Glass or plastic set in top of shelf. ¾" x 5" faceboard.

Hardboard or metal end returns. Side mounted channel. Lamp placed more than 2" above bottom of faceboard when slanted faceboard used.

1 Use fluorescent lamps of the same color and tube diameter throughout (preferably from the same carton). "Homeline" color recommended.
2 Exact position of channel relative to faceboard determined by actual viewing angle in use. Usually should be no higher than 2" above bottom of faceboard for good downward lighting.
3 For smooth uninterrupted line of light, paint back of faceboard flat white and use channels with white sockets back-to-back as shown below.

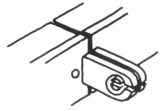

Low brackets are used for special wall emphasis or for lighting specific tasks such as sink, range, reading in bed, etc. Mounting height is determined by both seated and standing eye height of users.

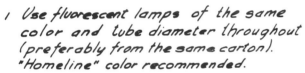

49

STRUCTURAL LIGHTING DATA SHEET·FLUORESCENT EQUIPMENT

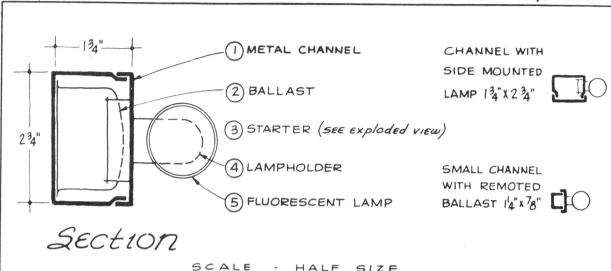

1. METAL CHANNEL
2. BALLAST
3. STARTER (SEE EXPLODED VIEW)
4. LAMPHOLDER
5. FLUORESCENT LAMP

CHANNEL WITH SIDE MOUNTED LAMP 1¾" X 2¾"

SMALL CHANNEL WITH REMOTED BALLAST 1¼" x ⅞"

Section

SCALE - HALF SIZE

1. METAL CHANNEL is required for fluorescent equipment used in structural lighting. Three recommended lengths for use with T-12 lamps (see item 5) are 48"-40-watt, 36"-30-watt, and 24"-20-watt. For uninterrupted line of light use type with lampholders mounted flush with ends of channel (see item 4).

2. BALLAST is required to stabilize lamp operation. Desirable features are "certified" label, "high power factor" and "A" or "B" sound rating. For quick starting use "trigger start" ballast with 20-w lamps and "rapid start" ballasts with 30-w - 40-w lamps

3. STARTER is required with conventional ballasts and lamps. Lamps start with a slight delay. Use FS-2 with 20-w lamps and FS-4 with 40-w lamps. Specify "certified" starters. Trigger and rapid start circuits need no starters.

4. LAMPHOLDERS should be flush with ends of channel so they will be back-to-back in continuous rows. White lampholders recommended

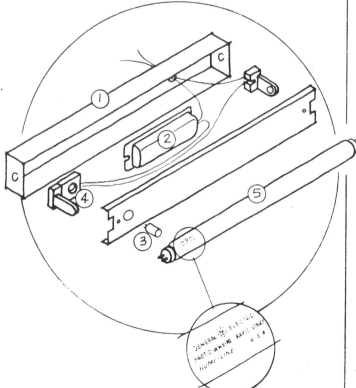

5. FLUORESCENT LAMPS used in structural lighting should be 1½" in diameter, (T-12 size). "Homeline" color recommended. For fast starting in 30-w and 40-w sizes use lamps marked "rapid start" and use with rapid start ballasts. Conventional 20-w lamp may be used with "trigger start" or conventional ballasts.

STRUCTURAL LIGHTING DATA SHEET • LIGHTED SOFFIT

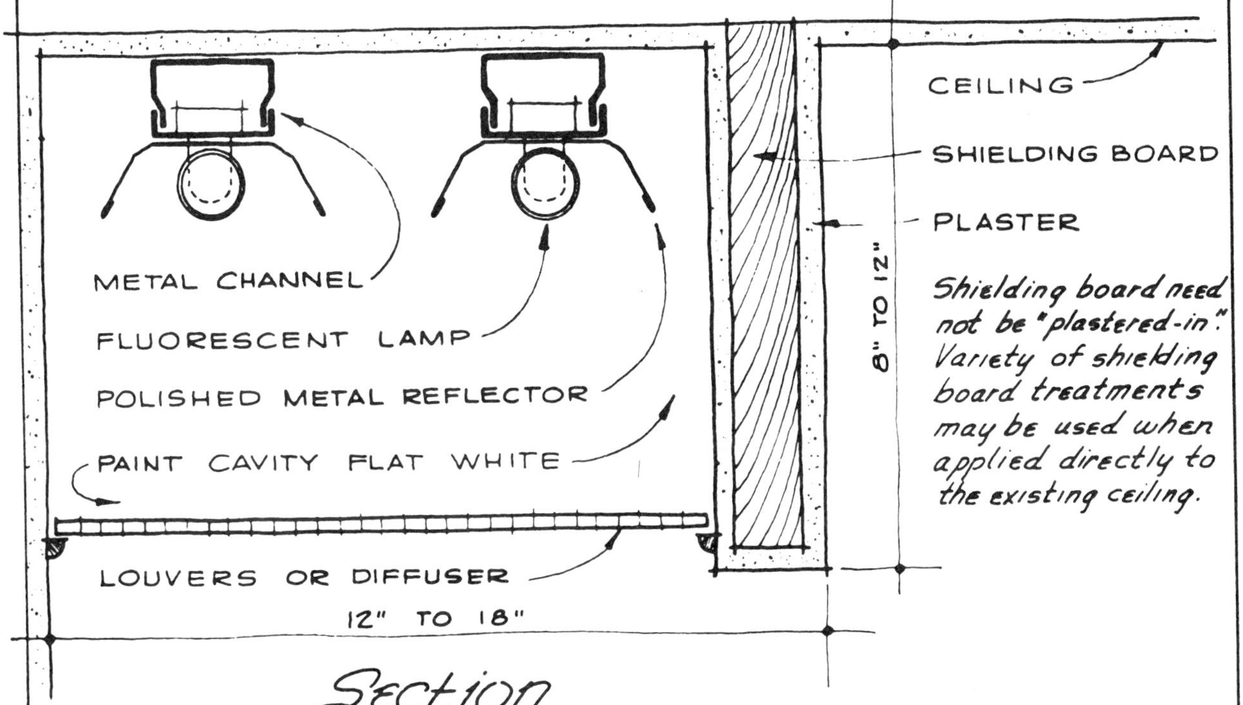

METAL CHANNEL

FLUORESCENT LAMP

POLISHED METAL REFLECTOR

PAINT CAVITY FLAT WHITE

LOUVERS OR DIFFUSER

12" TO 18"

8" TO 12"

CEILING

SHIELDING BOARD

PLASTER

Shielding board need not be "plastered-in." Variety of shielding board treatments may be used when applied directly to the existing ceiling.

Section

SCALE 3" = 1'-0"

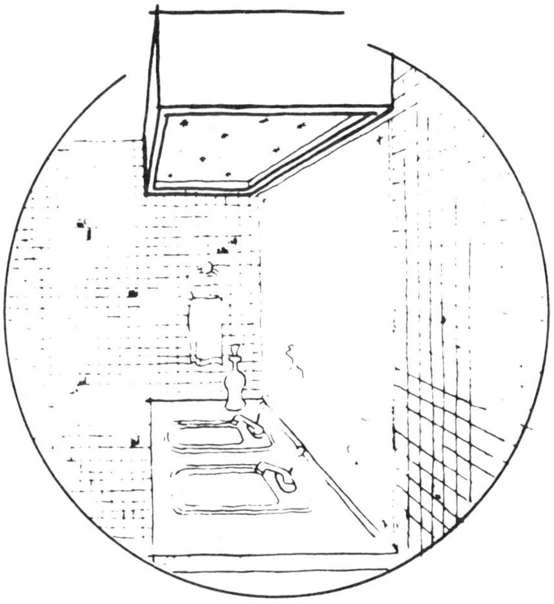

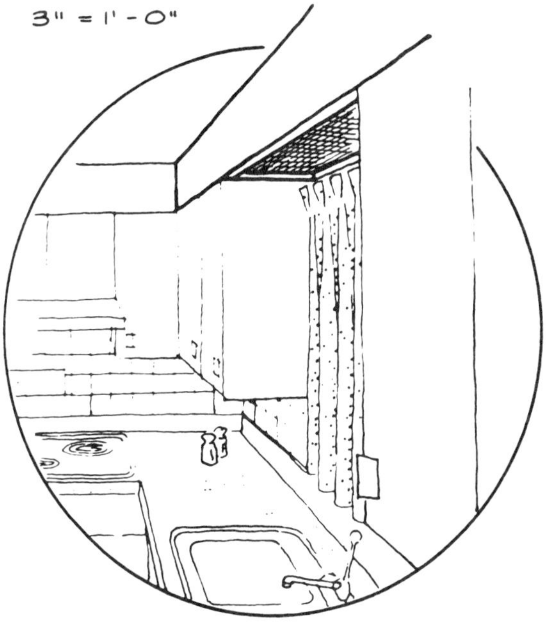

FOR PERSONAL GROOMING
Bath or dressing room soffits are designed to light users face. Therefore cover bottom opening with highly diffusing material which will scatter light toward face. Wide bottom opening (14" to 18") helps also. Light-colored counter top reflects light under chin.

HORIZONTAL TASK LIGHTING
Soffits over work areas are designed to provide high level of light directly below. Polished reflectors can double light output and increase comfort when used with louvers or very lightly diffusing glass or plastic in the bottom opening.

STRUCTURAL LIGHTING DATA SHEET • LIGHTED CORNICE

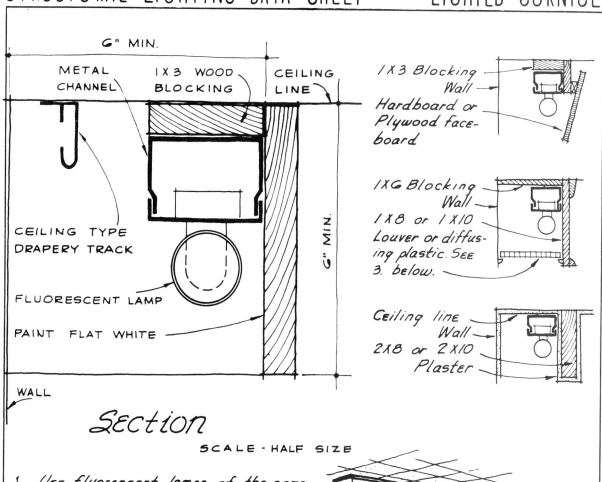

6" MIN.

METAL CHANNEL

1 X 3 WOOD BLOCKING

CEILING LINE

CEILING TYPE DRAPERY TRACK

FLUORESCENT LAMP

PAINT FLAT WHITE

6" MIN.

WALL

1 X 3 Blocking
Wall
Hardboard or Plywood face-board

1 X 6 Blocking
Wall
1 X 8 or 1 X 10 Louver or diffus-ing plastic. See 3. below.

Ceiling line
Wall
2 X 8 or 2 X 10
Plaster

Section

SCALE - HALF SIZE

1. Use fluorescent lamps of the same color and tube diameter throughout (preferably from the same carton). "Homeline" color recommended.

2. Place channel as close to faceboard as possible for best shielding. Bottom louver or diffuser is recommended when cornice is viewed lengthwise.

3. For smooth uninterrupted line of light, paint inside of faceboard flat white and use channels with white lampholders back-to-back as shown below.

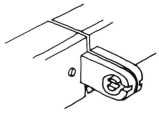

Cornices direct all their light downward to give dramatic interest to wall coverings, draperies, murals, etc. May also be used over windows where space above window does not permit valance lighting. Good for low-ceilinged rooms.

STRUCTURAL LIGHTING DATA SHEET • LIGHTED VALANCE

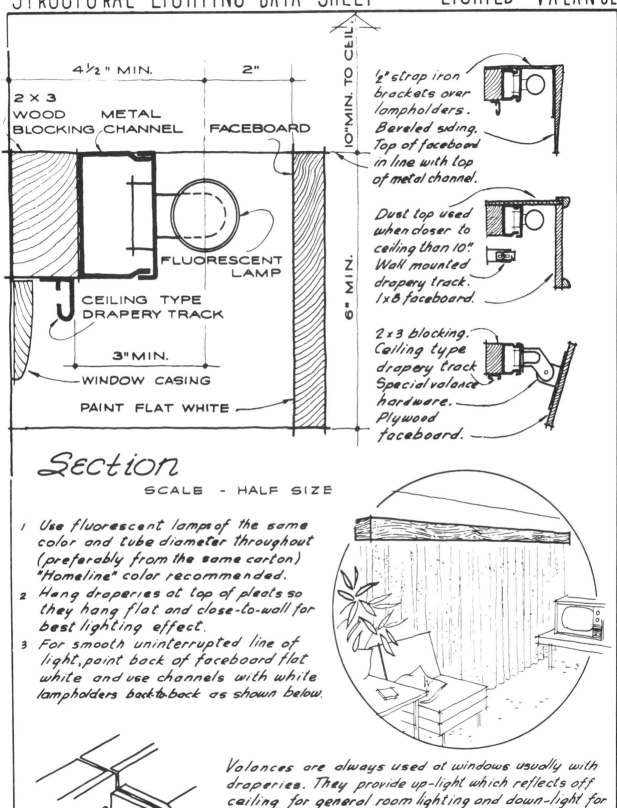

4½" MIN. 2"

2 X 3 WOOD BLOCKING   METAL CHANNEL   FACEBOARD

10" MIN. TO CEIL.

FLUORESCENT LAMP

6" MIN.

CEILING TYPE DRAPERY TRACK

3" MIN.

WINDOW CASING

PAINT FLAT WHITE

½" strap iron brackets over lampholders. Beveled siding. Top of faceboard in line with top of metal channel.

Dust top used when closer to ceiling than 10". Wall mounted drapery track. 1x8 faceboard.

2 x 3 blocking. Ceiling type drapery track. Special valance hardware. Plywood faceboard.

Section

SCALE - HALF SIZE

1. Use fluorescent lamps of the same color and tube diameter throughout (preferably from the same carton) "Homeline" color recommended.
2. Hang draperies at top of pleats so they hang flat and close-to-wall for best lighting effect.
3. For smooth uninterrupted line of light, paint back of faceboard flat white and use channels with white lampholders back-to-back as shown below.

Valances are always used at windows usually with draperies. They provide up-light which reflects off ceiling for general room lighting and down-light for drapery accent. When closer to ceiling than 10" use closed top to eliminate annoying ceiling brightness.

Cornice lighting directs all of the light downward onto the wall surface below giving emphasis to a mural, paintings and wall hangings. Because the wall is emphasized, the cornice gives an impression of greater ceiling height, as is sometimes desirable in basements and attics.

Soffit lighting is highly desirable in kitchen work areas above the sink and in bathrooms and dressing rooms above mirrors and vanities. Such applications should have two fluorescent lamps.

Literally thousands of different incandescent lighting fixtures are available for home remodeling. These units are designed in most instances for specific applications, such as pull-down pendants for use above a dining room table, or post lanterns for illuminating the driveway and entry to a house. Shapes, materials, finishes, styles and sizes create virtually unlimited selections.

Cove lighting involves units usually mounted high on the walls with all of the light being directed upward to the ceiling. This "indirect" illumination produces a soft effect. Coves are particularly suited to rooms with two ceiling levels.

Self-luminous walls and wall panels are another way of making rooms appear brighter and even larger. The best lighting results are obtained when a special cavity can be built 10 to 14 inches deep in the wall to give the front plastic diffuser an even distribution of light. In residential interiors, however, it is difficult to find this space and luminous panels have to be made to fit into the existing 2x4 and 2x6 inch stud spaces.

A number of practical dimmers are available for the control of fluorescent and incandescent lamps in residential applications. All will fit into 2x4 inch stud walls and are easy to install and operate, making it possible for you to dial just the amount of lighting you wish for your particular mood. It's advisable to follow the manufacturers' instructions for best results.

Luminous Ceilings

Luminous ceiling panels create an air of spaciousness and are often used in kitchens, bathrooms, entry halls and other areas of the home. The design varies with the room size and proportion and usually is applicable in rooms where high ceilings permit plastic diffusers to be dropped 10 to 12 inches. Manufacturers of these ceilings provide design and installation instructions for their specific products.

LIVING-DINING-FAMILY ROOMS, BEDROOMS AND FIREPLACES

LIVING ROOMS

Homeowners usually put their best foot forward in the living room. It's where guests are entertained, where conversation is at its best, and where the family presents its mode of living.

Unfortunately, in some older home designs the living room is also where guests first land complete with wet boots and rain gear, and where all family members enter to get from one area of the home to another. This is regrettable and should be avoided, if possible, in selecting a home.

Center-hall style homes and those with separate foyers help solve this problem, but many homeowners have to rely on the careful selection and placement of furniture to create a more practical traffic pattern for the home.

Living room furniture groupings are best arranged when they create conversation areas within a 10-foot diameter. Very large rooms often can accommodate several such circles, each independent yet related via a decorative scheme.

Elements of a good living room are many and vary with the personal tastes of the owners. A formal setting can be

Combination living room-dining room arrangements found in many older homes can be physically and visually separated with a partial room divider. This floor-to-ceiling partition was constructed with 2x6 wood members and durable plastic panels. Photo: Celotex Corp.

Paneling is one of the most used materials in remodeling family rooms. Once a full room visible from the kitchen, this setting now includes a divider wall which defines an informal dining area. Wrought-iron rails enhance the step-down from hallway (Photo: U.S. Plywood Corp.)

beautiful to one family, while another prefers a more modern arrangement. All types should have pleasant views and adequate wall space for furniture.

Arrangement of furnishings is the most important element of good interior design. The ideal arrangement is not always visually satisfying because of the placement of doors, windows, and other architectural features. However, it is usually possible to make any arrangement attractive through careful selection of color, pattern, texture, and attention to form and scale. Do not avoid an arrangement merely because it is unusual.

DINING ROOM

The relationship of the dining room to the kitchen is far more important than its relation to the living room. Preferably, the dining room should be somewhat secluded from the street and, again, should not be a room that is used as a footpath to all other areas of the house.

A pass-through opening between the kitchen and dining room is a convenient step-saver, but it becomes more attractive when it is unseen. This can be accomplished by installing a mirror wall around the counter, so that when mirrored doors are closed, the opening vanishes.

Living rooms that are entered immediately from the entrance can be modified to create a "separate" entry hall by means of partial room dividers. This not only simplifies day-to-day maintenance but also enhances the room setting. (Photo: Western Wood Products Association).

Multi-purpose family rooms can be created in minimum spaces such as this 12 foot 6 inch x 11 foot 5 inch area fashioned into a den "extra room". The bookcases surround the stereo center and repeat the textured grasscloth wall covering. The corner seating can be set up as a single bed (Photo: Magnavox Company). ➞

Framed and structural mirrors can do much for dining rooms that are short and boxy, or dining corners that suffer from claustrophobia. If one mirrored wall can double a room's dimensions, the joining of two mirrored walls will quadruple the apparent size of an area. Mirrored end walls greatly highlight dining room settings.

In planning any dining room remodeling give consideration to the placement of electrical outlets, decorative lighting fixtures that will beautify the room, and built-in cabinetry that can be used to display treasured china. Corner china cabinets are common to many older homes, and provide both functional and decorative appeal.

FAMILY ROOM

The family room may be a recent "invention" in the minds of some, but the area is one that has been around for a long, long time. It was located between the parlor and the dining room in the author's grandfather's home, complete with pot-bellied stove, library table and rocker. Seldom did we, as children, use the parlor, but the family room was there for all to enjoy.

Today's family room rivals the family kitchen for busy activity. It is the entertainment hub complete with television, stereo, game tables, fireplace, built-ins for collections and hobbies, wet bar for serving convenience, and many more features related to each given family's needs and likes.

Location of the family room in older homes can vary considerably. It may be the finished recreation room in the basement; an old sitting room that has been brought to life; an attached garage conversion; or even a new extension of the home or the enclosure of a side porch that heretofore could be used only several months of the year.

Family rooms can be sewing centers, children's play rooms, pool rooms, dens, studies, added dining space, an extra guest room — anything you make of them. And like the living and dining rooms, furnishings of the family room will reflect your way of living.

Mirrors and full-mirror walls can create the illusion of greater space in cramped areas such as hallways. The mirrored wall also reflects and increases natural light, diminishing the need for artificial light in a room. Framed mirrors are available in a wide range of styles to highlight any decor (Photo: PPG Industries, Inc.).

57

BEDROOMS

Once the domain only of the weary and sleepy and avoided during daylight hours, the bedroom today has become a round-the-clock living area. In selecting a new home for your family, careful attention should be given to bedroom needs and to basic improvements that can be made for the enjoyment of individual family members.

In a most extensive study on bedrooms, the Small Homes Council of the University of Illinois determined "the most efficient bedroom for a given set of needs is the smallest bedroom which will accommodate the required furniture and allow access to the furniture and adequate floor space for dressing, sleeping and cleaning."

Naturally, the master or primary bedroom of the house should be larger than secondary bedrooms usually inhabited by children. All bedrooms should have easy access to a bathroom, and it is an American preference that the master bedroom have its own bathroom whenever possible.

Over the years bed sizes have grown to catch up with the taller generation. The old double bed (54 inches x 75 inches) has most often been replaced by a queen size (60 inches x 80 inches) or a king (75 inches x 80 inches) and it's no wonder when you calculate that the standard double is just twice the width of the standard 27 inch x 48 inch baby crib.

HUD Minimum Property Standards, used as a guide in building new homes, requires at least one uninterrupted wall space of at least 10 feet in the primary (master) bedroom and a minimum "least dimension" of 8 feet in the secondary bedroom.

Usable bedroom space, of course, is dictated principally by the location of doors, windows and storage cabinets. Corner door placement is generally preferred as it doesn't break up a wall span. Likewise, corner windows permit better furniture placement and high ribbon-style windows should be avoided as they would be hard to get out of in an emergency.

Basically, an 8 x 10 foot bedroom will accommodate a single twin bed; a 10 x 14 foot 4 inch or 11 foot 8 inch x 12 foot 8 inch bedroom will take two twin beds; a 10 foot 4 x 11 foot 8 inch bedroom can accommodate a full-size bed. These dimensions are based on the use of standard-size dresser, night stand and chair, plus proper location of doors and windows which will permit placement of the bed to give a 28-inch wide space on one side, 40 inch wide space on the other side and at the end of the bed, and a 28-inch wide area between twin beds.

Master bedrooms in recent years have been substantially increased in size to permit the inclusion of desk, chaise lounge, coffee table and other furniture for such assorted pursuits as sewing, reading, record-keeping, telephoning, letter-writing, and watching or listening to TV, radio or stereo.

Designer William Pahlmann, FAID, created this bedroom for an active young boy. Built-ins simplify daily clean-up (Photo courtesy Venetian Blind Institute).

This bedroom remodeling created a master bath in one corner with a new wall serving as the headboard for the bed. Paneling, wood beams and a wood-burning fireplace further enhance the setting (U.S. Plywood photo).

Pine paneled wall with book cases has mantel of same material.

Bedroom storage minimums established by HUD call for 36 inch closet rods for one-person secondary bedrooms and 60 inch for two-person bedrooms. Closets should be a minimum of 24 inches in depth and have at least a 6 foot 8 inch height opening. Full floor-to-ceiling closets provide maximum utilization.

In general, homemakers are on safest ground when decorating a bedroom if they select one color that gives them and their families a particular lift — one they enjoy being with. A predominance of this shade should be used, and compatible supplementary colors should be worked in for interest and accent. Opportunities for interplay of colors can come through careful choice of such ingredients as paint or wallpaper, floor covering, curtains, bedspreads, lamps and pillows.

Lighting in the bedroom should be for decoration, illumination and illusion. While darkness obviously is necessary for restful and relaxing sleep, proper lighting is equally important for the many other activities ... dressing, grooming, studying, reading ... performed within these walls.

Both reading and sewing require good overall illumination plus supplementary light directed onto the page or fabric. Other activities, like watching TV, require only general illumination. Vanities with built-in overhead lighting keep the counter clear for cosmetics. Proper lighting in and around the closet aids in identification and selection of color-coordinated articles.

Dimmer switches that allow just the amount of illumination necessary are often desirable.

FIREPLACES

Fireplaces add to the charm and appeal of many older homes, most frequently being located in the living room, but also often found in a bedroom, dining room, basement, family room, den or kitchen. Regardless of location, careful inspection should be made to determine that the unit is structurally sound before lighting up.

Typical masonry units vary greatly in style yet have many elements in common including:

- a chimney that extends 3 feet above a flat roof or 2 feet above a roof ridge and is supported by concrete footings extending from solid ground below the frost line.

- an opening usually 2-to-6 feet wide, depending upon the type of fuel to be burned (cordwood units require a 30 inch wide opening to be most efficient), and a height ranging from 24 to 40 inches (the higher the opening, the more chance of a smoky fireplace).

- a hearth made of brick, stone, terra cotta or reinforced concrete. It should extend at least 20 inches from the chimney breast and should be 24 inches wider than the fireplace opening (12 inches on each side).

- back and side walls generally at least 8 inches thick and lined with firebrick or other approved noncombustible material not less than 2 inches thick or steel lining not less than ¼ inch thick. Such lining may be omitted when the walls are of solid masonry or reinforced concrete at least 12 inches thick.

• a lintel that extends across the top of the fireplace opening supporting the masonry and is made of steel.

• a damper, or hinged lid, which opens and closes to vary the throat opening of the unit and regulates the draft and, when closed, prevents heat loss from the home's heating system.

The conventional masonry fireplace is the most expensive to build and offers the homeowner viewing possibilities from one, two or three sides, depending upon placement and design. This type fireplace can be built as a "circulating unit" that directs heat into the room via registers which are

With all the appearances of a conventional wood-burning fireplace, this all-metal prefabricated corner model woodburning fireplace, complete with all metal flue and simulated brick chimney top, can be easily installed in any home without special footings, foundation or masonry. (Majestic)

part of the fireplace wall. While fireplaces are not recommended as the basic home heating source, they can supply supplemental heating and be used for a quick room warm-up in mild weather.

Factory-made fireplaces have become very popular over the past decade, primarily because of their low cost and easy installation. Offered in a wide range of sizes, shapes and finishes, the prefabs can be built into a wall or used free-standing. Most are metal and units can be secured for wood burning, gas logs or electric logs. They are the most economical for an exciting home, by far.

Electric and gas fireplaces now on the market more accurately resemble wood-burning fires than earlier models. These units require no special footings, yet supply heat much as an electric heater does. Gas models require a venting flue. Local building codes should be checked before purchasing and installing a factory-made fireplace and care should be taken to see that the unit carries the Underwriters Laboratory label.

Like brick walls, fireplace chimneys and surrounding in older homes may require pointing, or replacement of the mortar bond. A good mortar to use consists of 1 part portland cement, 1 part hydrated lime (or slaked-lime putty), and 6 parts clean sand, measured by volume.

Chimneys should be inspected every fall for defects. Check for loose or fallen bricks, cracked or broken flue lining, and excessive soot accumulation by lowering an electric light into the flue. Mortar joints can be tested from the outside by prodding with a knife.

If inspection shows defects that cannot be readily repaired or reached for repair, you should tear the masonry down and rebuild properly. If the old bricks are impregnated with soot and creosote, discard them and use new ones to prevent possible staining when dampness occurs. The creosote comes from burning wood in cold weather.

Chimney cleaning rarely is needed, but when it is you can either contact a professional "sweep" or tackle the job yourself using one of several different methods. You can fill an old burlap sack with bricks so that it fits into the chimney from the rooftop, lowering it a few feet at a time with a rope. The up-and-down action should loosen the soot.

If the chimney is capped and prevents use of the burlap bag method, a tire chain tied to a piece of rope can be lowered and rattled around to break the soot loose.

Chemical soot removers are not particularly recommended as they cause soot to burn, setting up a fire hazard. Some, if applied to soot at high temperatures and in sufficient quantity, may produce uncontrollable combustion and even an explosion.

Chimney Cap

Available precast for some standard flue sizes or cast in place. Note that the liner projects through the cap several inches.

Smoke Chamber

Together with the smoke shelf, this area is important to a smoke free fire. Both sides slope to the flue and it is important that they slope identically, otherwise the fire will burn on one side of the firebox only.

The entire smoke chamber and smoke shelf is parged with fire clay mortar (refractory mortar) or type "S" mortar one-half inch thick.

Throat and Damper

These parts are usually one and the same. The damper is capable of being opened and closed gradually to control the draft and keep out cold air when the fireplace is not in use. The opening in square inches should be at least 90% of that required for the flue.

Firebox

This is the area that comes alive with dancing flames and gleaming embers. To do this the firebox must be correctly proportioned, sealed, vented, and well constructed.

Hearth

The inner hearth is that portion within the fire area and is usually built of fire brick but may be other types of hard brick, concrete, stone, tile or other non-combustible heat-resistant materials. The outer hearth is built of the same type materials and should extend a minimum of eight inches on each side of the fireplace opening and sixteen inches in front. (Note: These figures are twelve inches and eighteen inches in areas covered by the Uniform Building Code.)

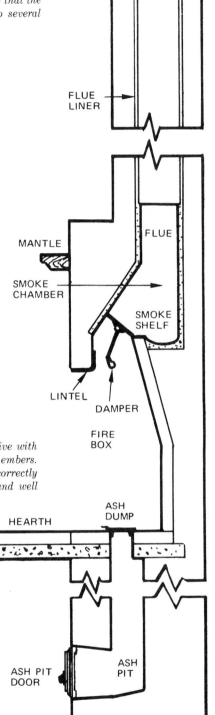

Flue and Flue Lining

The area of the flue should equal one-twelfth to one-eighth the area of the opening of the fireplace (width times height). Lining is supported on masonry.

Smoke Shelf

This is a horizontal shelf, usually concave and extended backward from the rear of the throat or damper to the rear flue wall. It directs cold air downdrafts which are present in the early stages of the fire, causing them to eddy and drift upward with the rising air currents.

Ashpit

This is the hollow space below the hearth into which ashes fall through the ash dump door located in the hearth. A metal door is provided in the ashpit for the occasional removal of ashes. In basementless homes, particularly those built on a concrete slab, it may not be feasible to provide an ashpit unless the hearth has been raised. In this case the ashpit door faces outside.

Foundation

Consult your local building code, since these codes differ according to existing soil and moisture conditions in individual areas. If total weight is needed to compute the depth and rise of the foundation required, figure brick at 130 lbs. and concrete at 150 lbs. per cubic foot. For cubic footage, figure the entire cross section volume including the open portion of the flue and firebox. The footing should extend at least below the depth of the greatest frost penetration.

As a general rule, footings should be of concrete at least twelve inches thick and should extend at least six inches on all sides of the foundation. Concrete should be poured on undisturbed soil.

Foundation walls should be a minimum of eight inches thick.

Electric fireplace unit is complete with hearth and mantel. Can be moved like furniture.

Showing how a compact gas-fired fireplace by means of a choice of available screen assemblies, can be given the illusion of a large size, realistic wood-burning fireplace when used in larger rooms. Lighted by push-button and vented with prefabricated metal flue. (Majestic)

THE KITCHEN

PLANNING

Homeowner studies show that the kitchen is the most-used room in the home and as such is redone or remodeled in some fashion about every seven years. Gone are the days of the pot-bellied wood-burning kitchen stove and the old-fashioned icebox. But in reality, many of the mid-1950 vintage homes fit perfectly into what has become known as the "Kitchen Generation Gap." Out-dated cabinets, appliances, surfacing materials, poor lighting—key elements have been passed by, yet kitchens still must cope with modern living.

Almost any kitchen remodeling project should begin with a critical look at the total package and a determination of how the scene meets several practical principles.

- THE ROOM SIZE ... Kitchens should be at least 100 square feet and usually not more than 160 square feet of usable floor space. The size of the home and the family, and the activities planned for the kitchen, will help determine this important dimension.

- ACTIVITY CENTERS ... There are several main centers that should form a work triangle measuring between 13 and 22 feet (see diagram). The three main centers are refrigeration, preparation-cleanup, and cooking. An optional center is the serving center, which should blend into the cook center and be located as conveniently as possible to the place where most meals are enjoyed.

- ADEQUATE LIGHTING ... No kitchen is complete without adequate lighting, both daylight and electric illumination where needed, both in general overhead lighting and localized lighting above each work surface.

The work sequence in a kitchen generally moves in an easy flow from storage to preparation, to cooking and serving. This is best accomplished by one of four basic floor plans — U-Shaped, L-Shaped, Corridor, and One-Wall. There are variations of each of these plans, caused by door and window locations, but nevertheless each basic shape retains its essential advantages.

The U-Shaped kitchen is quite attractive, adapting easily to efficient work patterns and, when properly designed, affords ample counter and storage space. To be effective, however, a U-Shape requires enough space for all major work centers to function well. It is often used with a breakfast bar or area, or family room, with one arm of the "U" as a room-dividing peninsula.

This U-shaped kitchen neatly divides the kitchen from the family room, with both areas having the same easy-care carpeting. A laminated wood block countertop is used for the sink center while plastic laminate surfaces are used for other countertop areas.

L-shaped kitchens afford ample storage area as well as space for a dinette set. This kitchen is fully equipped with Hotpoint trash compactor, food waste disposer, automatic dishwasher, smooth-surface range, range hood, combination refrigerator-freezer and large double oven.

There is plenty of space between the appliance walls of this corridor-style kitchen equipped with Hotpoint units. The "L" of the plastic laminate countertop helps direct traffic and serves as a convenient desk area.

Using two walls in L-shape fashion permitted great flexibility in the placement of Hotpoint appliances in this kitchen, as well as creating a breakfast area. The beams dramatize the extra-high ceiling and match the knotty appearance of the paneling and cabinetry.

The popular L-Shaped kitchen utilizes two walls and allows great flexibility in the placement of appliances and storage and eating. The arrangement usually allows space for a breakfast area. When the kitchen is used as a dining room, there is no separation of the dining and kitchen facilities.

The Corridor arrangement is a favorite for apartments because it adapts readily to efficient work patterns and is economical to install. Often part of one side is used as a snack bar or room divider. The Corridor kitchen sometimes has a door at each end, which often results in an inefficient traffic pattern through the work area. With careful plan-

ning, this problem can be eliminated. While the two-wall kitchen utilizes all its space, it may have too narrow an aisle or uncomfortable work patterns. Open appliance doors can block the aisle. The minimum aisle should be 48 inches wide for comfort and safety.

The One-Wall kitchen generally is seen in efficiency apartments and summer homes. It is a real space-saver since everything is within easy reach of the homemaker. While the One-Wall kitchen is adaptable to many types of main kitchen situations such as the "open" plan arrangements that have become more and more popular in modern homes, its main drawback is inadequate countertop space.

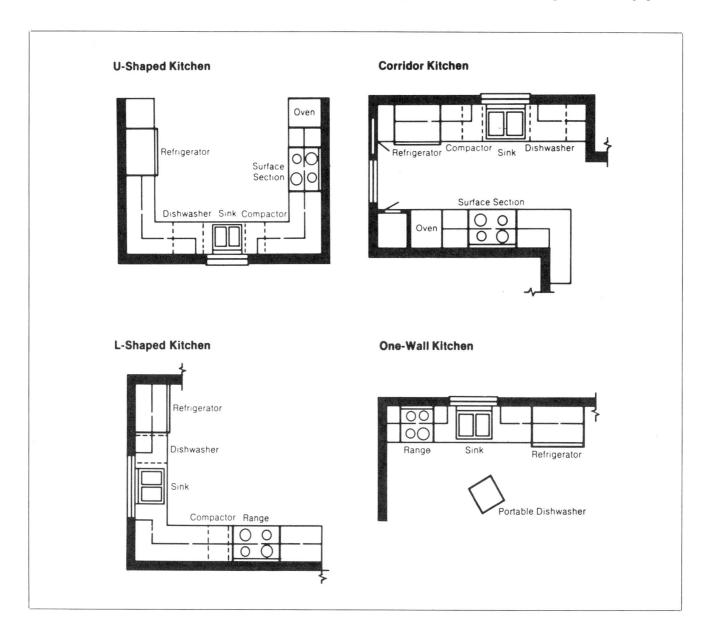

Depending upon available space, minor changes can be made in the basic design types of kitchen layout to accommodate additional appliances or include more cabinetry. These sketches show fundamentally sound floor-plan design for successful kitchens.

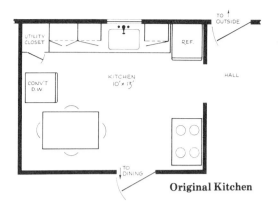

Original Kitchen

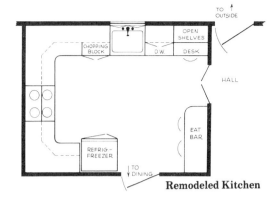

Remodeled Kitchen

Many older kitchens have generous floor space but poor storage and floor plan. This original kitchen remodeled by Maytag Co. experts was changed to a "U" design offering increased storage, adequate work surface space, an eating bar and a convenient desk-telephone center. Cafe-style doors were added to partially close the room off from adjoining areas.

For each of these four shapes one basic rule must be followed: the major appliances and sink must have adequate counter space available. Proper cabinet space next to each appliance also is important, so that utensils, foodstuffs and cleaning equipment can be located where they are first used. It's estimated that an average kitchen holds from 85 to 110 utensils, electric housewares, and miscellaneous items, so adequate storage is also a must.

Kitchen experts recommend the refrigeration center be located nearest to the service entrance or garage so that groceries can be unpacked and stored easily. This center should have at least 15 inches of countertop next to the refrigerator, with the refrigerator door opening on the side toward the counter. This also is an excellent area for baking and mixing, with a work surface and storage of all baking supplies. Plan a counter 30 to 42 inches if a baking area is desired.

The preparation-cleanup center area includes sink, dishwasher, food waste disposer and trash compactor. This area is used most frequently for preparing foods for cooking, drawing water for cooking and cleaning up after the meal. Fruits and other foods that must be soaked or washed should be stored here, as well as glasses, dishware and cleaning supplies. Try to allow at least a 24-inch work surface, 30 inches if possible, on each side of the sink.

The main cooking center includes the range, oven or ovens, range hood and portable appliance storage. Pots and pans, seasonings and cooking utensils may be stored in this center, which should be near the dining area. Try to allow 24 inches of countertop on the side of the range adjoining another activity center, and 9 to 12 inches on the other. Also allow at least 9 inches of counter near a built-in oven for setting pans and casseroles.

The optional serving center, as stated before, can be a separate center or located closest to the dining area. Plan for storage of ready-to-eat foods, serving platters, table linens and napkins. A 30-inch deep counter "snack bar" is convenient for serving meals.

In planning and placing these various work centers in the kitchen, no single arm of the work triangle should measure less than 4½ feet. If possible, place the centers so that traffic through the room does not pass through the work triangle. Plan adequate aisles between activity centers. Two people should be able to bend down, back to back, without touching. Between opposite work counters, allow at least 48 inches; if two or more people are likely to be sharing the kitchen, allow 54 to 64 inches. Placing unrelated appliances side by side, such as the refrigerator and oven, is a common planning error which overlooks the need for functional counterspace. If there is a built-in oven, the open door of the highest oven should be lower than the user's elbow. Mounting too high can make it difficult to remove roasting and baking pans. Install ovens and all appliances as recommended by the manufacturer's specification instructions.

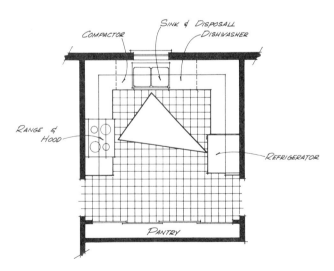

Remodeled kitchens should be based upon the widely accepted work triangle principal which "connects" the refrigeration, preparation-cleanup, and cooking centers. No single arm of the triangle should measure less than 4½ feet and the suggested total work triangle should measure between 13 and 22 feet.

Modern appliances are designed to fit standard cabinet dimensions. For example, single-oven models can be installed in 24- and 27-inch cabinets, and double-ovens will fit in 27-inch wide cabinets. Undercounter dishwashers occupy a 24-inch section, waste compactors fit into a 15-inch wide area. Replacement built-ins are easy to install and provide a wealth of new features.

Care should be given to selecting the right kind of base and wall cabinets for specific areas of the kitchen. These cabinets should be equipped with adjustable shelves and be installed at usable height. Unfortunately, too many kitchens designed for six-footers are most used by five-foot-two-inch homemakers. If space permits, include a walk-in pantry.

Many kitchen remodeling jobs combine the basic countertop materials. Heat-resistant tile or stainless steel is used in areas near the oven and range; a wood cutting board is used near the food preparation and clean-up center; and decorative plastic laminate is used for the remainder of the countertop surface.

Maintenance-free materials should be selected for walls, floor and ceiling. Washable vinyls are especially compatible with kitchen appliance surfaces. No-wax vinyl floor covering and good quality kitchen carpeting add greatly to the setting. Resilient carpet helps reduce breakage of those occasionally dropped dishes. It is also an excellent sound-reducing device and helps make the kitchen quieter.

Accessories, of course, play an important role in the final design and setting. New hardware for cabinets, shiny pots and kettles to hang on the wall, and colorful spice charts all can add sparkle. If you have reversible panels in your cabinets, you can reverse them or recover them with a new pattern.

Many homemakers have found the addition of a kitchen planning center to be most useful. Here you can maintain cookbooks, do your letter writing, converse on the telephone, plan budgets and the like, all at the comfort of a well-equipped desk.

Lighting the kitchen with fluorescent tubes is ideal because of the long slender shape of the tubes and their cool operating temperatures. They are available in a deluxe warm white color that blends well with the flow of incandescent bulbs. Fluorescents produce three to four times as much light per watt as incandescents, helping to keep the

A full-wall pantry with bi-fold doors enables the homeowner to have immediate full visibility of contents. The shallow-depth cabinets put both food and utensils just an arm's length from the work center.

kitchen cooler and conserve enrgy. As a bonus, fluorescent lights also last many times longer than most regular incandescent bulbs.

Each work center should have a light above it, so shadows aren't created. With well-lighted work areas, time is saved and the possibility of accidents is reduced. Remember to provide shielding for each light, so you never need look directly at a bare bulb or fluorescent tube.

Soft, overall general illumination will reduce the brightness contrast between work centers and surrounding areas, and provide light inside cabinets. Use ceiling-mounted or suspended fixtures, or for a rich custom effect at modest cost, use fluorescent built-in lighting around the perimeter of the kitchen. Other techniques, such as lighted beams and luminous ceilings, add to the distinctiveness and utility of the kitchen.

KITCHEN CABINETS

Kitchen cabinets are among the most efficient or inefficient storage elements of the home depending upon the type and number installed and their specific interior arrangement. You can choose from many kinds of woods, decorative plastic laminates, metal, finishes and decorative styles to achieve just the look you desire and the proper amount of storage for your family.

Standard base and wall cabinets are made in varying widths in 3-inch modules from 9 to 48 inches. Those manufactured in a factory usually have sides and backs plus adjustable shelves. Custom cabinets can be made at the job site, but in most instances today you can obtain fully finished furniture-style cabinets for less money when they are factory made.

Stock-size cabinets range in price from lower to upper medium and often fill all remodeling needs. Custom units, made to specific kitchen measurements and requirements cost more, yet afford the buyer a full selection of material, size and type. Fancy moldings, and special decorative finishes and interior fittings can increase the cabinet price.

Wood and plastic-laminate cabinets account for the largest share of the market today, with metal units a far-distant third. Manufacturers and kitchen specialists offer detailed literature on specific lines and local cabinet manufacturers will be pleased to show you samples and explain construction and use features.

There are four basic kitchen cabinet styles: Traditional, Colonial, Provincial and Contemporary. Each has a distinctive design that sets it apart and establishes the mood of the entire kitchen.

Traditional styling continues to be the most popular with American homeowners. These cabinets usually have a recessed or raised panel door and drawer styling.

Typical of the many styles of kitchen cabinets doors used by cabinet manufacturers are these designs fabricated from durable plastic laminates. In some cities, doors and face frames of cabinets are sold separately to give a new look to outdated cabinets that are still structurally sound.

Colonial or Early American styling can be knotty pine or more elaborate pegged and vee-grooved door facings. Distinctive hardware (hinges and pulls or knobs) further establish the period.

Provincial styling generally is French or Italian with delicate moldings on the face of the doors and drawer fronts. In some cabinet lines a routed groove is used instead of the molding.

Contemporary styling typically employs flush doors and clean lines. Often the doors have what is known as a reverse lip which eliminates the need for hardware pulls, and the hinges are "concealed," and not visible.

In addition, Mediterranean styling has become popular in recent years. Usually dark finished, the style is heavy and sometimes highly ornate.

Regardless of the styling, kitchen cabinets may be said to consist of five elements: (1) base units, (2) wall units, (3) drawers, (4) doors and (5) miscellaneous, such as bread boards, chopping blocks, pull-out vegetable bins, etc.

Base cabinets vary in depth anywhere from 22 to 24 inches, from the face of the cabinet to the wall, and are 34½ inches high without countertop. Most countertops are 1½-inches thick bringing the total base cabinet height to the recommended 36 inches. Dishwashers and most ranges are designed for the 36-inch counter height, although some range tops may be positioned two or three inches lower than its side rim. Some homeowners find it convenient to have a section of countertop area at a 33-inch height, usually at the end of a countertop run.

Base cabinets may be obtained with right or left-hand swinging doors or both; with drawers only; or with a combination of drawers, doors and shelves. Specific units are manufactured for single and double-bowl sinks, for corners where a revolving shelf arrangement makes full use of otherwise "dead" space, for built-in ranges, and for special accessory use such as pull-out bins and shelves.

Wall cabinets are 12 to 13 inches deep and are usually hung with the top line 84 inches above the floor to match the 84-inch height of utility (broom) cabinets. The height of the basic wall cabinet may be 30 to 33 inches, depending upon style. This gives ample clearance (15 to 18 inches) between the counter (36 inches from the floor) and the bottom of the wall cabinet.

If a wall cabinet is to be placed over a sink, allow 24 inches above the sink rim for the standard-depth wall cabinets. This space can be reduced to 16 inches if the wall cabinets are custom-made only 6 inches deep. Local codes should be checked in installing cabinets above the range. Usually there is a clearance of 27 to 36 inches and depth should allow for the range hood. Specific wall units are made for use over free-standing refrigerators and freezers.

Oven cabinets customarily have three drawers below the appliance and a two-door storage area above the appliance. Widths vary from 24 to 33 inches and in many floor-to-ceiling units the height can be cut from 84 to 82 inches if necessary.

Manufactured kitchen cabinets can be purchased with a number of "trim" items useful in filling an exact lineal or vertical dimension. Face molding, outside corners, trim molding, scribe molding, valence panels, and end cabinet panels frequently are required to complete the installation. Likewise, quarter-round and half-round shelves are available for full-view cabinet ends.

Among the many cabinet accessories offered for kitchen use are a metal bread drawer, cutting boards, combination soap and dishcloth rack, pan rack, suspended cutlery trays, extension towel racks, flour bin, spice racks, sliding storage bins, extension pan holders, extension wastebasket, tray base, vegetable base, food mixer mechanism and shelf assembly, full-depth drawer extensions, etc.

Kitchen desks or planning centers are offered in matching cabinetry. Units provide a center drawer and come with or without drawers on either or both sides. The kitchen desk should be installed about 29 inches off the floor, out of the traffic pattern and away from the spatter of the range or sink. Shelves can be installed above for cookbooks, etc., and frequently the telephone is located at this point.

Kitchen cabinet doors are of two principal types — flush and panel. The flush doors may be hollow-core or solid core, or simply a panel of plywood. If only a panel of plywood, it is generally ¾ inches in thickness. Some cabinet doors, either panel or flush, are rabbeted or lipped while others have a square edge. Self-closing hinges and magnetic catches are highly desirable.

Kitchen cabinet drawers generally vary in depth from 18 to 22 inches to satisfy the particular depth of the base cabinet. For greater ease of operation, drawers are often provided with metal slides and roller bearings or small wheels which run on metal tracks. Otherwise, drawers slide on wood drawer runners. Fronts are flush or lipped.

If kitchen space permits, the old-style walk-in pantry can be highly useful for the storage of canned and packaged foods, small appliances, dishes and glassware. When wall space is at a premium, use pull-out shelves that bring all the stored items within easy reach. Or you can hinge shelf sections on both sides so they will open like the pages in a book to make everything accessible. Slanting shelves, supermarket style, can also be used for canned goods storage with cans lying on sides so that a replacement rolls into position as one is removed.

Replacing Cabinets

The installation of new cabinets in an older home begins with the removal of the older cabinets. This will probably require the removal of the sink (so water supply must be shut off) and removal of electrical or gas appliances (so these sources must be turned off).

Begin the cabinet removal by first removing or having removed the countertop which is attached to the base cabinets. Next remove the wall cabinets and then the base cabinets. Also remove any baseboard and chair rail that may be in the area where new cabinets are to be installed.

In preparing for installation, decide if new flooring is to be installed, and if so, do this before installing the new cabinets. See the Flooring chapter of this book for additional suggestions. If you are retaining the existing flooring, chances are it is not perfectly level. Find the highest point, and from there measure 34½ inches up the wall and draw a horizontal line to establish the top height of your base cabinets. Then measure 84 inches up the wall from the same point and draw another horizontal line which will be the top height of your wall cabinets.

Cabinets should be attached to studs with screws, not nails. A stud finder will help locate the studs if you have not already encountered them in removing the old cabinets. Usually, the studs are located at 16-inch intervals, starting from the center of the wall.

Base cabinets should be installed first, beginning in a corner, and making certain that the first cabinet is installed at the highest point of the floor. Other cabinets can be brought up to that point using shims so that all base units are at the same height.

An electric drill can be used to drill through the top rail in the back of the cabinet at stud locations. Wood screws then are secured through the stile and into the studs.

Installing wall cabinets should again begin with a corner unit that is placed even with the top of the 84-inch line. Use wood screws to fasten the top stile to the studs. If only one stud is behind the cabinet, use another wood screw in the bottom stile. Don't completely tighten the screws at this point, as you may wish to make final adjustments to secure both level and plumb.

Since wall cabinets are installed at 7-foot height, there will be from one to two feet of open space above. This area usually is closed in flush with the cabinets or may be an extended soffit containing lighting. Both wall and base units should be secured to side-by-side units with wood screws through the vertical stiles found inside the door or drawer fronts.

Additional installation instructions can be obtained from individual cabinet manufacturers along with suggested cleaning and care ideas related to the specific cabinetry material and finish.

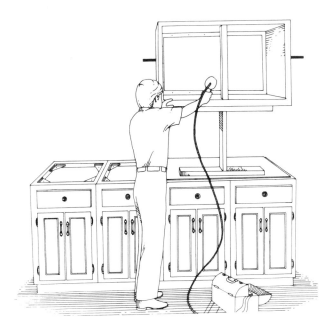

With base cabinets installed first, it's possible to use the lower units to support wall cabinets during installation. Here a T-support made of 2x4's sits atop a piece of polywood to position the wall unit at the correct height while the workman uses a power drill-screwdriver to secure it in place (IXL Furniture Co. drawing).

Cabinet Refinishing

If the wood is still in good shape, you can refinish rather than replace your cabinet doors and drawers. Many companies specialize in this, and can offer reasonable prices such as $10 per door, which includes the additional built-in cabinet area as well. Or, you can tackle the job yourself.

Refinishing kitchen woodwork is not an especially complicated or expensive project to do yourself, but be prepared for it to take quite a while, and to mess up your kitchen in the meantime. If at all possible get several people working on the detachable parts — doors and drawers — to cut down the amount of sanding and hours and sweat. The steps involved are: remove the doors from the hinges, and then take off hardware; apply varnish remover to the wood; scrape off the varnish remover and the old varnish; wash down with a varnish or lacquer solvent once both sides of the door have been stripped; sand down the wood so it is smooth and has an even grain (this is important to make sure the new stain takes evenly); stain, and lacquer or varnish. The tools required are: lots of newspaper on which to do your varnish removing and staining; rubber gloves; a scraper, about 3 inches wide with a sharp, flat edge; a brush to apply the varnish remover; fine sandpaper, rags to apply the stain; a brush to apply the final coat of varnish or lacquer.

These same steps (without the first two, naturally) apply to the built-in woodwork also.

Let's go through the steps more specifically:

1. Remove the doors from the hinges and then remove the hardware (knob pulls; leave hinges on doors). This is important to avoid leaving small patches on the edges of the door.

2. Lay the door or drawer down on several sheets of newspaper; or, if doing the woodwork, place newspapers along the floor. Always use rubber gloves. Brush on the varnish remover, making sure to cover all surfaces on the side facing up. Let sit about 10 minutes, and with a smooth motion scrape off the old varnish. It will peel off in clumps, but might require two or three coats to get all the way down to the wood at all points. Turn the door over and do the second side.

3. Rub with solvent to get any remaining varnish out of grooves.

4. Sand evenly and firmly with fine sandpaper.

5. Apply stain with long, brushing movements using rags. Make sure the stain has been well stirred, and that you have allowed enough time for the solvent, used to wash down the wood, to evaporate. Make the first staining a "wet" layer — heavy and dark. Let sit about ten to fifteen minutes, and then wipe off with a soft absorbent cloth, again with even strokes. Then wait an hour. Apply a second coat, but not as heavy, working it until you get ap-

HOW TO INSTALL PACKAGED PREFORMED COUNTERTOPS

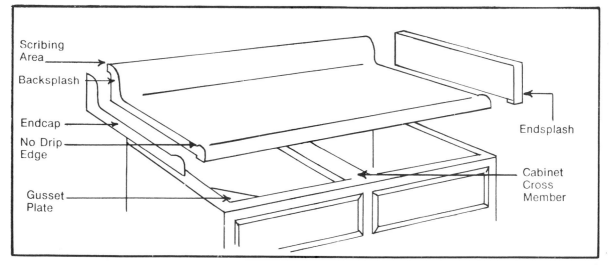

Components of a plastic laminate countertop

No special tools or skills are required to replace a damaged or worn countertop with a packaged preformed countertop of durable plastic laminate. Special finishing kits simplify the job and permit the homeowner to achieve a professional application.

The key components of the countertop are determined by the desired shape—straight, L-shaped or U-shaped. Endcap kits permit finishing the end of the countertop with matching laminate surface; endsplash kit provides a matching end or side splash for use when the countertop is placed against a wall or oven cabinet; the connector kit permits easy fastening of two top surface sections when an angle is involved, such as for an L-shape design.

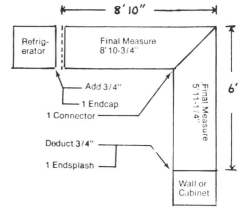

L-shaped kitchen drawing

Here are the basic steps in installing a preformed countertop:

1. Measure your present countertop and use a grid section sheet to make a scale diagram of your present plan. Measure along the wall at the cabinet top level to determine the length of each section. Countertop sections usually come in standard 6, 8, 10 and 12 foot lengths. Don't try to make your own miter cuts, have them prepared by the laminate supplier. If your current countertop measures longer than a given standard length, you'll have to order the next longer size and cut it to size. Also, keep in mind that normally the countertop is ¾-inch longer than the cabinet because of overhang.

Drawings courtesy of SUBA Manufacturing, Inc.

2. This typical L-shaped kitchen is used to show the materials needed for a new countertop: One 12' countertop with right-hand miter; one 8' countertop with left-hand miter; one endcap kit; one endsplash kit; one connector kit. You may also need a caulking compound and small ½ inch strips of wood for shimming.

3. Remove the existing countertop. If it is made of plastic laminate or linoleum, it probably is screwed to the cross members of the cabinet. Remove the top drawers of the cabinet to locate the screws. In some cases, such countertops may be nailed in place and will have to be hammered from underneath for removal. If the existing countertop is tile, a hammer and wrecking bar can be used to break the tile into small pieces (wear safety glasses) for removal. Also remove the craft paper, wire lath, mortar and tile adhesive which are part of tile tops.

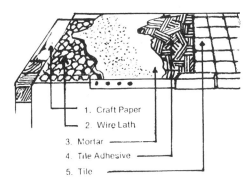

1. Craft Paper
2. Wire Lath
3. Mortar
4. Tile Adhesive
5. Tile

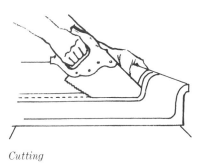

Cutting

backsplash, using a sharp 10-12 point hand saw. If a power saw is used, you must cut from the underside of the top.

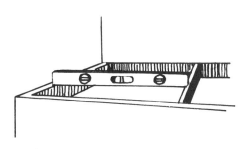

Leveling

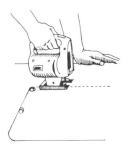

Sink cut-out

4. Make certain that your new countertop will be level when it is installed. Use a carpenter's level to determine that the cabinets are level both lengthwise and from front to back. If not, use small wood shims to level the top frame when installing the countertop. It is important that the countertop front edge hanging over the cabinets does not interfere with undercounter appliances or breadboards. If sufficient clearance is not provided, use small wood shim blocks to raise the height of the entire top, making sure these blocks are used around sink and range areas.

6. In cutting the countertop for sink or range holes, use the template supplied by the sink or appliance maker to mark the top side (or reverse side if using power saw) making sure the template is square with the countertop front. A hole is first drilled within the marked cutout and then a saw is used to follow the marking.

7. Miter joints are assembled next, placing the countertop on the floor upside down if space permits. If it doesn't, the top may be set atop the cabinets and bolted together from below.

SHIM BLOCKS

Shim blocks

Scribing

If cutting is required in fitting the new countertop to length, place the countertop on saw horses or other stable surface. Mark the countertop at the approximate place where it is to be cut. Place a strip of masking tape across the entire width of the top at this point. The tape will help to prevent chipping during the sawing process. Use a carpenter's square to redetermine the exact cutting line and to insure that it is square. Begin cutting at the top of the

8. The final fitting of the countertop to the cabinets may require a slight adjustment of the backsplash if the adjoining wall surface is irregular. This is done by using a scribe to mark the backsplash and a block plane or file to make the backsplash conform to the contour of the wall.

9. After the countertop is secured to the cabinet cross members with wood screws, caulking is used to seal the miter seam and the backsplash-wall joint. The sink and range should be installed according to instructions supplied with the units.

proximately the shade desired. Wipe again after ten minutes. If it still is not dark enough, apply a light final coat to darken with no excess to wipe off. Let sit 24 hours or more before applying lacquer or varnish.

6. To get a glossy finish, apply two or three coats of varnish or lacquer (follow directions on the can). To get a smooth, satiny finish, sand down the first coat after it has dried completely (fine sandpaper again), and then apply a second coat; sand again once completely dry and hard (or just use "satin" varnish).

COUNTERTOPS

Decorative plastic laminates continue to be the most popular counter material in the kitchen. Literally hundreds of colors, patterns, wood grains and textures are manufactured in a 1/16-inch thickness for horizontal application. Fabricators can provide either self-edging style tops for a squared-off look or pre-formed tops with a rolled nondrip edge at the front and a cove at the back. Most plastic laminate countertops have a ¾-inch particleboard core for dimensional stability. Plastic laminate countertops usually are installed with 4-inch-high backsplash of the same material, or with plastic laminate rising all the way from the countertop to the bottom of the wall cabinets. The plastic laminate tops can withstand the heat of a pan containing boiling water, but a hot frying pan may make a permanent mark. Among the current pattern favorites is butcherblock pattern in light or dark wood grain color.

Ceramic tile countertops are durable and heat resistant, but tend to be noisy and more care must be used to prevent dish breakage. Here again, literally hundreds of colors and patterns are available in various tile sizes and shapes.

Glass ceramic is a more recent development in countertop surfacing. This material is resistant to damage from heat changes or scratching, can be easily cleaned and is suitable next to a range or oven. The material comes in a range of sizes and is best fabricated in a manufacturing plant.

Still another countertop material is solid wood laminated in the form of a chopping block. Often sections of this material are used in combination with plastic laminate countertop surfacing.

The recommended total countertop thickness is 1½ inches and it is best to determine the material you plan to use before selecting your kitchen cabinets. This will permit you to have the cabinet manufacturer supply you with the base cabinets properly prepared for the specific type of countertop you will use.

SINKS

Many kitchen designers look to sink placement as a prime factor in the total kitchen scheme. With good reason they point out the sink is used more than any other part of the kitchen and it is here that the woman of the house will spend many hours standing or sitting.

Sinks frequently are placed below a window (which should be at least 40 inches above the floor level) that offers a pleasing view, hopefully not just the sight of automobiles passing up and down the street.

Still other homemakers prefer to have the sink located in an island work counter in the middle of the kitchen where it serves as the hub of activity. Still others like the placement in a peninsula dividing the work area from the dining area.

Most homemakers prefer two-compartment sinks, but a one-compartment unit is quite satisfactory if there is a dishwasher. Three-compartment units also are very handy. Dimension-wise, the single-bowl unit is 21 to 24 inches wide; the double-bowl 32 to 43 inches; and the triple-compartment 42 to 45 inches. Most sinks are 21 to 22 inches deep from front to back and the usual depth is 7½ inches for the deep compartment. Curved sink models also are available for use in a corner location, or if space permits, standard rectangular units can be used for this purpose.

Kitchen sinks are marketed with or without faucets and are of three basic construction types: stainless steel in 18 and 20 gauge; porcelain-on-steel; and porcelain on cast iron. The porcelain units come in a wide range of decorator colors, while the stainless steel units can be obtained with a bright or dull finish.

The newest self-rimming feature offered in all basic sink types eliminates the need for a separate installation rim which joins the sink to the countertop. Use of ceramic tile countertop usually requires supporting the sink from the underside of the counter and placement of tile for the joining surround.

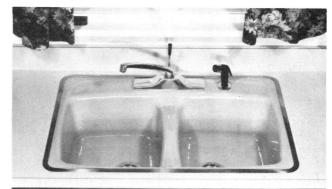

Stainless steel rings often are used to install sinks in plastic laminate countertops. This double-bowl design by American-Standard comes in a number of colors and is made of enameled cast iron.

Self-rimming sinks are made with one, two, or three compartments. This Kohler unit has a smaller compartment (9⅛" wide and just 5" deep) for waste disposer installation, and a 19¾"-wide and 9½" deep larger basin. The overall dimensions are 33x22". The unit can be easily installed without replacing existing countertops.

This exploded view of American-Standard's Aquarian kitchen fitting shows the heart of the leak-proof, washerless ceramic disc cartridge. The discs provide crisp, efficient water control, and are unaffected by sand, silt, grease or other impurities that frequently cause fitting failure.

A three-compartment sink usually accommodates the food waste disposer in the center section which is of less depth than the flanking bowls. This serves as a convenience in preparing vegetables and fruits, with the waste immediately dropped into the disposer. Some triple-compartment sinks are sold with hardwood cutting boards which again facilitate food preparation and permit food waste to be scraped directly into a central shallow food-waste disposer bowl.

Sinks can be purchased with any of several punched holes to accommodate conventional swing spout and control handles, single-handle faucets and accessories such as pull-out spray, lotion dispenser, and instant hot-water units for making beverages and soups. Be sure to know what accessories you will be installing before choosing a sink.

Designers recommend a minimum of 24 inches of countertop space on each side of the sink and suggest that the automatic dishwasher be located in the 24-inch area at either side of the sink. Be sure to avoid placement of the dishwasher at an immediate right angle to the sink, as it becomes very difficult to load and unload. If the dishwasher must be around the corner from the sink, place it 24 inches from the corner so you can stand at the sink and pivot to load the opened dishwasher.

APPLIANCES

Ranges

Kitchen improvement or remodeling often begins with the selection of a new range or oven and it's in this area that the homeowner has one of the greatest selections possible. It all begins, of course, with the source of energy — a 208 or 240-volt line for electric units or a gas line for gas-fired units. And from there, the choice seems endless.

Ranges include free-standing models from 30 to 42 inches in width, drop-ins, slip-ins and built-ins. Some models have exposed heating elements, even ones that are thermostatically controlled. Still other range tops provide the smooth cooking-top concept with the heating units positioned under a glass ceramic top that is extremely easy to keep clean.

Since its introduction in 1966, the smooth surface range has grown greatly in popularity. Several brands are now available, some of which require special ceramic cooking pots and pans and others which permit use of any pot or

Black see-through door is a feature of the Whirlpool set-in range, complemented here by the black acrylic panels of the refrigerator. The firm also offers built-in dishwashers and trash compactors with similar fronts.

pan with a reasonably flat bottom. Smooth-tops currently are available only in electric ranges.

One range top on the market allows great flexibility. Two sealed cartridges (each containing two surface units) can be removed and replaced with grille, rotisserie, griddle, french fryer, shishkebob or even a cutting board. An adjacent built-in exhaust handles smoke.

Controls on the newer range tops include the familiar dials as well as pushbuttons and solid state "touch" units that bring computer technology into your home.

Frigidaire's built-in wall oven incorporates solid state "touch" controls for all time-and-temperature settings. Accuracy is controlled within a few seconds. The system is easy to use — first touch the control marked "start time", then the numerals "300," which starts the oven at 3:00. Next touch "oven" and numerals "325" to set the roasting temperature. Then touch "stop time" and "600" which turns the oven off at 6:00, when the roast will be completed. The rest is fully automatic.

The big news in modern ovens is the choice in automatic cleaning systems, freeing the housewife of this messy chore. One system, pyrolytic or self-cleaning, is a high temperature process usually between 850 and 1050°F, that reduces food soil in the oven to a small residue of wipable ash. Cleaning time ranges from 1½ to 2½ hours and costs from 3 to 7¢ per cleaning.

The second popular method is the "continuous" clean where the porosity of underfired porcelain causes the food splatter to spread out as water does on a blotter. This thin film then burns off more easily at conventional oven-use temperatures each time you use the oven. Manufacturers still recommend placement of a sheet of aluminum foil on the bottom of the oven to catch spillovers from pies and casseroles. Both types of cleaning are offered in gas and electric ovens.

Frigidaire's Touch-N-Cook free-standing slide-in range has a smooth-top range surface, Electri-clean oven with see-through door and solid-state computerized programming.

Among the other popular features of modern ovens are over-and-under combinations that give two large ovens, lift-off oven doors, lighted control panels, visualite (see through) oven doors, and more automatic controls.

Black glass doors are very popular and permit the cook to see the oven contents when the oven light is flicked on. Speed broil is still another big attraction. It permits meat broiling on both sides at once without turning.

Microwave Ovens

The microwave oven keeps up with America's fast-changing lifestyle by providing quality meals in minutes, anytime of the day, for all members of the family with a minimum of effort.

As this book is being written, nearly one of every four new ovens going into an American home is a microwave unit priced from $250 to over $1000, depending upon size, style and location. These units generally come complete with a new recipe book geared to "instant" cooking with utensils made of paper, plastic, glass and glass ceramic.

General Electric's deluxe self-cleaning built-in wall oven costs no more to operate, on the average, than a conventional oven which must be cleaned manually, according to company studies. The cost of a self-cleaning cycle is about a dime. General Electric reports that the improved insulation system used to contain the heat during the cleaning cycle actually reduces the energy requirements during the normal baking and roasting cycles.

Over/under style combination range/oven units conserve space while providing eye-level cooking and control convenience. This unit by Whirlpool has a smooth glass ceramic cooktop, continuous-cleaning eye-level oven and lower oven with see-through black glass door, all in a 30-inch width.

You can grill indoors with the Jenn-Air convertible cooktop grill-range that takes but 20 seconds to switch from glass-ceramic conventional elements to the grill accessory. A powered ventilation system is built into the range where it is nine times more efficient than a similar power unit located 3 feet above the range. This type of cooktop also comes in drop-in style for countertop and island installations.

Tappan's over/under electric range combines a full-size microwave upper oven with an electric self-cleaning lower oven and a one-piece ceramic smooth top cooking surface equipped with four infininte heat cooking elements. All controls are at eye level, including the selector control for the microwave oven which enables the user to select microwave settings to roast, bake, defrost, stew, simmer and keep warm.

General Electric's Jet 83 microwave oven takes less than an hour to turn out a 6-pound standing rib roast. A built-in recipe guide on the control panel provides quick reference to defrosting and cooking times of many foods. The oven is sold with a 312-page cookbook containing 485 tested recipes.

You now have three basic styles of microwave ovens to choose from: (1) portables with interiors approximately 8 cubic feet and weighing about 60 pounds; (2) countertop units weighing 70 to 90 pounds with 1 to 1.25 cubic feet capacity; and (3) combination units in a choice of three configurations: over/under, built-in and free-standing.

Departing from the normal method of cooking with energy supplied by gas flame, electricity or burning charcoal, the microwave oven uses high frequency radio waves generated in a vacuum tube called a magnetron. This energy penetrates the food and is absorbed by water molecules to create heat within that cooks at an incredible speed. Bacon, for example, can be cooked in two minutes, a roast in 40 minutes, etc.

The microwave oven has become a natural tie-in with frozen foods stored in the freezer and pulled out at the last minute to meet an "urgent demand". Special controls and timers permit defrosting in a matter of minutes. The timer control also permits longer cooking times, up to an hour, for foods needing slower cooking.*

Range Hoods

Whenever possible the fumes from cooking should be vented to the outdoors. The most efficient arrangement is to have a hood and exhaust fan with a grease filter 24 to 30 inches above the range, with the shortest possible duct to the outdoors. The duct may go through the wall, but avoid directing cooking odors toward an outdoor sitting area. The duct also may go through the roof, but should never end in the attic.

There are two types of convenient range hoods — the model that has ductwork, and the ductless or nonvented unit equipped with washable aluminum filter or replaceable charcoal filter, or both.

Most vented range hoods have push-button control for an interior light and two-speed fan. These units should provide a minimum of 40 cubic feet per minute per foot of hood length to do the job efficiently and effectively. Some quality ovens and range tops are manufactured with built-in ventilating systems, but for the most part the hood installation is separate.

Range hoods come in many sizes (standard 30 to 36 inches in width), shapes, and colors to match kitchen appliances. Units can be obtained with three finished sizes for conventional installation or with all four sides finished for popular island cooking arrangement. Units normally require a 7 inch round duct.

A ceiling or wall fan located away from the range will draw the cooking fumes over the intervening surfaces, but will not be as efficient as the conventional range hood. Nonducted hood and fan will trap most of the grease and some of the odors, but none of the cooking heat and moisture.

Refrigerators-Freezers

Today's food storage appliances not only represent a better price value (most have continued to drop in price ever since 1950), but have larger capacity, better quality, more features and benefits, and are more sophisticated.

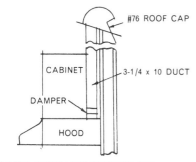

VERTICAL DISCHARGE THROUGH TOP
OF HOOD AND THROUGH CABINET

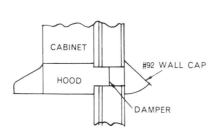

HORIZONTAL DISCHARGE THROUGH WALL

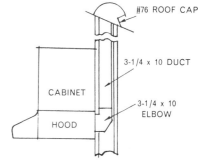

DISCHARGE THROUGH BACK OF HOOD
AND VERTICAL BETWEEN WALL STUDS

*For further specifics see Book of Successful Kitchens by Patrick Galvin.

Range hood installations can be vented through the roof or wall, depending upon room layout and location. These sketches show typical installations. (Sketch by Aubrey Manufacting, Inc.).

There are three types of refrigerators on the market today:

- The oldest, the conventional one-door refrigerator, has a freezer compartment that holds temperatures between 10 and 15°F. This compartment can be used for short-term storage of frozen food and must be manually defrosted.

- Two-door cyclamatic refrigerators maintain separate sections — fresh food is maintained at temperatures of 36 to 38°F and this section automatically defrosts; frozen foods are maintained at zero temperatures and this section must be defrosted manually.

- Frost-proof models (either with top or side freezer section) automatically defrost the food compartment and the freezer section.

The choice of styles available in today's units permits you to pick a single-door refrigerator, top-freezer model or side-by-side model. In each instance, the usable capacity has been greatly increased over the past twenty years, while requiring approximately the same floor space.

Three-door side-by-side refrigerator-freezer by Frigidaire includes a complete electronic message center built into the door. The push-button AM-FM radio, tape recorder and player is battery-operated and may be removed for use elsewhere without affecting the regular function of the freezer door.

Industry statistics show that 75 percent of refrigerators sold are the no-frost, top-mount style, while side-by-side units (costing more) account for approximately 20 percent of the market. Most top-mounted units sold are 15 cubic foot capacity, while the side-by-sides are larger 19 and 21 cubic foot models. Smaller units, of course, are also available.

Manufacturers today generally have limited the maximum height to approximately 66 inches, the width to a maximum of 35¾ inches and the depth to approximately 30 inches total, excluding the door handle. Installation requires an individual 120-volt, 15 amp circuit with a three-prong outlet. For an automatic ice-maker, a water hookup is also required.

In choosing a new refrigerator-freezer you will want to carefully determine that the unit can hold various size packages and bottles customarily used in your home.

Most refrigerators have cold meat storage, but it's important to determine if the drawer is a meat keeper that maintains temperatures around 30 to 34°F and will keep meat fresh up to seven days, or whether it is a meat storage compartment which holds meat at the normal refrigerator temperature of 36 to 38°F. This storage drawer would not be capable of holding fresh cut meats for more than a few days.

Reversible doors on this frost-proof Frigidaire permit left or right-hand swing. Twin storage compartments in the door accommodate spreads such as butter, and cheese and snacks.

Considerable improvements are to be found in today's refrigerators. Controls are better. Newer ABS plastic liners (replacing porcelain) are of one-piece construction and easier to clean (there are no cracks to catch spills and food). Plastic containers are more durable, lighter in weight, and never need rewaxing like metal ice trays. Foamed-in-place insulation assures better construction.

Some refrigerators on the market today permit you to change from a right-hand to a left-hand door should you move the refrigerator to a new location. Some units also are equipped with built-in base rollers which greatly simplify cleaning behind the unit. Other features include adjustable shelves, interior light, magnetic door gaskets, etc.

Separate freezers continue to grow in popularity with homemakers. Older chest models still must be defrosted manually, but newer vertical units can be frost-proof while maintaining zero temperatures. Vertical freezers require less floor space than chest-style units.

Ice makers — Aside from the popular automatic ice-maker in refrigerators, families who entertain frequently have found an automatic ice maker provides great convenience. This individual appliance needn't be confined to the kitchen as it often is used in conjunction with a built-in bar, in a pantry or other convenient nook.

Chest freezers can be placed in available kitchen space located in hallways, garage or adjoining room to reduce the required number of shopping trips. This Whirlpool model has convenient lift-out baskets, interior light, adjustable temperature control and power-interruption outside warning light.

Most available units are designed for either free-standing or under-the-counter installation requiring approximately 14 inches in width and 18 inches in depth, and 23 inches in height. Units require a ¼ inch copper tube supply line, 115V 60 cycle electric outlet and 1¼ inch trapped drain. Some units do not require a drain.

Front-panel controls enable the homeowner to select ice cube thickness from 3/8 to ¾ inches or make cubes 1¼ x 1¼ or cubelets ¾ x ¾ inches. The ice making is fully automatic with the unit shutting off as the bin fills to a predetermined level.

Dishwashers

Contrary to the belief of many, the automatic dishwasher will consume from 10 to 12 gallons of water during the normal cycles, or far less water than washing the dishes by hand. And the job is done better with less time involved.

There are five basic types of fully automatic dishwashers, each with advantages that should be considered:

- BUILT-IN undercounter types are permanently connected to water lines, drain pipe, and electric circuit. These units are unified with the surrounding kitchen cabinets, which tends to muffle the sound. And frequently the front panel of the dishwasher can be of the same material as the cabinets for appearance sake.

- PORTABLE units require a wall outlet for plugging in and a hose which connects to the spout of your kitchen faucet. The unit can be rolled to the table for filling and later moved to another room, if desired, for storage. Portables can be obtained for top loading or front-end loading on "convertible" models that may later be built into the kitchen.

- FREE-STANDING models are similar to the built-in undercounter models but are designed to go into an unused area or at the end of the counter. Units are offered with porcelain surround as well as with decorative panels of plastic laminate and hardwood tops.

- CONVERTIBLE automatic dishwashers are front-end loading type installed initially on casters with the idea that later the unit will be taken to a new home and installed as part of the cabinetry, either as an undercounter unit or a free-standing model.

- DISHWASHER-SINK models combine the sink top, bowl, cabinet, faucets and dishwasher all in one compact unit, usually metal.

When installing a dishwasher you will need a water supply which will flow at least 2 to 2.5 gallons per minute at a pressure of at least 15 pounds per square inch at a temperature of at least 140°F. Soft water is desirable but not absolutely necessary. Present-day detergents and wetting agents have done much to eliminate water-spotting problems.

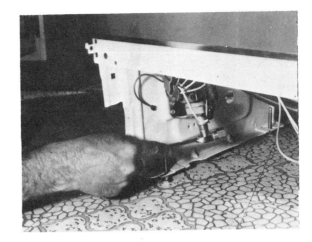

INSTALLING DISHWASHER

Replacing an out-of-date or leaking built-in dishwasher or adding a unit to your kitchen is now within the ability of many home handymen. Manufacturers have designed units for this purpose and supply them with easy-to-follow instructions.

General Electric's do-it-yourself replacement kit contains all the parts needed for a typical installation such as rubber drain hose and clamps, copper water line, brass elbows and unions, and electrical connectors. An electrical test light is also provided in the kit to determine that power has been shut-off before you begin.

Installation tools required normally include a screwdriver, wire cutter, tube cutter and crescent wrench. No soldering is necessary.

Detailed instructions, diagrams and illustrations on the backside of the kit will take you through the 17 steps of removal and replacement, with particular attention to safety and proper installation preparation procedures.

Steps 1-7 cover removal of the old dishwasher, starting with the water and electricity shut-off. The electric test light is used to be sure the correct circuit breaker has been thrown.

Removal is completed by disassembling electrical connectors, disconnecting the water supply line and drain hose, and removal of screws or fasteners that hold the dishwasher in place.

Steps 8-11 and the accompanying eight illustrations show how to alter the existing electric supply, hot water inlet plumbing, and drain connections. The remaining 6 steps outline dishwasher installation and final connection. All the dishwasher inlet and drain connections are made with quick and easy compression fittings and clamps from the kit.

The dishwasher is then leveled and fastened to the countertop's underside. After electrical connections are made, the replacement is finished. The unit is started and check is made for leaks after one completed cycle.

Many under-counter automatic dishwashers can be customized by removing the original color panel and inserting one to match the kitchen, either wood or a wallpaper covered panel (Whirlpool photo).

A power-saver option on the General Electric automatic dishwasher can save up to 40% of the power needed for a normal cycle. This unit has five pushbutton cycles and features 3-level washing action.

Automatic dishwashers are designed to do the whole job without scraping and prerinsing. Even pots and pans are handled easily. Many automatic dishwashers offer a good deal more than a normal wash and dry cycle, permitting you to select just the one needed for the task at hand.

For example, the normal wash cycle may include a pre-rinse or prewash with detergent, or two prerinses and main wash with detergent, and one to four after-rinses, plus drying. A rinse and hold cycle permits dishes to be rinsed and "held" until you have the full day's load in the unit.

A shorter cycle than normal wash, with shorter drying period, is excellent for fine crystal and china, as well as nongreasy dishes. Pots and pans may need longer cycles for washing and shorter for drying. And a rinse and dry cycle is ideal for seldom-used dishes which may have been stored for some time.

Perhaps the biggest change in dishwashers since the late 1940's is the method of moving water throughout the unit. Postwar dishwashers for the most part consisted of a tub with a propeller in the bottom that splashed hot water onto the dishware racked in circular racks above. Today, more and more units are offered with a spray arm that creates streams of water to scrub the dishware.

This newer approach consists of a pump, which draws water from a sump in the bottom of the tub and pumps it (usually at a rate of 50 to 60 gallons per minute) through one or more rotating or stationary spray arms where it is sprayed through openings or nozzles onto the dishes. The water then falls back into the sump to be circulated again.

A modern automatic dishwasher requires no special maintenance or attention. It should be used carefully, following the manufacturer's instructions and with recommended detergents. Units are sold with warranty protection. Prices begin in the neighborhood of $250.

Trash Compactors

The trash compactor has taken its rightful place beside the food waste disposer and automatic dishwasher in many American kitchens. This new unit is helping greatly to handle the approximately 5 pounds of trash created daily by each member of a four-person family.

Depending upon the size of the family, a typical trash compactor can handle a week's disposables (cans, bottles, cartons and papers) in one compact bag, instead of the customary three or four 20-gallon garbage cans.

Manufacturers currently offer the prospective buyer a number of different sized units to choose from — varying in width from 12 to 17¾ inches, in height from 22 to 34½ inches and all less than 24 inches in depth. Some units are made for built-in installation while others are free-standing models.

Simplicity of operation is the keynote. To use the compactor open the drawer (by hand or foot pedal), insert the trash, close the drawer, and push a start button. Some units even have front-end loading without opening the drawer.

All household compactors work basically the same. They employ mechanical pressure to compress the trash to about one-fourth its original volume in approximately 60 seconds. Mechanical means vary from one manufacturer to another — scissor-jack mechanism, belt-driven power screw, or chain-driven twin or triple screws.

Depending upon the make, compactors begin their compacting function anytime after a minimum of 2 to 7 inches of trash is put in the container. The trash bag used (costing 10 to 35¢ each) will hold about 25 pounds. Compacting pressure ranges from 2000 to 3000 pounds, depending upon model.

Manufacturers estimate the operation of a compactor for a year will require $2 worth of electricity and note that the accompanying noise is less than encountered in operating an automatic dishwasher or food waste disposer.

Safety is a key factor in operating a trash compactor. All models offer a key lock to keep the unit beyond the use of children. Some key locks disable the electric circuits and others lock the entire unit to prevent entry at any time.

Trash compactors come in a selection of colors to match or complement other kitchen appliances. Units are sold with a warranty and require a minimum amount of servicing. The entire unit should carry an Underwriters Laboratory approved label.

Food Waste Disposers

First introduced for public sale in 1938, the food waste disposer today comes in a variety of sizes and shapes priced at approximately $150, plus installation. All models consist of three basic elements — a hopper or container where the food waste is contained while being ground; a rotating device at the base of this area which moves the food waste against a sharp stationary object to grind it into small pieces; and a drain chamber where the water carries the ground food waste to an exhaust port in the disposer. Each unit, of course, is powered by an electric motor.

Two basic types of impellers are used in the operation of a food waste disposer. In one type the impellers are rigidly fixed to the fly wheel, while in the other they are free to swivel on a post which is attached to the flywheel. If fixed impellers are used and hard objects such as a bone or fruit pit gets between the impellers and the hopper projection or shredded ring, a jam can result stalling the disposer motor. To free this jam, a reversing feature is available on some models which causes the motor to reverse and rotate in the opposite direction either automatically, or by the user manually operating a switch on the disposer.

In the same potential jam situation, a swivel impeller will swing back and literally go around the hard object if the initial impact is not great enough to dislodge or break the object. On succeeding flywheel revolutions, the impellers continue to strike the object until it is finally broken up. Swivel type impellers keep jams to a minimum.

The two kinds of disposers from which you can choose: a batch feed type where the cover is the control switch and must be in place for the unit to operate; and the continuous feed type activated by a wall switch. The continuous feed unit has an antisplash guard designed to prevent waste from coming back out of the opening. Most manufacturers also recommend keeping a provided cover lightly in the drain when hard objects are being ground.

Cold water is used while grinding wastes to keep fats solidified and to prevent their solidifying further down the drain line and clogging it. The water flow rate should be great enough to keep wastes moving down the drainline, or enough to fill a quart container in 10 seconds.

Most food waste disposers will easily handle all food wastes including bones, fruit rinds and seeds. Fibrous matter like corn husks and artichokes may grind more easily when mixed with other food wastes. They should be fed slowly and with good water flow.

Manufacturers caution that you should never pack wastes into a disposer and that the unit is not designed to dispose of metals, glass or china. If odors are ever noticed, running an orange or lemon rind or some ice cubes through the disposer usually will solve the problem.

When installing a new unit in your home for the first time, it is well to check with your local building department. Some cities still have antiquated codes which prevent the use of disposers due to fear that sewers cannot handle the waste.

Kitchen Aid's line of food waste disposers features a "quick click" mounting system.

BATHROOMS

Bathrooms, like kitchens, are semi-permanent arrangements that become expensive to change and thus should be planned carefully from the start. Not only should you consider current needs, but also keep in mind the use of this room by family members as they grow older.

In approaching bathroom remodeling in the older house it's well to have a very clear idea of who will use the room and what type of bath facilities will meet their needs. Should it be a "family" bath common to all the bedrooms, as it has probably been for the life of the house? Should it be converted to a master bathroom with a new accessway to a particular bedroom? Should it be compartmentalized to provide better usage by more than one person at the same time? Or should the remodeling simply be replacement of an outdated fixture or two and a general sprucing up of the walls, plus better lighting?

While you will look at the bathroom in its entirety, a better way may be to take each phase of bathroom planning by itself for the sake of making a working plan that is within reality.

The age of your family members and their number will help you determine whether your bathroom facilities are sufficient, in the correct location, and equipped to handle their particular needs and desires. The room arrangement may be such that you can't change it without major structural changes, or it may be large enough that you can consider more efficient rearrangement within current confines.

Among the specific types of bathrooms to consider in remodeling are: master suite units, children's baths, garden baths, compartmented baths, lavatories and powder rooms, and special baths such as those designed for a handicapped person or baths incorporating saunas or steam bath facilities.

In bathroom remodeling, give special attention to the existing floor plan and how it can be made more efficient. Is it possible to remove a wall and substantially enlarge the room to the point of compartmentalizing? Would you be able to use one tub-shower fixture in the new setup and gain a second bath with the addition of just another lavatory and water closet?

FIXTURES

The least expensive fixture arrangement places all of the plumbing in one "wet" wall — both supply and drain lines for the tub, lavatory and toilet. Likewise, adding another bathroom back-to-back with the existing bath can produce installation savings. Relocating the toilet is more expensive than relocating either of the other fixtures.

Plumbing fixtures on the market today offer a wealth of remodeling possibilities. No longer are you forced to be satisfied with plain white fixtures so common to the older home. You can choose from a rainbow of colors, many of them special to the particular manufacturer.

LIGHTING

Regardless of size, shape, or age, every bathroom needs two types of lighting — general and directed. In a very small bathroom or powder room, a single light in the ceiling or above the mirror or medicine cabinet may provide sufficient general and directed lighting, but mirror side lights are also recommended. Lighting engineers recommend 30 footcandles of illumination for the bathroom. This is the equivalent of 3.5 to 4 watts of incandescent lighting per square foot of floor area, or 1.5 to 2 watts of fluorescent lighting.

The greatest need for directed lighting in the bathroom is for shaving and make-up. A ceiling fixture above the mirror and a light fixture on each side of the mirror will illuminate the face without shadows. All three fixtures are usually wired to and controlled by one wall switch.

Incandescent lamps are generally preferred for use in areas where women apply make-up as this type of illumination is most like sunlight in color. Always choose white bulbs for reading. Electrical outlets should be carefully placed in the bathroom to accommodate the use of an electric razor, hair dryers, electric comb, toothbrush, etc. These outlets, of course, should be grounded.

Here are some basic "rules of lighting" as set down by General Electric experts:

LIGHTING SMALL MIRRORS—use three fixtures, wired to one switch.

Incandescent. Ceiling unit should be centered over the front edge of the lavatory bowl or countertop. The fixture should be a minimum 12-inch diameter with two 60-watt bulbs. Wall brackets should be centered on the mirror, 30 inches apart and 60 inches above the floor. At the minimum a 6-inch diameter should have one 75-watt each, and preferable for a 5 to 6-inch diameter, spacing should be 16 to 24 inches with two 60-watt or four 40-watt bulbs. Pendants of equal or greater diameter should be similarly spaced.

Fluorescent. Use deluxe warm white tubes with trigger start ballasts, located and wired to one switch. Ceiling fluorescents should be two to four-tube units (20 watt) 24 inches in length and shielded. Fluorescent 20-watt wall-bracket units should flank the mirror with the center of the tube located 60 inches above the floor.

LIGHTING LARGE MIRRORS—mirrors 36 inches or greater in width should be illuminated with a double row of deluxe warm white (30-watt, 36 inch; or 40-watt, 48 inch) fluorescent tubes in a recessed fixture or custom built into a soffit. Recommended soffit dimensions: 16 inches front to back; 8 inches deep; full length of counter.

THEATRICAL EFFECT—exposed-lamp fixtures across the top and sides of a mirror should include four to six lamps per fixture. Decorative 15 watt or 25 watt bulbs are recommended. Side strips should be 30 inches apart.

Lighting in separate compartments of the bathroom should be a minimum one 75-watt, R-30 type unit recessed in the ceiling, or 8-inch diameter 100-watt surface mounted fixture or wall bracket. Fixtures used in the shower or tub area should be recessed vapor-proof type for 75 to 100-watt, with a switch outside of shower area. A bathroom night light can be either a 15-watt switched wall bracket or plug-in type units with 4 or 7-watt bulb.

TUBS AND SHOWERS

Bathtubs used in remodeling need not follow the traditional rectangular style, nor need they be built in. You can obtain square units for use in a corner or niche, and you can get free-standing tubs which sit on four feet much as they did when bathtubs were first introduced in the United States.

Rectangular tubs range from 4 to 6 feet in length, just under 3 feet in width and from 12 to 16 inches in height. Some have body contour design, slip-resistant bottoms and built-in safety handles of polished metal. Square tubs typically are 31 to 48 inches long, 42 to 49 inches wide and 12 to 16 inches high. Many double as shower receptors.

One of the newest applications of the bathtub is the built-in, sunken look which can be accomplished by using a tub with drop-in top flange. The unit can be set into a raised deck to give the appearance of being sunken without cutting through the floor. And, of course, you can go through the floor in some locations and have a fully sunken tub, but this approach becomes much more expensive when remodeling, as opposed to doing it in new construction.

Lightweight fiberglass tubs are very popular for remodeling as they add considerably less weight to the structure than their 200 to 500 pound cast iron counterparts. Steel tubs, weighing approximately 100 pounds, also are remodeling favorites.

Packaged, four-piece baths specifically designed for remodeling applications make possible the addition of a combination bath-shower in an existing 5-foot alcove. Made of fiberglass, the package includes tub and three-piece surround which when assembled becomes a one-piece waterproof unit.

Other packaged shower stalls feature similar assembly and are so designed that all components can be easily moved into the existing room without having the ceiling open, as happens with one-piece units installed in new construction.

Numerous kits on the market permit tub recess remodeling, either using the existing tub or installing a new one. These materials are applied with waterproof mastics and require no further finishing. They are maintained much like plastic laminate countertops.

Soaking tubs of heavy-duty fiberglass are made with molded-in seat to provide comfort and relaxation. This model by American-Standard fits into any 40x40" area and is finished on all four sides for flexibility in location.

Packaged ceramic tile surrounds by American Olean can be installed in one hour or less. Each consists of large sheets of glazed ceramic tile which have been factory-grouted with flexible, waterproof silicone rubber, plus internal corner trim strips which permit slight size adjustments. The only cutting required is to accommodate pipes and the receptor curb.

Also available for improving a bathtub are several styles of enclosures which replace old-fashioned shower curtains and make possible shower bathing. The enclosures include both solid and flexible door styles for one or more sides of the tub.

LAVATORIES

Old-fashioned pedestal-style lavatories are making a comeback, along with bathtubs on decorative feet, so hesitate a moment before you plan to discard such units. If they are damaged, however, you may wish to consider replacement with a built-in style lavatory bowl or perhaps two bowls to ease the morning rush-hour traffic.

Bowls can be recessed in a number of ways, the method being determined by the type of countertop you select. Self-rimming styles are the newest and easiest lavatories to use, as they merely set into a prepared countertop opening and are secured into position with clamps supplied with the bowl.

Under-the-counter styles and flush-mount bowls require special handling of the surround and are somewhat harder to keep clean because of dirt-catching joint lines. A metal rim is required for the flush mount installation in plastic laminate tops. Wall-hung and pedestal-type lavatories usually rule out the use of a vanity top.

Four shapes of lavatories are common to remodeling installations: oval, circular, triangle and the well-known rectangular. In addition, there are specialty units such as shampoo centers with spray fittings and swing-away faucets.

Lavatories usually are installed 31 inches from the floor to the top of the bowl rim, but may be located from 34 to 38 inches off the floor if children will not be using them. A minimum of 12 inches is maintained between bowls in double-bowl installations, with 20 inches preferred.

Recessing kits for up-dating the wall surfaces surrounding a bathtub are offered in several easy-to-install materials including fiberglass, ceramic tile, synthetic marble and prefinished hardboard. The kits usually come complete with all materials for a standard 5' tub recess area including panels, moldings, nails, caulking and adhesive.

The completed installation is professional-looking and can be easily maintained by damp wiping. Full instructions are supplied with each kit.

1. The Marlite tub recess kit installation begins by establishing guidelines for edge moldings, caulking the tub rim along the wall and installing the moldings.

2. The 5'-wide back panel is fitted and adhesive applied to the wall and the back of the panel. Next, the handyman fits and applies the top edge and two inside corner moldings, and caulks the moldings.

3. The side panel with openings already cut for plumbing outlets is applied in the same manner with adhesive applied to both the wall and the panel back. Tub and corner moldings are caulked and edge moldings fitted. Additional caulking weatherseals all plumbing openings.

4. The remaining Marlite panel is coated with adhesive and fitted into place. Harmonizing tub and corner moldings are caulked, edge moldings fitted and applied, and plumbing fixtures and handles replaced.

5. Completing the final step in the installation, the homeowner wipes clean excessive adhesive and caulking. Virtually maintenance-free, the soilproof, heat-resistant Marlite requires only an occasional cleaning with a damp cloth.

6. The fully remodeled bathroom includes a recessed lavatory-vanity installation and large windows opening onto a private garden court.

Photos: Marlite Paneling

Decorative lavatory bowls by Gerber come in drop-in self-rimming and under-the-counter styles. Most self-rimming lavatories have holes for faucet sets while suspended bowls require placement of the fitting in the countertop surface.

Most toilets are made of vitreous china but half of the unit here, the lightweight tank, is made of injection-molded ABS plastic and contains a special thermal inner liner that prevents tank condensation. The unusual corner is the flush tab which replaces the customary handle. This tank can be used with most of Universal-Rundle's water closet bowls.

TOILETS

Four basic types of water closets, or toilets, are manufactured, but in many areas only three of them are accepted by local codes. The one excluded is the washdown which is the noisiest and least efficient, and the one often found in older homes. Next up the line in cost and functions is the reverse trap which has a smaller water area, passageway, and water seal than the better siphon-jet and siphon-action models.

The siphon-jet toilet with its larger trapway is also quieter than reverse trap and washdown units, but not as quiet as the top-of-the-line low-profile siphon-action, a one-piece toilet that has almost no dry surfaces on the interior bowl.

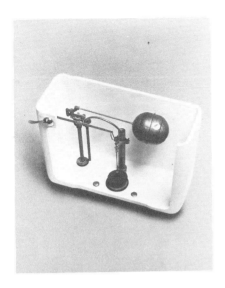
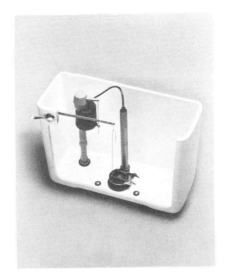

HOW TO REPLACE A TOILET BALLCOCK

Older toilets frequently have leaky, worn out, old fashioned ballcocks that cause water to continually leak into the toilet bowl and create high pitched noises when the toilet is flushed. Replacement of old ballcocks is easy with a new unit that adjusts in height to fit virtually all sizes of toilet tanks and is fully anti-siphon code approved.

The Fluidmaster 400-A provides a fast and positive water shutoff. There are no troublesome float balls or rods to buy. The ballcock is made of stainless steel and Celcon plastic for corrosion-free operation even in salt water conditions.

The unit has internal thread design which permits adjustment merely by twisting apart upper and lower portions. There are no nuts to loosen or tools needed to adjust the height.

(View 1) Conventional ballcock uses mechanical leverage from the float ball and rod to hold back water pressure. As the valve wears, leaking occurs, causing water to be wasted down the overflow tube.

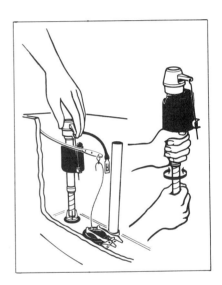

(View 2) The Fluidmaster 400-A valve works with water pressure, not against it, with mechanical leverage. It fills the tank faster and with less noise and the water pressure is actually redirected to hold the valve closed. The stronger the pressure, the tighter the seal.

(View 3) After turning off the water supply to the tank and removing the old ballcock, the Fluidmaster 400-A installation is begun by attachment of a rubber refill tube to the ballcock nipple and positioning the new ballcock to determine proper height.

(View 4) The ballcock can be lengthened by turning counterclockwise and shortened by turning clockwise. It is adjusted so the inside tank lid just clears the top of the ballcock. The unit is then pushed down into the base and tightened in place with nuts.

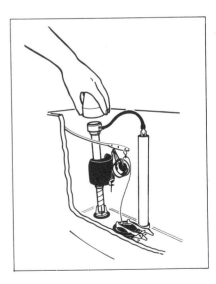

(View 5) After the refill tube has been clamped to the overflow pipe and the water is turned back on, hold down the cup of the unit tightly for the first cycle to fill the tank with water. Then turn the water off, remove the cap, flush the toilet, and turn the water on and off a few times to flush the line of rust, pipe chips and debris. Replace the cup and the unit will be ready for regular use.

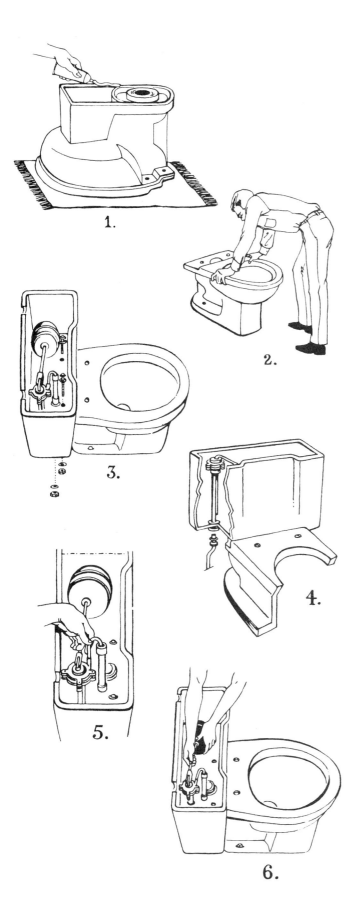

1.

2.

3.

4.

5.

6.

Installing the Toilet Tank and Bowl

Replacement of an existing toilet tank and bowl or installation of this fixture in a new bathroom begins with a thoroughly clean floor surface where the bowl is to be located.

The fixture is placed upside down on a protective soft material to prevent scratching (Figure 1) and a warmed wax ring is applied to the circular recess in the base of the bowl. This is where the fixture will be connected to the waste line previously plumbed through the floor. A setting compound is then applied to the outer rim of the bowl to assure a continuous seal to the floor.

The bowl is then carefully set atop a metal flange previously attached to the floor. The toilet bolts fit through holes in the base of the fixture (Figure 2) ready to receive washers and nuts which should be secured snugly. They should not be force-tightened.

Following placement of large donut-shaped washers on the threaded tank outlet, the tank is placed on the ledge (Figure 3) of the bowl and aligned for placement of bolts downward through the bolt holes of the two parts. Again the bolts should be carefully tightened, alternating from side to side to prevent breaking the tank or bowl.

The cold water line is then connected to the tank with a straight or angle stop (Figure 4), and the ballcock inserted into the tank and secured in position. This latter unit (Figure 5) varies in style with appropriate installation instructions detailed on the package.

Water is turned on by opening the angle or straight stop located beneath the tank. The tank should fill to the "water line" indicated inside the tank. If not, the brass rod supporting the float ball (Figure 6) should be bent until the tank stops filling at the water line.

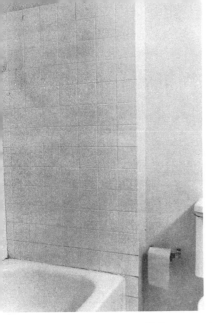

Ceramic tile can be installed over previous ceramic tiles as illustrated here. The "before" view shows mildewed and cracked grout. Following the preparation of the surface (by cleaning all soap film and hard water deposits off the existing tile), adhesive is spread using a notched trowel and then applying pregrouted sheets. New grout lines created between adjoining tile panels are caulked with silicone rubber grout that is highly stain and mildew resistant.

Redi-Set pregrouted ceramic tile sheets, approximately two square feet each, are easily put into place over gypsum wallboard. Grout joints are filled at the factory with a flexible silicone rubber grout which will not mildew, stain or crack. After all sheets are put up, the same grout material is used to finish the installation (American Olean photo).

Toilet styles and tank mechanisms vary from manufacturer to manufacturer, but most bowls are round or elongated and most tanks operate with a ballcock attached to a valve by means of a rod or arm (see sketch). This mechanism often requires replacement in older toilets and frequently is the cause of toilet leaks, and squeaks.

FITTINGS

Often the replacement of bathroom fittings on lavatory bowls and in the tub or shower will help to change the bathroom decor and provide better operation of these fixtures. Lavatory fittings have been greatly improved in recent years making the compression valve somewhat of an outdated unit in the modern home (see adjoining page).

Single-handle lavatory and shower controls simplify both water and temperature control, especially for children. The units come in various finishes, with a variety of decorative handles made from plastic, crystal and metal.

Shower heads, too, have been greatly improved in recent years. You can now obtain units that provide a "massage" and have finger-tip controls for quickly changing water patterns. Some personal-style shower units can be attached to existing shower head arms or tub spouts to provide the benefit of a hand-held unit (for further information, consult *Book of Successful Bathrooms*, by Joseph F. Schram.)

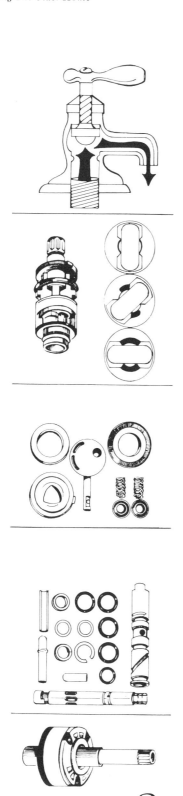

Standard Compression Valve (1)

As illustrated on this page, two-handle faucet sets operate with threaded stems controlled by the handles. The stems screw out to open the supply port and screw in to seal the supply ports. Known as a compression valve, this type faucet has been around for nearly a hundred years.

Disc-to-Disc Type (2)

A newer, two-handle type of faucet uses disc-to-disc contact and has no threads. The lower disc is movable, controlled by a standard handle, and the other disc has ports that are exposed as the cover disc is turned. The more you turn the handle, the more the port is opened and the greater the flow of water. Full-off to full-on is accomplished by only a quarter-turn of the handle. This type faucet has no threads, washers, or packing and the o-ring is not exposed to friction or wear.

Ball-andSocket Units (3)

Single-handle-control faucets, which have grown greatly in popularity over the past decade, include a ball-and-socket type that operates something like an automobile stick-shift. The lever is moved up and down to control volume and left or right to control temperature. As the lever is moved, the holes in the ball line up with those in the socket.

Cartridge Type (4)

Another type of single-lever faucet works with a cam that is pulled out to control water flow, and turned right or left for temperature control. The tapered shape of the cam controls the flow of the water by direct sealing of the ports. The interchangeable cartridge has no metal-to-metal friction and is self-adjusting and self-lubricating. If the faucet requires maintenance, the entire cartridge is replaced.

Tapered Cam Mechanism (5)

Still another of the newest types on the market is the single-handle unit with a cam that is pulled out to control water flow. The tapered shape controls water volume by opening and sealing ports. Here again, turning the handle left or right controls temperature. This kind of faucet is easy to operate, is permanently lubricated and its single moving part is completely isolated from water to provide years of maintenance-free usage.

When you purchase a faucet, ask the seller for a written warranty. Quality faucets, like other appliances, have written warranties to back them up.

LAUNDRY FACILITIES

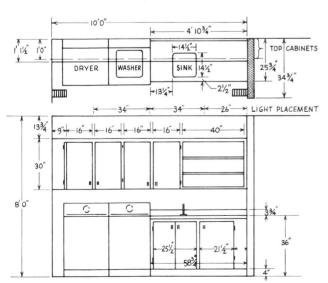

A home bar has been combined with the laundry center at one end of a family room detailed in this drawing. Storage cabinets hide laundry supplies and liquor. The bedroom laundry plan below includes washer, dryer and sink plus storage, all of which can be concealed by 18"-wide folding doors (Plans: Maytag).

While the laundry is located in the basement of many older homes, studies show this to be a most inconvenient location and one that should be avoided if at all possible. One study conducted by Kansas State University shows that an upstairs location can reduce footsteps by as much as one-half. Carrying heavy loads up and down the stairs adds to the inconvenience.

Among the possible locations for a home laundry are:

- The bedroom-bath area, where soiled clothing and linens accumulate and where they are returned after being cleaned. Laundry units often can be installed in a bedroom hallway, or in a larger bath being remodeled.

- The kitchen area is preferred by some as this location combines the two busiest work centers into one. A utility room right off the kitchen keeps the mess from view and is highly convenient.

- The family room is another possible location. Here the laundry units can be concealed behind a folding wall when not in use.

- A patio, breezeway, carport or garage is still another possible location, particularly in warm climates. However, here again the mess of piled clothes becomes highly visible, often when least desired.

Both side-by-side and stackable washer and dryer units require but a minimum amount of space and often can be recessed into an existing closet, under a countertop or in a small area.

An automatic washer requires a drain, plumbing lines for both hot and cold water, and a 115-volt 60 HZ electrical outlet, preferably on its own circuit. An electric dryer requires its own 230-volt, 60 HZ, three-wire circuit, while the gas dryer needs a connection for either natural or LP gas. A gas supply line of rigid pipe or flexible copper tubing is standard, depending upon local codes. A gas dryer also requires a 115-volt, 60HZ connection for the motor (this outlet should be on a separate circuit from the washer). It's well to consider the addition of other wiring and outlets for ironing, sewing machine and the like. And all laundry appliances should be grounded.

All standard-size, air-flow type automatic dryers, gas or electric, should be vented to the outside. Nonvented standard dryers inevitably add to dust accumulation and high moisture content of the exhaust air creates problems of humidity control if not vented.

93

Whirlpool automatic dryers can be hung on the wall or stacked on a rack above a matching washer that rolls easily on sturdy casters. This type of installation requires only 24 inches of floor space and is ideal for containing the units in a closet.

Frigidaire's "Skinni Mini" home laundry center is designed to operate on regular 120-volt household current instead of the usual 230-volt circuit. This makes it possible to install the units near a bedroom, in the kitchen, hallway closet, or other area equipped with a standard electrical outlet. The combined unit is 24 inches wide and 65¾ inches high.

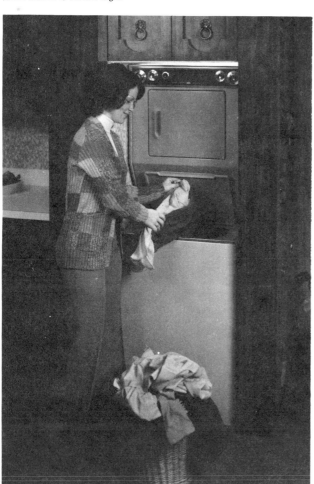

Maytag laundry specialists say venting distance should not exceed 30 feet (minus 5 feet for each elbow) and should not include more than two elbows. Some dryers can be vented through either side, through the back, or straight down. Rigid aluminum vent tubing is recommended, but flexible tubing often is used for greater installation ease. The exterior vent hood should be at least one foot above ground level.

Among the ingredients of a successful laundry center are storage for accumulated laundry, adequate glare-free lighting, countertops and shelves, floor and wall surfaces requiring little care, and safe cabinets for detergents and household cleaning aids.

Countertops and shelves should be at a comfortable level, geared for your own height. Counter-work surfaces 36 inches above the floor allow women of average height to maintain correct posture and avoid fatigue while working. Shelves should be adjustable. Cabinets above the laundry units should allow for opening the appliance tops.

If at all possible, storage for soiled laundry should consist of several smaller containers, rather than one large hamper. If clothing is sorted as it accumulates and put with other items that will be laundered in the same manner, you don't have to re-sort every time you want to wash a load of clothes. The number of containers needed depends upon the type of laundry the family accumulates, and the size of the family.

Slide-out and removable hampers often are the best answer to soiled clothing storage. Plastic tray-style or wire baskets can be stacked vertically on shelves in a tall closet or can be placed side-by-side on a shelf or under a counter.

Some additional suggestions in planning your laundry:

- Select appliances that are designed for front-end servicing and units with back panels that permit flush installation against the wall.

- If you choose colored appliances, pick a color that you can live with for quite a few years and use it as part of your decorative theme.

- Be sure to check the volume of the automatic appliance you are buying. "Pounds" are a meaningless way to judge a washer, as five pounds of nylon curtains take up much more space than five pounds of bath towels. Select a model large enough to handle the loads you normally wash, but engineered to handle other size loads — small, medium and large.

- Check warranty conditions closely to see if the price includes installation, delivery and service.

ATTICS

With the square-foot cost of living space increasing almost daily, it makes considerable sense to look at unused attic space as a potential living area when you are cramped for space. Converted attics can be used for bedrooms, a study or sewing center, children's play area, or even a private apartment within a house.

Most attic conversions involve many of the basic construction details outlined in this book — framing, door hanging, insulation, paneling, painting or wallpapering, installing a lighting fixture and convenience outlets, ventilation, storage and built-ins and other decorative touches.

This converted attic bedroom with its sloping ceiling and walls was redone by designer Ethel Samuels, NSID. The headboard wall was "straightened out" by building a storage compartment under the window, covering the window with folding shutters and lighting the window alcove with fluorescent tubes hidden from view. Masonite shale white paneling and contrasting dark woodgrain paneling were used effectively in combination with a bold print wallpaper. The opposite end of the room was transformed from an uninteresting arrangement to a large walk-in closet with folding doors covered with prefinished paneling. The desk was moved to this area of the room and adjustable shelves installed. The houndstooth wallpaper in the closet is matched by the carpeting.

Wasted attic space was turned into this combination den-guest room with fold-down hanging desk, wall-hung shelving, cabinets built in under the sofa-bed and other storage fit into the lower part of sloping walls. Western wood 1x8" v-groove paneling visually lifts the walls (Photo: Western Wood Products Association).

Some attic conversions are accomplished without breaking through the roof while others become more desirable by the cutting through an area and installing a dormer or skylight for natural daylighting. Where feasible, plumbing can be extended to provide a small bath with shower stall, lavatory and water closet.

Before undertaking an attic remodeling, carefully sketch all existing details which will have a bearing on your possible floor plan and layout. For example, if the chimney runs directly through the center of the attic you may wish to frame around it with shelving for open storage on each side, or you may wish to use the chimney area as the divider wall for establishing two rooms. Chances are the possibilities of moving the chimney will prove costly.

While sloping ceiling and walls of the attic can be a decorating problem, consider the use of built-in bunks, desks,

clothes storage and other compartments or cabinets to enhance the finished setting and save space.

Second thoughts should be given to finishing an attic that has a pitched roof which will not permit a ceiling height of at least 7 feet in the center portion. While beds and other low furniture can be placed on either side of an "aisle", there must be adequate headroom in the walking area if the finished room is to be put to practical use. Likewise, an attic which must be reached through a trap door and does not have space to add stairs, is not an efficient area to be used for other than storage purposes.

A shed dormer can be added to the front or back of the house by raising the roof slope and framing in new outside walls. This type of dormer is preferable to the gable dormer, as it results in more usable floor space through increased head room.

Once the maid's quarters on the third floor of a Northwestern region home, the dated appearance was transformed into a hideaway studio. Remodeling included enlargement of the window opening with installation of a floor-to-ceiling unit, elimination of a corner closet and nearby crawl door to attic eaves, and installation of a skylight.

Walls of the studio and the ceiling were surfaced with Western cedar beveled paneling and new landing railing was added to the stairwell. The original door leading into the room was painted and remains equipped with the original lockset. Carpeting and pull-up fabric blinds add to the setting. (Photos: Western Wood Products Association).

BASEMENTS

Large basements can provide the space for another entire living center. Or smaller basements can provide a family recreation room, game room, hobby center or series of rooms to make your home more functional and enjoyable.

Aside from being a catch-all storage center, the basement usually is home to the heating and cooling system, which makes it an economical area to maintain, temperature-wise. In fact, many furnaces have register outlets on the side for just this purpose.

In remodeling a basement into living area attention should be given to possible traffic patterns, location of key elements such as furnace, support columns, plumbing controls, laundry units and the like. Make several sketches and keep an open mind as to possible room arrangement. Heating ducts often can be incorporated into a dropped ceiling or decorative soffit; pipe columns can be boxed with paneling or gypsum wallboard or even concealed as part of a new wall; ceiling framing can be hidden from view by an acoustical ceiling containing luminous panels; and walls can be furred vertically or horizontally and then covered with attractive prefinished paneling.

Various patching compounds available from paint and building materials dealers make it relatively easy to seal cracks in a concrete floor or you may prefer to put down 2x4" "sleepers" and install a totally new floor above the concrete. Various grades of resilient tile may be used at basement level, as well as carpeting and wood-finish flooring.

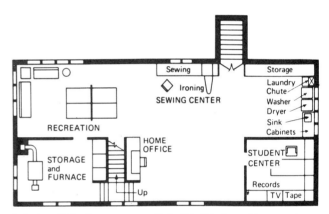

Only two distinct rooms are walled off in this "open" basement arrangement, permitting the housewife to keep an eye on toddlers while performing her laundry chores. The student center reduces possible irritation of stereo volume.

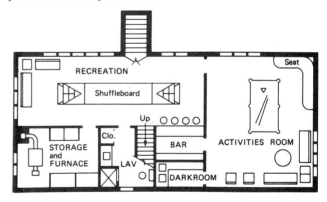

Distinctive areas created in this basement arrangement accommodate varied activities. A laundry on the floor above removed the need for appliances in the basement.

Basic 2x4 framing with studs 16 inches on center added to the masonry walls of this basement, as the first step in remodeling the area into usable living space. Insulation batts were then applied between the studs and the walls are shown here ready to be covered with prefinished paneling (Photo courtesy of Marlite).

Floorplans: Bilco Company

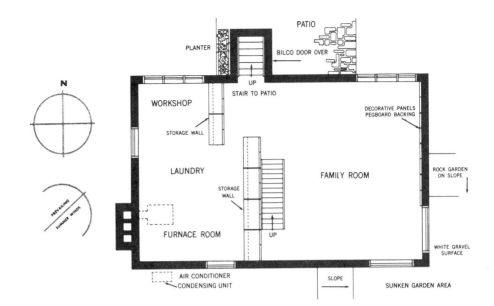

This basement plan with a southeast sun exposure shows deep windows at the corners of the house to catch summer breezes. A storage partition serves as a sound barrier while open planning insures excellent ventilation.

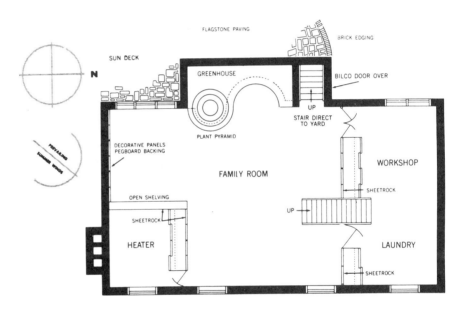

With the installation of a longer window and centralized basement entrance, this basement provides indoor-outdoor living with access to the patio and greenhouse area.

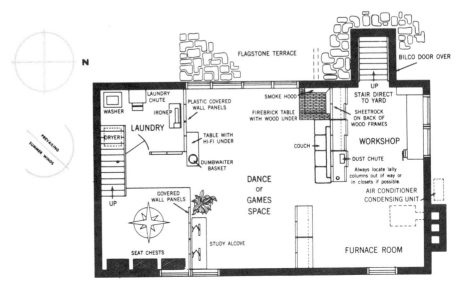

Outside entrance provides access to workshop, cleanup rooms and dirt-associated areas. The fireplace is vented through the ground to an outdoor barbecue.

Unattractive basement columns can be hidden in several different ways, including this arch approach built with lumber and Z-Brick decorative brick. The arches can be adapted to fit any room and ceiling height.

A fireplace can be the center of attention in a basement recreation or family room. This remodeling included resilient flooring and a suspended acoustical ceiling with built-in lighting panels. Storage cabinets and bookcases occupy the entire wall area flanking the fireplace (Photo: Conwed Corp.).

Basement entryway stairs in new or existing installations are easily installed with heavy, 14-gauge steel stringers nailed to the areaway sidewalls.

Standard 2x10" lumber treads slide into slots in the stringers and are anchored with nails. The treads may later be removed if necessary (when bringing large bulky items into the basement) to provide a whole areaway free and clear.

While the indoor basement steps provide the main access to the lower location in most homes, you may wish to consider an additional entrance from the outdoors. In such installations, a sturdy metal basement door conceals stairs framed in a masonry block or concrete well area. Exterior doors range from 3 feet 11 inches to 4 feet 7 inches in width to provide a convenient traffic flow to the yard area without going through first-floor rooms in the house. Lawn furniture, bikes, garden tools and the like can be easily moved in and out as desired. Packaged stair stringers can be purchased to avoid the need for constructing concrete steps. Installed in minutes, these steel unit have removable treads to facilitate moving bulky items (ping-pong tables, billiard table, etc.) in and out of the basement. The treads are cut from standard 2x10 inch lumber stock.

Remodeling of basement areas often can double the usable space in a home. The basement pictured here in the "before" stage is really only half the total basement area. The stairway from the floor above comes down to a point at the far left of the picture. The same area in the second view has a large refreshment bar as a focal point. Designer Terry Regnier used Marlite wormy chestnut paneling and accented it with bright splashes of color in the furnishings and accessories. A built-in charcoal broiler and oven is located at the extreme left. The third view of the room shows plenty of space for billiards and a comfortable game table. The paneling used for the remodeling is 16-inch by 8-foot prefinished planks applied with adhesives and concealed metal clips to furring strips. No finish is required.

Light and ventilation are two other key elements of good basement design and layout. Maximum natural daylighting is desirable and often can be increased from a minimum beginning by means of additional grading away from the home. Basement windows need not be small and widely spaced; group them for bright and airy settings.

Dampness in a basement in the summer is frequently caused by condensation of moisture from the air. This moisture problem occurs when warm, moist air from the outdoors comes in contact with cool basement walls and floors, and with uninsulated cold-water pipes. The water then condenses on the cool surfaces.

Dampness caused by condensation can usually be cured by warming the basement, through ventilating, insulating.

or heating, or by reducing the amount of moisture in the basement by dehumidifying.

By opening basement windows in dry weather, the walls and floors can be warmed in the summer. An exhaust fan installed in a basement window and operated during the day is helpful in circulating air through the basement. However, ventilating alone is not a very dependable cure for moisture problems.

The amount of moisture in a basement can be reduced by a mechanical dehumidifier which extracts the moisture and deposits it in a tank or allows it to run down the drain. The mechanical dehumidifier is essentially a small refrigeration unit, and the moisture in the air condenses on the coils since they are colder than any other surface in the basement. Some heat is given off in the operation of a dehumidifier, which further helps to control condensation.

Walls can be kept above the temperature of the ground by insulation. When the walls are warmer, the moisture in the air will not condense readily on them. Moisture-resistant insulation and built-in vapor barrier must be used.

To reduce the amount of water collecting on cold water pipes, insulate them with a formed or wrapped insulation.

Try to keep work areas separated from play areas. Use of storage walls as dividers between the two areas helps to deaden sound from one to another. Likewise, darkrooms and other hobby centers requiring plumbing should be located as close as possible to water source and drain.

Basement storage needn't be unattractive. Three-sided "wedge" cabinets in unused corners can be equipped with doors to conceal contents. Under-the-stairs spaces can be enclosed or compartmentalized for canned foods or seasonal storage items.

The basement is an excellent location for a "mud" room or small bath area with stall shower, lavatory bowl and water closet. Some sauna kits are designed for use in a basement. Not only can the room be used by children after a long day of play, but also for mom when she is doing the laundry or dad after he has finished with the gardening or working in his adjacent workshop.

HOW TO REPLACE AN EXISTING BASEMENT DOOR ENTRANCE

Old wooden basement doors often mar the appearance of an older home as well as cause problems with rain and snow leaks. Such doors can be replaced by the homeowner with packaged entrance units that are weathertight and virtually intruder-proof. This series of photographs solves this common basement headache with a steel basement door by Bilco Company.

(1) Old-fashioned wood basement doors frequently show their age and have hardware so installed that a burglar could easily gain entrance.

(2) Removal of the old doors is accomplished with a crow bar. If concrete surround is in good condition, mounting framework for the new unit is a simple matter of locating and drilling holes for the hardware. If concrete is poor, knock it off and recap the area.

(3) Bricks are used to prop the assembled door frame in position while marking and cutting the siding to accept the header which secured the unit to the house. Flashing and caulking waterproofs the joint.

(4) The brick and stone used to prop up the unit now become a part of the new concrete surround poured into a simple wood frame erected around the unit.

(5) Before completing the capping, make sure the frame is square by assembling the doors to the frame. Bottom edges of both doors should form a straight line. Concrete should not go above the metal.

(6) Concrete is allowed to set before engaging the torsion bars. Forms are then removed and caulking applied around the outside where the door joins the masonry. Finish with an alkyd-base metal enamel will give you the color of your choice.

(7) The completed installation provides doors that open and close effortlessly. Automatic safety catches lock the doors open against accidental closure, yet release with a touch. An inside bolt locks the doors securely (Photos: Bilco Company).

1

2

3

4

5

6

7

WALLS

GYPSUM WALLBOARD

Gypsum wallboard is an excellent material for room remodeling and room additions. Panels are produced in thicknesses of ¼, ⅜, (⅜ inch or thicker panels provide the necessary sound insulation), ½ and ⅝ inch in a standard 4-foot width with lengths of 7, 8, 9, 10, 11, 12, 13, or 14 feet. The material comes with a standard finish sheeting on each side, with a foil back for vapor barrier use in exterior walls, and with a water-resistant surface which serves as a base for ceramic or plastic wall tile in bathrooms, kitchens and utility rooms.

You can install gypsum wallboard two ways — apply it horizontally across studs or joists, or apply it vertically (parallel) to studs and joists. The preferred method is horizontally, as it will require the least lineal footage of joints that require taping and finishing.

Gypsum manufacturers recommend purchasing a material length that will run the entire length of the room wall if this is possible, and it is in rooms up to 14 feet long. Doing this places the only vertical joints in the corner or outside edge of the wall. Most walls in today's home are 8 feet to 8 feet 2 inches high, an ideal dimension for using gypsum wallboard.

Gypsum wallboard is easy to cut with a standard trimming knife or sharp utility knife. The material should be carefully measured, marked and then scored with the ivory-colored side face up. A straightedge should be held firmly against the panel while the knife is pulled through the paper and part of the panel core. Hold the knife at a slight angle away from the straightedge to prevent cutting into the board edge.

Once the score has been made, you can easily break the core of the gypsum panel by snapping away from the scored face paper. The cut is completed by carefully running the knife through the back paper. The cut edge should then be sanded with coarse sandpaper wrapped around a hand-sized block of wood. Be sure to keep panel edges as square as possible.

Recommended nailing of gypsum wallboard calls for 1¼ inch annular-ring nails when using panel thicknesses of ¼, ⅜ and ½ inch. Use 1⅜ annular-ring nails for ⅝-inch thick panels. With either size nail, space nails a maximum of 7 inches apart on ceiling and 8 inches on walls and at least ⅜ inches from the edge of the panels.

You should begin nailing a gypsum panel in the center. Hold the material tight against the framing and complete the center nailing. Nail the perimeter of the panel last. Be cautious to not overdrive or countersink nails as this results in breakage of the paper surface. Just leave a small dimple at the nailhead which will be covered with taping compound.

Exterior corners of gypsum walls should be protected by a metal corner bead nailed every 9" along each edge in holes provided along the flange. Be sure to drive the nails all the way to below the nose of the corner bead and tightly into the flange. Here again, they will be covered by taping compound.

When installing panels horizontally, apply the top panel first, tight against the ceiling panels. Use the vertical application when the ceiling is over 8 feet 2 inches high.

If a new gypsum ceiling is needed in the room, apply the ceiling panels first with the aid of another person. If you are totally alone, use of T-braces made of 2x4's (with the long end ½ inch longer than the floor-to-ceiling height) will enable you to support the panel firmly against the joists while you nail.

Taping wallboard joints requires the use of 4, 5, or 6 inch and 10 inch-wide joint-finishing knives available from paint and building material dealers. These tools are used to apply joint compound and wallboard tape. The 4-inch knife is used for taping and embedding; the 6 inch knife for second and third-coat application; and the 10 inch knife for flat joints and exterior corners.

The first step in finishing joints is to spread wallboard compound across the joint, leveling it with the surface of the panels and being careful not to leave any bare spots. Wallboard tape is then immediately applied, using the knife to embed the tape in the compound. Excess compound is removed during this process.

With the tape centered over the depression and firmly embedded, another layer of compound is spread across the tape (with 4" knife). Tape should not be overlapped at tapered joints. Nails should then be covered with compound making certain that no metal head remains above the surface.

The joint taping and nail-covering first coat should be permitted to dry for at least 24 hours before the second coat application. Begin by smoothing the surface lightly with sandpaper and then apply the compound extending 2 inches beyond the taping coat. Feather the edges of the compound flush with the panel and allow to dry. Cover nail head a second time.

Gypsum wallboard can be cut with a utility knife, using a 4-foot T-square to assure an accurate cut.

In horizontal wall application of gypsum wallboard, the top panel should be installed first, pushing it flush to the ceiling.

Paper tape and joint compound are applied with a wide knife.

Photos: Georgia-Pacific Corporation

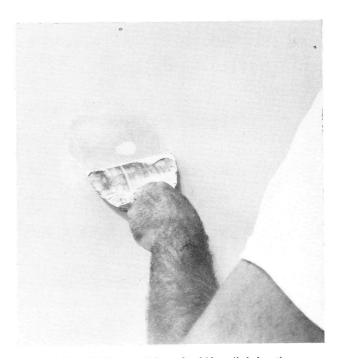

A 4-inch joint finishing knife is used to hide nails below the wallboard surface.

The third coat is applied in the same fashion, feathered another 2 inches beyond the second coat. Give final sanding with a fine-grade paper, taking care not to scar the face paper.

Wallboard panels can be smooth painted or textured with sand-finish paint or textured paints. More about this is covered in the section on painting.

PANELING

Paneling a room is one of the quickest and best ways to add a new and attractive appearance to an older setting that would otherwise reflect both its age and use. Applying paneling is relatively simple and a project that can be undertaken by the homeowner with most gratifying results.

Antique-style paneling can increase the attractiveness of an older home without changing the original mood of the house. Here the decorative paneling features an authentic crazing and distressing complete with worm holes and random-spaced beaded double grooves (Photo: Masonite Corporation).

Wood paneling blends well with other basic interior building materials including stucco, brick, gypsum wallboard and flexible wallcoverings. A disastrous blight which all but eradicated one of the most beautiful trees from the North American continent gave us the rare and distinctively marked wormy chestnut wood veneer shown here (Photo: U.S. Plywood Corporation).

Literally thousands of prefinished panels are now available from building materials dealers for use in both new construction (add-ons) and remodeling. Your particular taste will help to determine what is best for you, best to achieve the setting you are planning (style of furniture, carpeting, drapes, etc.) and best for finishing and future maintenance.

Prefinished, factory-made paneling is by far the biggest seller and the most easy to use. It is finished the minute you drive the last nail or apply the last panel and matching moldings with special panel adhesive. And from there, it's just an occasional wiping with a damp sponge, water and possibly mild detergent. Available panel sizes range from 4x7 feet (used for mobile homes) to 4x16 feet in ⅜, 3/16 and ¼ inch thicknesses. Prefinished hardboard also is available in convenient 16-inch wide planks with tongue-and-groove edges.

Light, medium and dark-toned wood paneling species also are offered in 1 inch thickness in nominal widths of 4, 6, 8 and 10 inch-widths, with square-edged or tongue-and-groove edged patterns. Many of these patterns are architecturally shaped and machine-molded to provide handsome shadow lines. This type of paneling needs finishing, but offers the advantages of board-and-batten and board-on-board applications in the contemporary home. Random-width wood paneling is also easy to install horizontally or in herringbone patterns to produce an interesting design, and is excellent for wainscoting a period room.

A tour of your local building material dealer's showroom will quickly give you an idea of the tremendous number of species, patterns, colors and styles of paneling from which to choose. Once you have made your selection, it's time to begin the installation.

Like all remodeling projects, your work should be planned carefully, in advance. It's well to sketch the job before you begin and once you have the material, place the panels around the room to obtain the most pleasing effect in color and grain. Then number the panels in sequence before piling them out of the way when you begin the fitting process.

Manufacturers will supply you with specific instructions for their brand of paneling. Usually, these instructions will give you two application choices: nailing or adhesive application. In new construction, the panels can be applied (if building code permits) directly to wall studs; in existing construction the materials can be used over plaster and other nonmasonry walls without furring strips. The application of ¼-inch plywood paneling over existing plaster or new ½-inch gypsum wallboard makes the resulting wall less vulnerable to fire. Some codes require this.

In new construction, it's best to use a ⅜ inch gypsum wallboard or 5/16 inch plywood underlayment, but 1x2 inch framing lumber or ⅜ x 1⅞ inch plywood strips may be used for furring attached to the studs. The same furring also is required for applying paneling to masonry walls such as those found in the basement. All furring should be applied with the face grain running at right angle to the direction of the panel application. Shimming with cedar shingles or other material often is necessary to obtain a true wall surface. Shorter vertical furring strips are applied to masonry walls at 48 inches on center, while the longer strips are spaced horizontally 16 inches on center.

Be sure to follow the specific instruction on the adhesive cartridge when using this installation method. All surfaces to which the adhesive is applied should be clean and dry (wallpaper should be removed), and both the adhesive and room temperature should be between 60 and 100 degrees. As shown in the accompanying Royalcote photos, a ⅛ inch-thick continuous ribbon of adhesive is applied to furring or other surfaces where panel edges are to be bound. Intermittent ribbon beads are 3 inches long and spaced with a 6 inch open area between. All four edges of the paneling should be attached to the furring.

Paneling applications should begin in a corner using a scribe to mark the first panel before it is cut to assure a plumb fit. Manufacturers recommend that on long spans of paneling a small space be allowed at the end of the wall for possible expansion. Likewise, a ¼ inch clearance should be allowed at the ceiling and base (often this is covered by a molding strip).

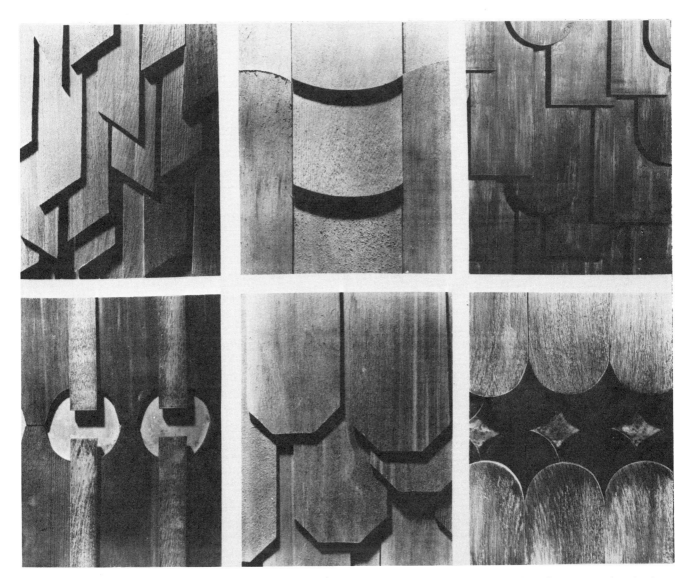

Siding shingles can be used to create highly distinctive interior wall surfaces. These six possibilities employ fancy butt patterns in red cedar (Photo: Red Cedar Shingle & Handsplit Shake Bureau).

Paneling over an existing wall sometimes requires furring strips to obtain a level surface. Here the 1x2s are spaced 16 inches apart and are nailed to studs.

1

A ⅛ inch thick continuous ribbon of adhesive is then applied to the clean furring strips and other surfaces where the panel edges are to be bonded. Adhesive is applied according to manufacturer's instructions.

2

Prefinished panel is then moved into position over the furring strips and immediately pressed into position. Uniform hand pressure is used to press the panels firmly into contact with the adhesive bead.

3

Two nails are used at the top of the panel to maintain its position. Heads remain exposed for easy removal later.

4

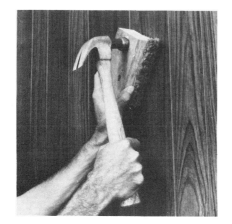

A padded block of wood and hammer or mallet are used, after a 15 to 20 minute interval, to reapply pressure and provide the final bond.

5

A scrap of carpeting is used under the hammer to protect the paneling surface while the top nails are removed (Photos: Masonite Corporation).

6

When using the nailing method, all panel edges should be joined over a stud regardless of whether an underlayment material is used. Two-inch finish nails are used (with underlayment) and 1¼-inch nails are used with furring strips or solid surfaces. Specifics on placement will be contained in the paneling literature and manufacturer's instructions.

Nominal 1x4 inch furring also is used for the application of random-width, 1 inch lumber paneling. Here the material, if tongue-and-grooved, is blind-nailed along the tongue edge as each piece is applied to conceal all nails in the finished installation. Panels are checked each step of the way for plumb and can be adjusted slightly until plumb is corrected.

Horizontal use of lumber paneling will make a room seem longer or larger and a ceiling lower. Furring strips usually are located vertically on 3 foot spacing for this type installation.

This living room is highly typical of many others found in older homes being purchased today. The decorating goal: to achieve the most dramatic change at least cost.

Before paneling, the walls of this living room required painting at least every two to three years. The owner's small children necessitated constant wall cleaning and maintenance which wore paint away.

After paneling, the living room takes on a warm quality. Maintenance has become practically nil and heating costs less because of the insulative value of the redwood material (Photos: California Redwood Association).

The application of just two sheets of distinctive prefinished paneling resulted in this dramatic change. The paneling simulates hand-laid oak panel inserts, highlighted by a beautifully detailed inlay strip, all on a single 4x8 sheet of durable hardboard (Photos: Masonite Corporation).

Moldings

Newly paneled rooms can be given the professional look by completion with the appropriate moldings — for finishing door and window openings, at inside and outside corners, where paneling meets the ceiling, as a cap to cover exposed panel edges (such as the top of wainscot panels) and at the floor line to cover the gap between the bottom edge of the paneling and an uneven floor.

Standard molding patterns are available in various species of wood including ponderosa and sugar pine, white fir, douglas fir and larch. Pine moldings are also available in many areas in specified length finger-jointed moldings for use in applications where the surface will be covered with an opaque finish.

As well as unfinished wood moldings sold by most lumber and building material dealers, prefinished moldings are offered in colors and woodgrains to match or harmonize with various wood panels. Some of these moldings have a vinyl outer skin that never needs refinishing while still others are embossed cellular vinyl with the color going all the way through the material.

Standard moldings have particular applications in finishing a room as shown here. Specific shapes are made presinished and unpainted for job-site finishing. Other molding patterns also may be obtained from some companies on special order.

Standard patterns

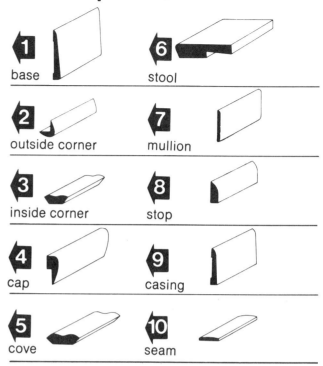

1 base
2 outside corner
3 inside corner
4 cap
5 cove
6 stool
7 mullion
8 stop
9 casing
10 seam

Standard moldings have particular applications in finishing a room as shown here. Specific shapes are made prefinished and unpainted for job-site finishing. Other molding patterns also may be obtained from some companies on special order.

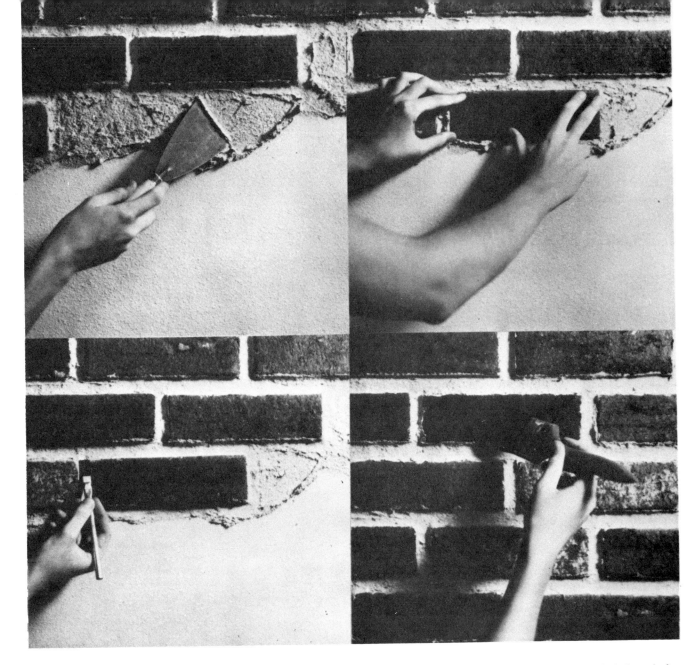

DECORATIVE BRICK

Decorative brick wall covering is an efficient and relatively easy material to use in restoring older homes. Applied with an adhesive mortar which is troweled onto the surface to be covered, the nonceramic mineral material is lightweight and easy to handle.

Z-Brick, the oldest of substitute brick materials, looks just like real brick but is only ⅜ inch thick. It is fireproof and comes in two traditional, standard-shape types — with a smooth surface or with a texture that gives a rustic weathered look. Colors range from reds and golds to buffs, grays and white. Styles with the look of used brick are also available.

There are no special corner pieces required with this material as the bricks are easily cut with a hacksaw. At corners, the bricks can be butted or mitered for a clean fit. In addition, the bricks can be tapered along their length for use in arches.

Because Z-Brick is applied one brick at a time, a number of interesting effects are possible. For example, the brick can be set in herringbone, basket weave, and stack bond patterns. White, natural or black adhesive mortar can be used to create an unlimited number of design patterns.

As shown in the accompanying pictures, mortar is troweled onto the surface to be covered. The bricks are then slid into place with a side-to-side, wiggling motion. At corners, windows or doors, the bricks are cut to fit with a hacksaw, with the edges dress cut with a file. After the brick is in place, the mortar between the bricks is smoothed. The final step is brushing on a coat of protective sealer.

This material is weatherproof and also may be used for exteriors, around fireplaces, barbecues, for landscaping, and the like.

View 1

View 2

STUCCO

Applying stucco used to be a job strictly for the professional. But a new acrylic-base version has changed all that and you can create a boldly textured stucco ceiling or accent wall without running the problems of conventional powdered stucco.

The new material, called Z-Ment Stucco, is a thick, premixed adhesive that can be easily troweled on, even over bumpy or badly cracked walls. The material fills in deep cracks and pits without sinking or cracking and because it is resilient, it will not crack from shrinkage.

Z-Ment Stucco comes in white, black and natural colors and provides a 16-to-20 foot coverage per gallon. Application begins by troweling the material on the surface (view 1) then texturing it (view 2) with a heavy texturizing brush or smoothing it with a wood float. After the stucco has had an hour or two to stand up, a second application of Z-Ment mortar is troweled on with a random smoothing to give it a "patched" look (view 3).

Mediterranean effects are easily achieved with white Z-Ment Stucco which can be applied directly to existing walls and ceilings. The material is premixed, requires no water and provides rough textures and shadows.

View 3

HOW TO BUILD AND FRAME PARTITIONS

A room or area may be divided or changed in shape by the construction of a simple nonbearing partition. Because nonbearing partitions do not support the floor above, their construction is lighter and easier than that of load-bearing partitions.

Nonbearing partitions generally are constructed of 2x4-inch studs, set either 16 or 24 inches apart. The bottom of the studs are nailed to another 2x4 called the sole plate, which is nailed to the floor. A top plate, also 2x4, is nailed to the ceiling, or in the case of an unfinished basement or attic, directly to the ceiling joists or rafters.

To align the new partition, measure its location from an existing wall and then, using a chalk line (1) mark a straight line on the floor. The partition sole plate is then set against the chalk line (2) and nailed to the floor.

Using a level to insure the partition being level, (3) nail the first studs to the existing walls. Once these end studs are in place, set the top plate (4) by nailing it to the bottom of the ceiling joists or the ceiling. Place the studs on 16-inch (or 24-inch) centers and toenail (5) them on both sides to both the sole plate and the top plate.

Where ceiling heights and clearances permit, it is possible to assemble the partition on the floor and then tilt it into place. Studs should be doubled at the sides and tops of all openings, and never be notched (for wires, pipes, etc.) more than one-third their depth (Photos: Georgia-Pacific Corporation).

WALLPAPER

Wallpaper does much more than just cover the wall, it lets you achieve special effects, give more depth to a room, emphasize the motif of any kind of furniture, add warmth or coolness, and express your individual taste. You can easily create new dimensions with patterns and textures and unusual color combinations.

Anyone who has spent time selecting a wallpaper pattern will quickly tell you that the options are truly limitless. You can choose from thousands of different wallpapers including florals, geometrics, damasks, brocades, flocked and embossed papers, papers especially designed for kitchen, bath, living room, dining room, family room, bedroom and hall. Every conceivable color is offered and some textures including authentic grass cloth from the Orient.

Scenic wallpapers available today include mural treatments for a single wall or an entire room. These wallpapers are best used in rooms where drama can be expressed, such as dining rooms. They should be selected with considerable care and assigned to the right place.

Many wallpapers are plastic sealed to protect against wear and tear and can be washed. Others are made of vinyl and can actually be scrubbed. One type requires you to apply the adhesive, while another comes prepasted for faster application.

Problem walls that may need covering — concrete, cinder or cement block, grooved paneling, old plaster, etc. — can now be finished with decorative wallcoverings without the bother of filling cracks. A special Wall Cover lining bridges minor cracks and recesses. The 24-inch-wide material is applied with ready mix vinyl adhesive and in turn is covered with decorative wallcovering (Photos: Imperial Wallcoverings, a Collins & Aikman Co.).

113

You can easily estimate your room requirements and then multiply the number of rolls required by the cost per roll or material you select. First, add up the lineal footage around the walls of the room to be prepared. Then multiply this figure by the height in feet of the wall from the baseboard or chair rail to the ceiling. Divide this by 25 and you will arrive at the number of rolls needed.

A roll of wallpaper is a unit of measure usually containing 30 square feet, but wallpaper is sold in double or triple roll bolts depending upon its width, which ranges from 30 to 54 inches. This is to give you the maximum number of full strips from each bolt. You divide by 25 to allow for matching and pattern. Deduct two single rolls for every three doors and windows.

Many local wallpaper shops have free movies which customers can watch at their convenience to pick up the many "tricks of the trade" in hanging wallpaper. They also usually permit taking sample books home over night for easier selection in the actual room to be papered.*

*For additional information consult *Wallcoverings and Decoration* by Abel Banov, a Successful book.

HOW TO HANG PREPASTED WALLCOVERINGS

1. One strip (less ½ inch) to the right of the door, fasten plumb line from ceiling. Chalk the sring and, holding it near the bottom, snap a line onto the wall.

2. Measure ceiling height. Allow 3 inches extra at top, 3 inches at bottom. Cut one strip. Match pattern, cut two more, hang before cutting more.

3. Fill water tray. Hold bottom edge, roll up the strip, pasted side out. Weight the strip with table knife inside, submerge in the water.

4. *Pattern side down, pull slowly from water. Fold as shown, paste-to-paste. Set aside to soak at least 5 minutes if wallcovering in strippable. If not strippable, hang immediately after folding. Prepare second strip.*

5. *Unfold top part of strip only. Position near ceiling, leaving 3 inches to trim later. Line up the right edge of the strip with the plumb line.*

6. *Wet with sponge, smooth strip, working from center to edges. Unfold bottom, align with plumb line, smooth. Small bubbles disappear with drying.*

7. *Use ruler with knife or razor blade to trim top, bottom and around door frame. Wipe off paste with wet sponge. Sponge entire strip. Roll down edges with a seam roller. Don't use roller on flock wallcoverings. Tape seam with sponge to avoid matting flock pile.*

8. *Dip and hang succeeding strips. Carefully match pattern at left edge of new strip with previous strip. Butt edges, sponge, and roll edges.*

9. *Measure edge-to-corner at top, middle and baseboard. Take widest measure. Add ½ inch. Cut vertical strip this width. Apply, overlap corner. Measure remainder of strip. Add ½ inch. Drop plumb this distance from corner. Follow plumb, apply, match and lap at corner.*

10. *Measure to frame. Add 1 inch. Cut vertical strip to this width. Apply so it extends over top of frame 1 inch. Trim around frame. Match pattern; use short lengths above, below frame.*

11. *Alternate method. Use drop cloth. Place water box at baseboard. Slowly unroll throughly wet strip. Align with plumb line. Follow steps 6 through 10 (Photos: Imperial Wallcoverings, A Collins & Aikman Co.).*

FLOORS AND CEILINGS

FLOORS

A new floor is just as good as the job done installing it, and today's homeowner has more choices and flexibility than ever before. Manufacturers have made considerable strides in producing materials geared for the nonprofessional, materials that are easier to install, longer lasting, and require a minimum of care and maintenance.

All flooring material should be installed according to the specific instructions of the manufacturer of the material. Finish flooring must be firmly fastened (with a few exceptions) to the underflooring to avoid buckling or cracking. Adhesives are used to fasten asphalt, cork, linoleum, rubber, vinyl, wood block and ceramic tile floors. The latter can also be set in a bed of cement mortar, as are brick, cement tile, flagstone and slate. Nails are used for strip wood flooring, and nails and screws for plank flooring.

In order that adhesives can attain their full bonding strength, all underflooring must be thoroughly dry and free from grease, oil, wax, paint and varnish. These can be removed by sanding, scraping, or using a chemical solvent. Be sure that all traces of solvent are removed before the adhesive is applied.

To secure a good adhesive bond on concrete subfloors, remove all loose particles and concrete dust by wire-brushing. Use crack filler to close up cracks and small holes, and resurface badly damaged concrete with a mastic underlayment or a smooth, troweled cement finish.

A very thin asphalt "cut-back" cement, which is especially alkali and moisture resistant, is recommended as a primer to seal porous and dusty concrete subfloors, to coat concrete floor slabs which show signs of dampness, and to prepare concrete subfloors for adhesive when asphalt or vinyl asbestos tile is used. Surface oil or grease should be removed from concrete subfloors with an alkali-type cleaner or a solution of tri-sodium phosphate. The floor should be rinsed with water and dried thoroughly.

Always use the adhesive recommended by the manufacturer for the particular type of flooring material and its condition of use. The general types of adhesives commonly used are water-soluble paste, asphalt adhesive, asphalt emulsion, waterproof cement, flooring mastic, and ceramic tile adhesive.

Hardwood floors

Famed for its beauty and durability, oak flooring is in a sense like a fine watch. No matter how perfect the component parts, they must be properly assembled in order to render the expected superior performance.

For years people have been attracted to the beauty of hardwood floors. The rich, natural lines in the grain of the wood. The solid textures. The feeling of warmth. Hardwood floors never fail to catch the eye and some are still serviceable in historic castles and mansions after several centuries of use.

The 20 species of oak trees used for flooring are grouped as either white or red, differing slightly in coloration, but not at all in quality and usefulness. This durable material is available in a wide variety of styles, grades, sizes and finishes. The basic types are strip, plank, unit block and parquet. Its cost depends on the type selected, grade, whether it is plain or quarter-sawed, and whether or not it is prefinished at the factory.

Tongue-and-grooved oak strips have been the most popular hardwood flooring in U.S. home construction. Strip flooring 2¼ inch wide by 25/32 inch thick is most used, but ½ and ⅜ inch thicknesses and 1½, 2 and 3¼ inch-widths also are available. Strips (except those 5/16 inches thick) are tongued on one side and grooved on the other for strength in application.

Hardwood floor planks are wider than strips, ranging from 3 to 8 inches wide. Where wood pegs once were used to fasten them to the subfloor, today the pegs are simulated to give this appearnce. Tongue and groove edges conceal actual nailings.

Unit blocks appear very similar to parquet flooring, with each block made up of several short lengths of carefully selected pieces held together at the back by metal splines or other fasteners to produce square or rectangular blocks. Parquet geometric patterns such as squares, rectangles, herringbone and basket-weave have remained the most popular designs. Units are installed in the same manner as ceramic tile.

Unit blocks come in ½, 25/32 and 33/32 inch thicknesses, with individual pieces measuring 1½, 2 and 2¼ inches wide. Squares from pieces 2¼ inches wide are 6¾ x 6¾ inches or 9x9 inches or 11¼x11¼".

Prefinished hardwood flooring costs slightly more than unfinished, but eliminates the on-site cost of finishing and makes it possible to immediately use the new or remodeled room.

Hardwood flooring can be installed in houses built on concrete slabs or those with conventional wood joist construction. Block and parquet flooring are widely used over slabs, but can also be installed over subfloors on wood joists. Some types and brands of hardwood flooring may be laid directly over linoleum or old resilient tile, but not rubber tile. Manufacturer's instructions should always be carefully followed.

Refinishing Hardwood Floors. Even if an oak floor has received extremely heavy wear or has been neglected for many years, its original gleaming beauty can be recaptured by means of sanding and refinishing. Professional craftsmen who specialize in reconditioning floors can be hired, or you may prefer to do the job yourself.

The first step is sanding. This rubs off the old finish and restores the original smooth surface, free of scratches, stains and other marks that may have appeared over the years.

Electric sanding machines can be rented in most areas and generally are used in combination with a small hand sander which gets closer to walls, into corners and small closets. The National Oak Flooring Manufacturers Association recommends three trips across the old floor.

1. If the old finish is varnish, use No. 4 open coat sandpaper for the first sanding which may be across the grain. No. 3 closed coat sandpaper is suitable for removing other finishes.

2. The second cut is made with the grain using No. 0 sandpaper.

3. The final cut is made with No. 00 or No. 000 sandpaper.

Squeaky Floors. The chief causes of squeaks in hardwood flooring are: inadequate fastenings in the subfloor and/or finish floor; the loosening of fastenings as the result of expansion and contraction of the wood under changing moisture conditions.

If there is access to the underfloor construction from a crawl space or basement area, you can undertake certain steps that are usually effective. If there is no such access the corrective efforts must be attempted from the surface side of the floor.

If you do have access from underneath, first check to determine if the subfloor is tightly secured to the joists. This can be done by pushing up on the subfloor with a heavy pole or 2x4, or having someone of substantial weight walk across the floor while you are observing it from below. If the subfloor is loose, it can frequently be tightened up by driving shims, on which glue has been spread, between it and the joists. Wood shingles make ideal shims.

In most construction, bridging is used between joists and, if butted together, the strips may rub against each other to

cause squeaks. The bridging pieces can be separated by running a saw between them.

If it appears that the flooring strips are not securely fastened to the subflooring, it can frequently be corrected by driving screws of an appropriate length from the underside of the subfloor into the surface floor, to draw it down tightly, using a stress strip.

Sometimes squeaks are caused by the rubbing of one flooring strip against the other and can be silenced by lubrication. You can simply sift powdered soap into the cracks between strips. If this doesn't work, try a few drops of liquid soap in cracks at the squeaking area. Do not use a petroleum lubricant, which will stain the floor.

Sometimes waxing with a liberal amount of heavy bodied liquid wax helps. It should be a spirit wax and not one containing water. If the floors are still noisy, face nailing is the next step.

First, locate the spots where the flooring strips are nailed by passing a commercial magnetic stud finder along the cracks between strips. When such a finder is passed over a nail head the magnet will be activated.

Now drill a pilot hole next to the spot and then nail through the surface floor with a 2 inch finishing nail that will penetrate through the surface floor and into the subfloor, countersinking the head. Fill the resulting hole or holes with plumber's putty or plastic wood colored with a raw sienna or burnt umber to match the surrounding area. The face nailing should be repeated throughout the squeaky area.

Structural deficiencies such as sagging floors can also cause squeaks and may indicate that more extensive repairs are required (see Section One on identifying sagging floors).

Resilient Flooring

Most homes built since the turn of the century have resilient floor covering in one or more rooms, usually the kitchen and, in some post World War II homes, in every room in the house. The water-resistant materials come in sheet form (rolls) and tiles are known by the given ingredients: asphalt, vinyl, vinyl asbestos, rubber, cork and linoleum.

Linoleum is the oldest of the group and long has been a popular kitchen flooring material. It is available in solid colors, or with inlaid, embossed or textured patterns simulating wood, stone or tile. Rolls are 8 feet wide or larger offering large expanses without dirt-catching cracks and crevices. Linoleum is very resilient, wears well, is easy to clean; it also comes in tile form.

Asphalt tile gained great popularity in postwar building tracts but has since been replaced in many areas by more luxurious flooring. It is still used for basement family rooms and on concrete slabs on grade. Normal tile size is 9x9 inches with ⅛ inch thickness. The material is somewhat brittle and less resilient than other materials.

Vinyl floor covering is made chiefly of polyvinyl chloride, resin binders and pigments. Plastic through and through, the material can be installed anywhere. The wear surface extends through the entire thickness of the tile. Sheet vinyl has a backing surface.

Vinyl-asbestos tile is a blend of asbestos fibers, vinyls, plasticizers, color pigments and fillers. Tiles without backing are 9x9 or 12x12 inches in thickness of 1/16, 3/32 and ⅛ inch. Marbelized patterns are offered along with textures simulating stone, marble, travertine and wood. The material is semiflexible and is highly popular with do-it-yourselfers. It can be obtained with a peel-and-stick backing.

Rubber tile is a popular choice for foot comfort, springy resistance and extra quietness underfoot. It is noted for its lustrous, plate-smooth surface, but requires frequent waxing and buffing to maintain the high gloss. The surface also becomes slippery when wet. Standard sizes are 9x9 and 12x12 inches in 3/16 and ⅛ inch thickness.

Cork tiles likewise offer exceptional foot comfort and sound control, yet they wear rapidly and do not resist impact loads well. Maintenance sometimes becomes difficult as this material becomes broken down by grease and alkalies. Thicknesses range from ⅛ to ½ inch.

There's a type of resilient flooring to fit virtually every need, each with its own special characteristics, some of

Vinyl asbestos tile with a self-adhesive back simplifies installation for the homeowner. Once the protective backing has been removed, the extra holding power of the adhesive allows the tile to be installed, with ease above grade, over wood, linoleum or concrete subfloors (Photo: GAF Corp..).

which have been detailed above. And they all share these mutual advantages: color and decorative appeal; the ability to spring back into shape after indentation; a smooth splash-resistant surface that is easy to clean; and years of wear when installed and maintained properly.

Homeowner installation of resilient flooring increases each year with improved products being offered by flooring manufacturers. Self-sticking tiles greatly simplify this type of installation while even newer decorator package kits of 12 inch vinyl tiles make it possible for the do-it-yourselfer to create custom floors that once were the sole province of skilled tradesmen. The 1/16 inch thick material is easily cut with a scissors or knife and can be installed over almost any clean, stable surface.

No-wax resilient flooring is now available in tile as well as sheet goods to eliminate this common household chore. The finish is permanent and retains its original beauty for years to come.

Shown in accompanying illustrations, sheet goods of cusioned vinyl can be bought "folded like a blanket," unfolded in your room and installed with a perfect fit over any existing floor — with the homeowner doing an expert job.

Colonial brick solid vinyl tile in a choice of colors includes two styles in Colonial brick—flat and edge brick. The matte-finished bricks are surrounded by a mortar-like grout which is an integral part of the 9x9x⅛ inch tile (Photo: Kentile Floors, Inc.).

Available in 12-foot and 6-foot widths, Armstrong's Tredway cushioned flooring is easily moved into position and can cover most rooms without seams. Here the material is being laid over an existing vinyl floor. It can also be installed over plywood particle board, concrete, and most other floors.

Staples are spaced at 3-inch intervals. A heavy-duty staple gun shoots the staples into the material with little effort on the installer's part. The staples are concealed when the molding is replaced.

Excess material is cut away with a utility knife and a carpenter's square or straight edge.

Tredway is fastened at the floor edges with staples or cement — cement in places a staple gun can't reach. Where there's no molding to hide staples, or when stables can't penetrate the subfloor (concrete). The installation kit has a squeeze bottle with a nozzle that spreads a five-bead strip of cement.

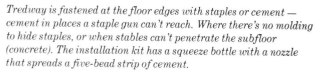

Tredway cushioned vinyl is the first flooring to "forgive" an amateur's mistakes, up to a point, If slightly undercut, the material can be stretched. If cut a bit too loosely, bulges or wrinkles will disappear as the material gently contracts. Cost of the material is in the mid-price range (Photos: Armstrong Cork Company).

Ceramic tile

New application techniques make it possible for homeowners to install ceramic tile floors and walls without the assistance of a professional. Ceramic tile has a long history in new home construction and remodeling, augmented yearly by numerous new decorative colors and patterns.

Ceramic tile is made of clays pressed into shape and fired at high temperatureses in kilns to a very hard surface. Colors achieved in this process do not fade and the tiles last for years.

Three basic kinds of ceramic tile are offered for remodeling.

GLAZED TILE — a clay "body" on which a glaze is sprayed before firing. This kind of tile can be found in sizes ranging from 1 inch square to 12 inches square and a vast variety of shapes. Gloss, matte and crystalline glazes are suitable for interior walls and vanity tops. Crystalline and certain other glazes may also be used for residential floors. Thicknesses range from ⅜ to 5/16 inch.

CERAMIC MOSAICS — small unglazed solid chunks with color through the body of the tile, these come in 1x1 inch, 1x2 inch and 2x2 inch sizes. Thickness is usually ¼ inch, and the tiles are usually mounted into sheets, 1x2 feet, either on paper or back-mounted. Ceramic mosaics are suitable for interior and exterior floors and walls.

QUARRY TILE — usually unglazed with color integral throughout the tile body, this material ranges in size from 4x4 inches to 8x8 inches and a number of shapes are available including hexagon, octagon, and provincial shapes. This tile is ¼ inch thick and is suitable for residential floors.

The newest application technique, which puts ceramic tile in the do-it-yourself realm is a pressure-sensitive method called Press-N-Set. Pressure-sensitive sheets with a dense asbestos felt core may be used with glazed tile, ceramic mosaics or quarry tile and can be applied over plywood, concrete, existing ceramic tile, hardwood floors or resilient flooring, if sound. The adhesive sheets add approximately 1/32" to the floor elevation and measure 19-11/16 inch x 29 17/32 inch to cover four square feet.

Among the residential applications recommended for this method are home entryways, kitchens, family rooms, powder rooms and bathrooms.

Installation is simple. A bottom release paper is peeled, the sheet is pressed onto the surface (it may be cut with a scissors or utility knife), the top release paper is then peeled and tiles set in place and grouted.

Still another variation of this method is the Easy-Set method which can be used around bathtubs, showers, on bathroom, kitchen and laundry room walls, and for back-splashes and on vanity tops. Here the material comes in sheets of tile pre-grouted with polyurethane and is applied to the surface with emulsion-type adhesive spread with a notched trowel. Tubes of silicone rubber sealant are then used to grout between panels. This grout, importantly, resists stains and mildew, is permanently smooth, resilient, white, waterproof and easy to clean.

Grouting spaces between sheets of tile and along the tub edge are filled with silicone rubber using a simple caulking gun. A special tip on the cartridge is shaped to fit the joint (Photos: American Olean Tile Company).

Sheets can be cut with a simplified kit including a carbide tipped scribe, and straight edge. After the line is scored, the scored line is placed over the raised metal strip shown at right and hard force is applied to either side.

Easy-Set sheets of pregrouted ceramic wall tile are applied to surfaces with adhesive spread with a notched trowel. Tile nippers are used to notch tiles where required.

Conventional cement mortar and "thin-set" dry mortar methods also are widely used by tile setters to obtain perfectly flat vertical surfaces and square, plumb corners. The cement mortar bed requires the use of expanded metal lath, while the less-expensive thin-set method requires only a ⅜ inch application of portland cement material for bonding the tiles on the backing materials such as concrete, cement mortar, concrete block, brick and sometimes gypsum board. This method is not generally recommended for wet areas (such as tubs, showers and countertops) unless waterproof grout joints such as silicone rubber are used.

No coating or sealer need be applied to glazed tile. Cement grout joints may be sealed, however, with silicone or acrylic sealers to prevent joint discoloration and to facilitate maintenance. An acrylic sealer is suitable when applied in thin, uniform coats.

Some quarry tiles, particularly imported varieties, are porous and require a penetrating sealer or finish to protect the surface. Cleaning is done with a neutral detergent such as Hillyard's Super Shine-All.

Cleaning methods for ceramic tile vary with the type of tile and area where it is used. A tub recess or shower, for example, is subjected to much use. Hard water film will form on any surface but is generally easier to remove from ceramic tile than from other surfaces. The best method is to prevent buildup of soap accumulation by washing frequently with a soap-free detergent such as Fantastik or Hillyard's Clean-O-Lite and drying with a towel. If hard water scale is present, there are several satisfactory mild acid cleaners, such as Tile-Glow for crystalline glazes and Hillyard's CSP for all other tiles. For heavy-duty cleaning, use a cleaning pad such as 3M Scotch-Brite with Fantastik Clean-O-Lite, Tile-Glow or CSP.

Carpeting

Carpeting is now common to every room in the house including the kitchen and bathroom and can be found on patios of many homes throughout the country. Materials on the market permit installation below grade as well as above and some types of carpet are specifically designed and manufactured for do-it-yourself installation.

In determining where and what type carpeting to use in a home it's well to have a good idea of how much traffic the carpet will carry. Carpet in a living room, kitchen, family room or near an entrance usually gets more wear than one in a bedroom or guestroom.

Flooring specialists recommend a good quality carpet that wears well for heavy-traffic areas and point out that you can get by with a lesser grade for little-used rooms.

Carpet is offered in two basic types — room-size rugs sold in standard sizes such as 9x12 and 12x15 feet, and room-fit carpet for wall-to-wall semi-permanent installation. Rugs, of course, are the easier material to install, can be taken up

for cleaning, and may be shifted to equalize wear. Room-fit carpet usually requires professional installation, cannot be easily shifted for wear, and becomes more difficult to clean.

The eight basic types of fibers used in the manufacture of carpet each boast special properties and often are sold by trademark names adopted by the manufacturer. No one fiber is best for all purposes, and carpets frequently are made from a combination of fibers.

Here's a brief run down on the various fibers:

NYLON—used in nearly half the carpeting made in the U.S., has good resilience and excellent wear resistance, good colorfastness and is priced from $5 to $12 per square yard.

POLYESTER—has about a fifth of the carpet market, soft and luxurious appearance for living rooms and bedrooms, good wear resistance and colorfastness. Priced from $7 to $15 per square yard.

ACRYLIC — used for about 12 percent of all carpet pile fiber, has a soft appearance, good resilience, colorfastness and wear resistance. Priced from $7 to $14 per square yard.

MODACRYLIC — generally used with acrylic fibers to increase flame resistance. Has fair to good wear resistance and moderate resilience. Priced $7 to $14 per square yard.

WOOL — has declined in use since advent of man-made fibers, gives soft, warm appearance, excellent resilience and good resistance to showing soil and wear. Priced $10 to $28 per square yard.

POLYPROPYLENE — also known as "olefin", principally used for indoor-outdoor carpeting as it has excellent resistance to moisture, water-based stains and is highly colorfast. Priced $4 to $10 per square yard.

RAYON— the least expensive man-made fiber, usually found in bathroom and scatter rugs, has poor resilience and fair resistance to wear and stains. Many rayon rugs are washable. Priced from $4 to $9 per square yard.

COTTON — usually found in scatter rugs, has poor resilience, good wear resistance and fair soil resistance. Like rayon, may be washed. Priced from $4 to $10.

Government regulations require that a carpet label must show the percentage by weight of each fiber in blend combinations and less than 20 percent of any fiber would not be enough to affect carpet and quality and should be looked upon as chiefly a selling point.

A great variety of carpet textures include level loop pile, cut pile or plush, level tip shear, multilevel loop, random shear, sculptured or carved, shag, and frieze or twist. These textures are produced by tufting, weaving, knitting, needle-punching and flocking and are best understood by personally inspecting the materials in a carpet store.

Wall-to-wall carpeting is sold by the running foot and is made in 6, 12 and 15 foot wide rolls. Carpet squares also are available permitting easier homeowner installation. These 12x12 and 18x18 inch units also simplify the replacement of a damaged or worn area.

Carpeting should have a strong backing and many times requires a layer of padding that will lengthen the life of the carpeting and provide more comfort underfoot.

Highland Plaid is one of the do-it-yourself carpet patterns offered by Armstrong Cork Company. The textured nylon plush of the cut pile softly interrupts the rigid geometric lines of a plaid with a dual yarn system. This carpeting has a built-in foam backing that eliminates the need for additional padding. The material can be cut with a heavy shears to fit along room edges.

Sculptured shag carpet squares with dense foam rubber backing are self-sticking units that are easy to apply over an existing floor surface. The carpet squares show no seams in wall-to-wall installation (Photo: Armstrong Cork Company).

CEILINGS

Acoustical Tiles

For years, homeowners have used acoustical tiles to solve a multitude of ceiling problems. To conceal cracked or broken plaster or add a ceiling to an unfinished room, the standard method of installation has been to nail up wood furring strips on 12 inch centers and then staple tongue-and-groove tiles to the strips.

The difficulty with this method is that wood strips have a tendency to absorb moisture from the air and warp — or sometimes split with age — causing unevenness in the finished ceiling. Also, the method takes considerable installation time. As many as 260 nails may be required to "fur out" an average 12x12 foot room.

Suspended Ceilings

To combat this problem, manufacturers have developed a better way of attaching ceiling tiles to plaster, drywall or exposed joists, eliminating the furring strips altogether. One method employs a suspended grid system for lay-in type ceiling panels. Another method is a full suspension system where all members are integrated into the ceiling itself and totally concealed in the finished surface.

Armstrong's Colonial Sampler ceiling tile combines with a rough-hewn beam cornice and rough stucco walls to give an Early American "tavern like" appearance to this residential study. The stucco covers wall cracks and the ceiling tile covers ceiling cracks.

Developed by Armstrong Cork Company, the Intergrid full suspension system is adaptable to any room size and shape and requires no special tools. All grid components are adjustable to provide a built-in margin for error (see installation photo series) and specially fabricated tiles butt tightly together to form a continuous, unbroken surface of pattern or texture.

Besides eliminating the cost of ceiling removal, this installation method produces a double ceiling which affords extra insulative value and improved resistance to transmitted noises from the floor above. Accessibility to areas above the ceiling is gained fabricating special access panels where needed. To do this, remove tongue-and-groove joint on the access tile, then screw the tile to slots in the supporting cross tee. To remove the panel, simply unscrew it from the tee and lift it out of the ceiling.

Armstrong's Intergrid ceiling: begin with wall molding, nail at desired height on all four walls. Either metal or wood molding may be used. Measure the room's dimensions to determine the number of panels and suspension system parts needed. If either width or length is less than a full panel's width, cut border panels equally at each end of a row. Establish the elevation mark and chalk line around the perimeter of the room ¾ inches above the intended ceiling height.

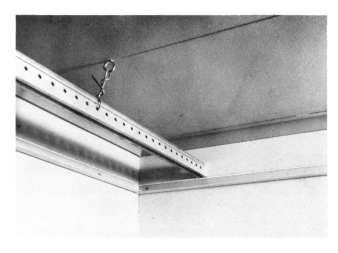

Intergrid main runners are installed with hanger wires. The first runner is always located 26 inches out from the sidewall; remaining units are placed 48 inches on center, perpendicular to direction of joists. This system, unlike others, requires no complicated measuring or room layout.

After all main runners are in place, begin installing ceiling tile in a corner of the room. Simply lay the first four feet of tile on the molding, snap a 4 foot cross tee onto the main runner, and slide the tee into a special concealed slot on the leading edge of the tile.

Continue across the room in this manner, inserting tiles and cross tees. Note how all metal suspension hangers are hidden from view in the finished portion of the ceiling.

The finished ceiling comes out looking as if it had been installed in one piece. There are no metal grids to mar the wall-to-wall texture.

A special recessed fluorescent light fixture may be purchased with this system. Available in a choice of 2- and 4-lamp models, the unit mounts easily on the intergrid main runners. The system can also accommodate conventional hanging fixtures.

Ceiling tile manufactures for use with this suspended system offer design motifs ranging from Modern to Early American; from French Provincial to Mediterranean. There are also several "natural" patterns for informal rooms of the home.

Lay-in style suspended ceiling systems have long been used in commercial buildings where access is required to reach in-the-ceiling lighting fixtures, telephone wires, and other utilities. This type system also is popular with homeowners for remodeled attics, basements, garages and other rooms.

The suspended ceiling grids are usually painted steel fastened to the existing ceilings or joists with metal straps or wire. Various size ceiling panels, including 2x2 foot and 2x4 foot units, are easily tipped into position with no stapling, nailing or adhesive required.

Tiles

Brush-on ceiling cement and adhesives continue to be used to apply ceiling tile directly to smooth, level existing ceilings. This method requires a surface that is sound, clean and dry, and on which the mastic will not loosen the old surface.

The stapling method usually is combined with wood furring strips, 1x3 inch pine boards, nailed at right angles to the joists. This approach often is taken where the existing ceiling is so badly cracked that it will not support the weight of the tiles if cemented directly to it.

Regardless of installation method selected, finished ceilings look best when the tiles along opposite borders are the same size and at least 6 inches wide. Proper size and placement of border tiles is determined before beginning the installation and in accordance with specific instructions provided with each system. Ceiling tiles are easy to cut with a sharp utility knife and a square edge.

Accents

Real and imitation wood beams can give ceilings additional beauty. The rustic, hand-hewed look is possible even with suspended ceilings by attaching lightweight polyurethane reproduction beams to the exposed metal grid.

Ceiling cornices made of expandable polystyrene offer still another means of creating a distinctive ceiling. These units come in various designs including gothic, contemporary, French Provincial and Mediterranean. They are easy to cut with a hand saw and miter box and are applied with adhesive.

Sculptured polystyrene ceiling cornices give an added touch of distinction to this room. The lightweight material looks like wood once painted, stained or antiqued (Photo: Creative Packaging Corp).

Before moving into this 30-year-old house, the new owners solved a cracked ceiling problem by installing decorative and noncombustible ceiling tiles with a concealed suspended grid system. The cabinet seen in the adjoining room is actually a radiator cover (Photo: Armstrong Cork Company).

COMFORTABLE, EFFICIENT,
& ATTRACTIVE INTERIORS

INSULATION

It's a well-proven fact that a well-insulated home requires only about half the fuel as one without insulation. And half the fuel means half the cost to the homeowner.

Approximately 40 million existing homes in the United States are presently in need of some thermal protection improvement — and chances are, your new home is among them. Most homes have some insulation, but usually not enough to make the structure comfortable the year 'round, with minimum heating and cooling.

In appraising your home's insulation you should look into the many items you may not have considered to be insulation. First, weatherstripping of doors and windows can help to "tighten up" your home; storm windows and doors (or double-paned insulating glass) can cut heat loss through glass; caulking around door and window frames can prevent air infiltration and heat loss; carpeting on the floors can reduce heat needs; insulated heating ducts and pipes can be made more efficient; drapes and blinds can help to save fuel.

But with all these and other insulation practices in use, your home still needs the basic and fundamental attic, wall and floor insulation that makes the major difference in residential climate control. Attics should have a minimum of 6 inches of insulation, walls should be insulated over or between the studs or in both places, and floors and unheated crawl spaces should be insulated.

*SOME FEATURES OF A LOW ENERGY PER MONTH HOME

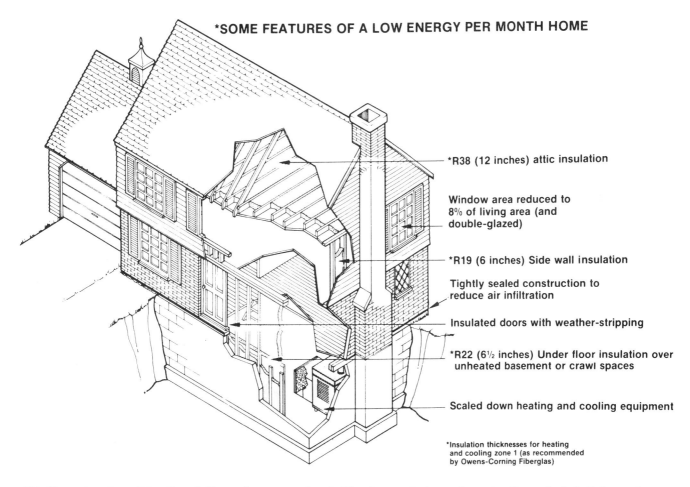

*R38 (12 inches) attic insulation

Window area reduced to 8% of living area (and double-glazed)

*R19 (6 inches) Side wall insulation

Tightly sealed construction to reduce air infiltration

Insulated doors with weather-stripping

*R22 (6½ inches) Under floor insulation over unheated basement or crawl spaces

Scaled down heating and cooling equipment

*Insulation thicknesses for heating and cooling zone 1 (as recommended by Owens-Corning Fiberglas)

This illustration of a traditionally styled home shows areas where builders have made changes in construction methods, both for new homes and remodeling, to reduce the amount of fuel needed to heat or cool a home. The modified framing technique, using 2x6 studs on 24 inch centers, enables thicker batts of building insulation and reduces costs as less lumber is needed than in conventional 2x4 walls. Vapor bariers reduce air infiltration.

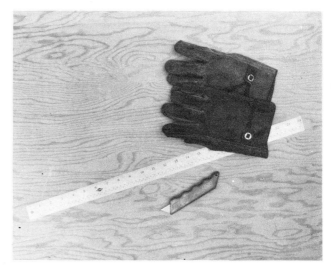

Loose-fil insulation can be pneumatically blown between attic floor joists and wall stud cavities in the older home. Contractors specializing in this service are listed under "Insulation" in the Yellow Pages.

There are products on the market today to solve almost any conceivable insulating problem. All aspects of the use and application of insulation have been exhaustively studied by the individual manufacturer and various educational institutions.

Insulation materials are now produced in uniform quality and density and the thicknesses and sizes are controlled. There are bulk-type materials that can be used as a filler or blown into ceilings or walls during or after construction; the batt, blanket and reflective types can be used for walls, floors and ceilings; and structural fiberboard can be used in sheathing, plaster base, interior finish and roof insulation; plus polystyrene insulation boards can be used for floor, perimeter, wall, plaster base, and other types of insulation.

The effectiveness of home insulation is expressed in terms of "R" or thermal resistance. The higher the "R" number, the higher the insulating value. To meet FHA Minimum Property standards, your house should have R-11 insulation in floors and outside walls. Minimum R-22 insulation is required in ceilings (R-19 for areas with less than 8000 degree heat days)*. Keep in mind that one brand of insulation might be thicker than another, but if they're marked with the same "R" number they'll resist heat flow equally well. "R" numbers are plainly marked on packages and vapor barriers and your local weather bureau or building materials dealer can give you the number of degree days and specific minimum insulation specifications for your particular area.

How you plan to use a given area of your home has a bearing on how you should insulate it. For example, if you have an attic that is not used for living area, you can place loose fill insulation, batts or blankets between the joists of the unused attic floor. If the attic is to be used as a room in itself, the walls and ceilings around the attic space should be insulated. If a vapor barrier insulation is used, the vapor barrier should face into the room to be heated.

Installing attic insulation is an easy do-it-yourself project that can reduce home energy and fuel waste up to 30 percent. The only tools needed are a sharp knife, a straightedge and measuring rule, and a pair of gloves. Actual installation is simply a matter of unrolling the insulation, cutting it into the required lengths, and then placing the material between the joists on the attic floor.

*EDITOR'S NOTE: Degree-days determine the amount of fuel needed to heat your home. Subtract the mean temperature outside from 65 degrees to determine how much heat will be used that day. If the mean outside temperature is 30 degrees you will have a 35 degree-heat day.

If you are remodeling your basement into a room or combination of rooms, it's well to first insulate the walls. First fasten 1x2, 2x2 or 2x4 furring strips in place vertically on 16 or 24 inch centers. Then install the insulation batts. Basement ceilings can be insulated with batts or blankets between the floor joist, or insulating and sound-deadening tile board may be used for the horizontal surface.

Crawl-space houses should have insulation under the floor and the ground should be covered with a suitable vapor barrier. Be sure to also provide at least one square foot of ventilating area per 150 square feet of floor area.

For homes built on concrete slabs, particularly in colder climates, slab edge insulation is very important. If the home you have purchased does not have adequate insulation, it can be added. Always put a vapor barrier such as polyethylene film under a concrete slab.

Special insulation materials are available for use with existing insulation you may find in your attic. It's recommended that if you don't find at least 6 inches of blanket insulation or 8¾ inches of loose insulation, you add this insulation for maximum efficiency. One re-insulation on the market simply rolls between joists and is lightly pressed into place above existing insulation.

Figuring your needs to insulate a ceiling, wall or floor area is relatively simple. Multiply the total area (length by width) by .90 if framing members are 16 inches apart, or multiply by .94 if framing members are 24 inches apart. Example: 1000 square feet of ceiling with joists spaced at 16 inch intervals would require 900 square feet of blankets or batts.

Door and window weatherstripping and caulking help greatly to reduce home heating and cooling costs. Newer windows come with built-in weatherstripping, and prefabricated thresholds with flexible weatherstripping can be used to update older doors.

Foil-faced fiberglass insulation provides a built-in vapor barrier with a small flange on each side for fast stapling to wall studs.

If you are going to use pouring insulation in the attic floor, usually there will be a bag label that will tell you how many square feet a bag of that material you'll need for a desired "R" number and thickness. Divide that number into the number of square feet you want to cover and you'll know how many bags to purchase.

Few tools are required to install insulation — a measuring tape, knife, gloves, and if no illumination exists, a portable light such as the mechanic's trouble light with extension cord. If loose insulation is used, you'll need a small rake. If batts are used, you'll need a staple gun.

Manufacturers caution that in placing batt insulation over existing insulation you should use an unfaced (without vapor barrier) material. If you must use a vapor barrier material, slash the material freely (vapor barrier side) and place this side down.

Here are some other insulating tips.

- In attic installations, always work from the outside edge to the center of the room, as it's easier to cut and fit where you have more space to work.

- Patch vapor barrier of the insulation if it becomes torn.

- Don't insulate on top of lighting fixtures, motors or other heat-producing equipment that protrudes into the insulation area.

- Don't cover eaves or vents with insulation.

- Cover vapor barriers with gypsum wallboard or other noncombustible material.

- Cracks around windows and other framing should be stuffed by hand if necessary and then covered with a vapor barrier.

- Batt insulation left exposed in basement ceilings can be held securely in place with chicken wire attached to the bottom of floor joists.

- When confronted with a cross-bracing in ceiling or floors, cut the insulation to fit tightly around cross members.

- When pipes are installed in a wall, place the insulation to the outside of the pipe to prevent freezing.

- When insulating walls, begin at the top and place staples no more than 8 inches apart.

- When insulating an unfloored space, put down boards or plywood over the joist for walking.

For specific energy-saving measures you can take throughout your home, see *How To Cut Your Energy Bills* by Derven and Nichols, a *Successful* book.

STORAGE

No home — new or old — ever has too much storage space. Those without basements and attics put still further emphasis on finding a suitable place for household items not used on a day-to-day basis.

The older home frequently will have untapped storage areas that can be finished to make the total house more enjoyable. For example, some basements have unexcavated rooms or partially finished rooms beneath porches. By completing these areas, you can obtain valuable storage area.

In planning storage and storage units, emphasis should be placed on maximum accessibility of all items stored, efficient use of space for storage, economy in construction and flexibility in the use of storage units.

In planning desired storage space, first prepare a list of all items for which you will need storage and decide where the items should be stored so they will be most convenient to the point of use.

Think in terms of putting lazy walls to use; they can house bookshelves and cabinets. Look for out-of-the-way areas that aren't being used; under-stair areas can be extremely handy for storage. Use drawer and cabinet organizers; rubber and plastic accessories often can double the amount of items you can efficiently store in a cabinet space.

Adjustable shelves are recommended for new or improved storage units because the types of articles, as well as the number, vary with different families. The height of the tallest item to be stored sets the distance between the floor of the unit and the first shelf. Articles of similar height are usually stored on one shelf, in one drawer, or in one compartment.

Whenever possible, storage units should have a full-front opening for accessibility. Bedroom closets, for example, are more efficient when they have bi-fold style floor-to-ceiling doors that afford total access.

By standardizing storage units to three depths — 12, 16 and 24 inches — it is possible to simplify construction and to reduce costs. Items which are often stored in 12 inch deep units include dinnerware, books, magazines, and toys. Units 16 inches deep are used for business papers, desk supplies, bathroom supplies, musical instruments, sports equipment, cleaning equipment and supplies, and work and play clothes. Clothing, bedding, luggage, table linens, sewing equipment, and infants equipment are usually stored in 24 inch-deep units.

Well-planned built-ins not only solve storage and space problems but can be a source of visual enjoyment. A handsome background can be bold or quiet, informal or elegant, dramatic or joyous. Room dividers can provide storage accessible from both sides, as can island dividers.

Specialty equipment for home office and study centers requires different types of storage. This home center includes a video tape recorder (center), tape recorder and architectual drafting setup. Cabinets have a durable plastic laminate countertop (Westinghouse Photo).

Home entertainment centers make it possible to use storage space as a design element of the room. Here the lower shelf provides record storage, AM-FM Stereo and swing-down record player. The second shelf includes television and home projection equipment. Upper shelves house speakers for the stereo system and space for books and mementos (Westinghouse Photo).

Floor-to-ceiling poles with recessed standards make it possible to erect a combination room divider-storage wall. And the entire arrangement can be changed at will. This unit has hand rubbed walnut-finished shelves (Photo: Grant Pulley & Hardware).

    Plans for literally hundreds of build-it-yourself storage units are available from local lumber and building material dealers.*

*For additional information on built-ins and storage, see *Successful Space Saving at Home* by Patrick Galvin.

PAINT

Color-in-a-can is not the technical definition of paint, but it is the mental image most of us have when we bring out the brushes and rollers. But a successful painting job is really a combination of factors including:

- Selection of the color or colors to create the appearance you wish to present.

- Determining the proper paint to purchase for the surface to be coated.

- Preparation of the surface — before you open the paint bucket — to insure the longest possible paint life and a continued good appearance.

- Application of the paint in the most efficient and economical method using accepted safety precautions.*

In selecting a color for exterior or interior use, use a color wheel so you can compare numerous color schemes. The color wheel presents the primaries (red, yellow and blue), secondary colors (green, orange and purple) and intermediates (red-orange, yellow-orange, yellow-green, blue-green, blue-purple and red-purple).

Color tints are produced by adding white. Light colors reflect more light, and make areas seem larger. A shade of a color is produced by adding black, making it darker. These darker colors absorb more light, making areas seem smaller. A tone is produced by adding both black and white (which is gray) making the color appear more subtle or muted. Pink is a tint of red. Maroon is a shade of red. Rose is a tone of red.

In dealing with paint stores you are certain to come across the term "hue." It's often used as another name of color, but really means a color family. Pink is a red hue. Lavender is a hue of purple.

Colors are also classified as warm or cool. The warm colors (reds, oranges and yellows) seem to advance toward you. They convey warmth and are emotionally stimulating. Warm colors are recommended for rooms that have northern exposures or are windowless. Deeper shades of warm colors will give intimacy to very large rooms.

Cool colors (the blues, blue-greens, blue-grays and violets) seem to retreat from you. They are cooling and relaxing. Cool colors are suggested for rooms with southern exposures. Light tints of cool colors will further the illusion of size for small rooms.

In choosing a paint color it is well to understand that there are four basic color patterns or color schemes:

*For an in-depth discussion of these factors, see *Book of Successful Painting* by Abel Banov.

- Monochromatic — based on tints, tones and shades of one color. An example of a monochromatic scheme would be a room decorated in pink, rose and red.

- Analogous or Related — is a color scheme using related colors, such as blue, blue-green and green.

- Complementary — a scheme using colors that complement each other. An example of a complementary color scheme would be a decor based on chartreuse (yellow-green) and mulberry (red-purple).

- Neutral — this fourth basic color scheme employs neutral colors, the beiges, tans, grays.

Determining the proper paint to use on the surface you wish to coat is of key importance. Using the incorrect paint will prove a waste of time in most instances and could lead to time-consuming removal. Most paints fall into two categories, depending upon the vehicle used for carrying the paint's pigment or color: they are oil and latex-based paints.

Oil-based paints usually are made with vegetable-drying oils. There are specific oil-based paints for inside and outside surfaces. Some painters feel that oil-based paints have slightly longer life than others, that they hide previous coats better, and that they bond better because they have stronger solvents to penetrate the surface more deeply.

Latex or rubber-based paints have either solvent or water thinned mediums for carrying the pigment and can be used inside or out. Latex paints, particularly water soluble types, are easier for homeowners to handle. Some persons feel they have better color retention, are less likely to be affected by air pollution, and are easier to remove from brushes after the job is finished.

Another unique advantage of latex paint is that it can be applied over a damp surface without affecting either drying time or results. The "breather-action" of latex paint allows moisture to escape from walls, which helps to lessen two common paint headaches — peeling and blistering. But understand that serious moisture problems cannot be solved by paint alone.

Preparation of the surface to be coated is also highly important. A careful inspection of the surface will reveal areas where paint problems already exist or are brewing. Scratches, mars and cracks should be repaired with compounds formulated for this purpose. If working on the exterior, caulking may be required at window and door frames and surrounding areas, at the bases of columns on porches and entryways, at steps, siding, downspouts and under-eave areas — basically anywhere that moisture is likely to collect. The amount of surface preparation needed for exterior painting depends on the surface. If it's sound, dry and not too dirty, all that's needed is a good brushing down to remove surface dust. If it's extremely dirty, it may require a washing with soapy water and then a thorough rinse.

Look before you paint is the advice of major paint manufacturers who recommend moisture and other problems first be corrected. Peeling and chalky paint is then removed, dirt and dust brushed off, and a quality paint applied with brush, roller or pad applicator (Photo: PPG Industries, Inc.).

Mildew forming on painted surfaces is the result of prolonged warm and damp conditions. Treat these areas before painting with a mixture of tri-sodium-phosphate, detergent, and household bleach. Then thoroughly rinse with clear water and allow to dry. Many paints on the market help prevent these conditions.

In preparing masonry surfaces for painting, a wire brush is handy for removing dirt, loose particles and other extraneous materials. Efflorescence, a white, salt-like material caused by the reaction between moisture and salts in alkaline materials, must also be removed. This can be accomplished by washing with diluted muriatic acid solution. Detergent and water or a commercial cleaning agent will eliminate grease and oil. As a final step, use a grout coat or fill-coat before painting porous surfaces. The combination of fill-coat and finish coat will provide a good seal against moisture, plus a smooth, attractive finish.

Exterior painting is best done when the temperature is neither too hot nor too cool. Clear, dry days between 60°F and 70°F are ideal. Exterior surfaces should not be painted with latex paint at temperatures below 50°F, or painted with oil-base paints at temperatures below 40°F. Start at the top of the house and work down and around the shady side of the house. Avoid painting in direct sunlight during hot weather.

Begin interior painting preparation with a careful inspection of the surface and repair of any holes or dents in walls or ceilings. Spackling putty is good for this purpose when the walls are plaster or gypsum wallboard. Newly plastered walls and ceilings should be permitted to dry out for three to four weeks and should be thoroughly brushed before painting.

Latex paints can be used over a previous coat of oil base,

but if the surface is glossy, a light sanding with fine paper will assure a better bond and lasting finish. Semi-gloss paints that can take repeated washings are most used in halls, kitchen and bathroom. And there are numerous textured paints on the market for custom designing walls and covering minor blemishes.

Bathroom and kitchen walls require washing with household detergent before repainting. Wallpaper that is firm with no loose seams usually can be painted with one or two coats. However, painting over wallpaper will make it difficult to steam off and remove the paper at a later date. In cases where the wallpaper is badly worn or loose, it should be removed completely before painting..

Tools and Techniques

Homeowners have a choice of painting tools to help simplify and speed the job. Besides the wide range of brushes available, you may choose from various rollers, pad applicators, and spray guns. Many jobs can be completed with the use of any one of these four types, whereas some surfaces will be obviously better suited to one particular method of application.

Regardless of the type or size, quality brushes will last longer, hold more paint, and give a smoother coat than do cheaper ones. Select the size and style brush according to the surface and type of paint with which you will be working. Man-made fiber brushes and rollers are best when using water-base paints while natural bristle brushes and mohair roller covers are best for enamels, varnishes and oil-based paints. Look for brushes made with split-end bristles, as this is a mark of quality in brushes.

A 4 inch brush size is most popular for flat surface exterior painting and a 1½ or 2 inch angled sash brush for trimming. Don't dip the brush bristles more than half way into the can and tap off excessive paint. Don't wipe off paint on the sharp edge of the can, as it will cause the filaments to clump together. Paint with bristles flat against the surface, using long steady strokes and light pressure. Smooth out runs as you go along and at the end of each stroke lift the brush slightly to feather the edges. In any case, don't use the brush to stir the paint and don't wipe paint with the narrow end of the wall brush.

Paint rollers are available in various sizes and with handles of different lengths. There are rollers for use in corners, on fences and for irregular surfaces, but the most common is that used for painting large, flat areas such as walls, ceilings and floors. An extension roller handle may eliminate the need for a ladder when painting a ceiling or will let you avoid stopping when painting the floor.

The best size roller for walls and ceilings is the 7 or 9 inch model, while the 3 inch model is best for finishing woodwork, doors and trim. The fabric on the roller should conform with the type of paint to be applied. Check the label of the roller cover. Lambswool rollers are excellent with oil-based paints, but they should not be used with water-thinned latex paints. Mohair rollers can be used with any type interior flat paint but are recommended especially for applying enamel and whenever a smooth finish is desired.

Rollers made from synthetic fibers can be used with all types of flat paint, inside and out. A handy rule to remember is the smoother the surface you are painting, the shorter the roller's nap should be; the rougher the surface, the longer the nap. And this writer usually takes a long nap after using either type!

When using a roller it is well to first brush a strip of color along the ceiling line and in the inside corners when doing walls, having put masking tape on adjoining surfaces. The roller then will not accidentally touch the adjoining surface. With a newly loaded roller, always begin by rolling upward. Start a short distance from the finished area and work toward it. After an area about two feet wide by three feet deep has been coated with up and down strokes, use the roller in a horizontal back-and-forth direction.

At the bottom of walls, use a brush to paint areas the roller can't reach. Use a cardboard guard when painting next to woodwork.

When painting a ceiling, work across the width rather than the length of the room. This enables you to begin a second lap before the first has completely dried. Never try to paint a strip more than two feet wide both for lapping and safety purposes.

Paint pad applicators were originally developed for applying paint and stain to shingle siding. Now these handy units come in a range of sizes and are highly efficient tools for painting smooth or rough surfaces. Like the roller, the paint pad applicator has a removable pad for easy cleaning. The painting surface is mohair fabric, flocked filaments or lambswool laminated to a foam backing. The pad applicator is used with a roller tray and is handy for edging and painting lap siding and flat surfaces. It is cleaned with water or paint thinner.

Spray paint equipment ranges from the large pressure types (fed by air compressors) to the small aerosol can used for coating small items. Before deciding to spray paint, be sure to consider whether the time gained will be consumed in the extra work of masking more windows and covering surrounding areas.

Airless spray equipment can be rented in many cities or you may prefer to purchase a small unit if you anticipate annual repainting of lawn furniture and the like. Self-contained spray applicators require no compressors, air hoses, strainers, etc. and operate from standard household electrical current. The pressure-actuated spray gun is attached to a plastic paint container and may be used with a variety of nozzles. Commercial-style spray units locate the paint supply at the point of the compressor so the painter holds only the spray gun itself connected to a long hose.

ROOFING & SIDING

REDWOOD SIDING

Redwood is widely used for siding throughout the United States because of its desirable physical and aesthetic qualities. Redwood heartwood is naturally durable, with a built-in resistance to decay and insects. Properly seasoned and applied, it will lie flat and resist deterioration from weathering in all climates, even without a protective finish.

Two redwood grades are best suited for exterior siding: Clear All Heart, and Clear. Either should be certified kiln dried and the California Redwood Association recommends that they be pretreated with a water repellent. This will improve performance no matter what type of finish is specified.

Redwood siding is manufactured in a variety of styles, including: Plain bevel, rabbeted bevel, shiplap V rustic, tongue and groove, channel rustic and board and batten. Stainless steel, aluminum or high-quality hot-dipped galvanized nails are used for application.

While all woods provide a relatively high degree of insulation, redwood is one of the leaders. This is due to its low density (a high percentage of air spaces in ratio to wood substance).

In insulating value, a redwood board 1 inch thick is equal to approximately 6 inches of brick, 7 inches of glass, 9 inches of concrete block, and 14 inches of concrete or stucco, or over 1700 inches of aluminum. Redwood's insulating protection against both heat and cold helps keep homes comfortable the year round.

HARDBOARD SIDING

Hardboard siding offers the best properties of wood, but eliminates many of its unwanted characteristics. The engineered material has no knots or other defects, won't split, and is practically dentproof. Hardboard adds great strength to any construction and permits finishes that withstand unusually severe weather conditions.

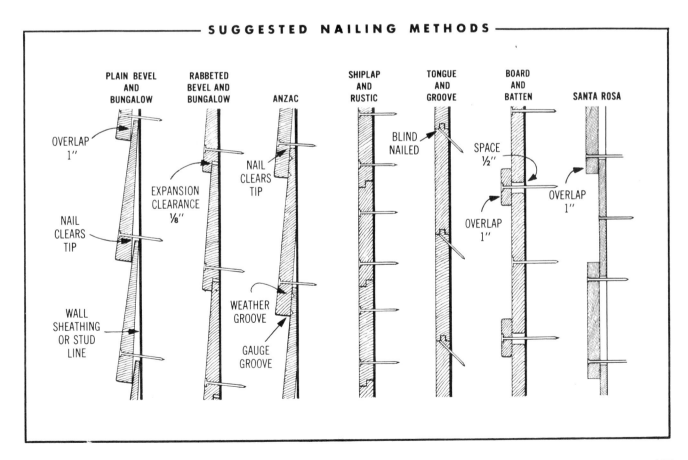

SUGGESTED NAILING METHODS

PLAIN BEVEL AND BUNGALOW — RABBETED BEVEL AND BUNGALOW — ANZAC — SHIPLAP AND RUSTIC — TONGUE AND GROOVE — BOARD AND BATTEN — SANTA ROSA

OVERLAP 1″
NAIL CLEARS TIP
WALL SHEATHING OR STUD LINE
EXPANSION CLEARANCE ⅛″
NAIL CLEARS TIP
WEATHER GROOVE
GAUGE GROOVE
BLIND NAILED
SPACE ½″
OVERLAP 1″
OVERLAP 1″

Tongue and groove redwood siding often is used in a diagonal manner to create contemporary exteriors. Four and six-inch widths are offered for blind nailing; wider boards are face nailed (Photo: California Redwood Assocation).

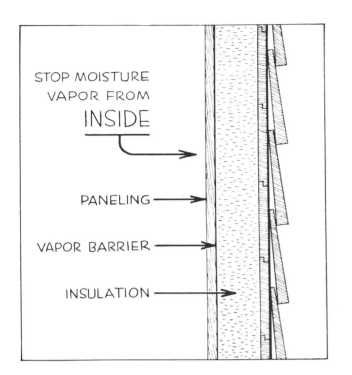

STOP MOISTURE
VAPOR FROM
UNDERLINE INSIDE

PANELING →

VAPOR BARRIER →

INSULATION →

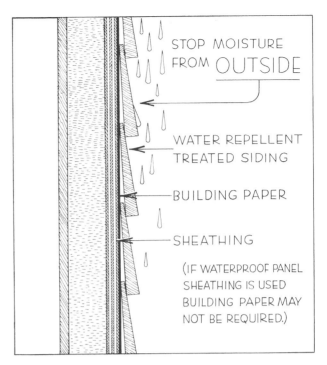

STOP MOISTURE
FROM OUTSIDE

WATER REPELLENT
TREATED SIDING

BUILDING PAPER

SHEATHING

(IF WATERPROOF PANEL
SHEATHING IS USED
BUILDING PAPER MAY
NOT BE REQUIRED.)

BEFORE: typical older, unimproved home found in major cities throughout the country, this three-level structure had a space-stealing staircase, unsightly exposed plumbing, and dated windows and siding.

AFTER: the entire house was opened up to indoor-outdoor living with the use of redwood balconies and deck. Sliding windows and doors were used to increase usable floor space. Note the fire-protection ladder well on the second level (Photos: California Redwood Association).

Hardboard siding holds paint longer than lumber sidings and may be applied over sheathed or unsheathed walls. Manufacturers recommend for residing applications that the old siding first be removed. If this is neither possible or practical, a flat level plane must be developed by applying furring strips or plywood sheets.

Proper performance of any wood siding product requires that a continuous effective vapor barrier, such as polyethylene or aluminum foil, be present near the warm (inside) surface of the wall to prevent condensation from taking place. When the wall being resided is also to be reinsulated, a proper vapor barrier can be installed at that time. If no vapor barrier is present or it is ineffective, warping of the new siding may occur.

Hardboard siding is factory-primed and backsealed or prefinished in a selection of long-lasting colors. It is offered with smooth or textured surface in both lap siding and panel sidings.

Hardboard lap siding is 7/16 inch (nominal) thick and comes in 16-foot lengths. Widths range from 6 to 12 inches. Panels for vertical application are 4 feet wide and 8, 9 or 10 feet long. Thickness is 7/16 inches (nominal). These panels come in a variety of grooved patterns and frequently are used with battens.

PLYWOOD SIDING

Plywood siding is real wood with all its natural versatility and warmth. It is manufactured in various species and dozens of textures. These range from the smooth, even surface of medium density overlaid panels to the deep grooves and resawn texture of reverse board-and-batten patterns.

The built-in bracing ability of plywood delivers strength and stiffness. In U.S. Forest Service tests, walls sheathed with ¼ inch plywood proved twice as rigid, and over twice as strong as similar walls sheathed with diagonal 1 inch boards. This type of siding is strong enough so that panels can be applied directly to studs, with the single layer performing both as the structural sheathing and finished siding.

Plywood siding panels are manufactured with fully waterproof glue in standard 4x8-foot panels and also are available in 9- and 10-foot panel lengths and in lap siding to 16-foot lengths. Panel thickness varies from ⅜ to ¾ inch depending upon style.

Various plywood sidings come in redwood, Douglas fir, cedar, Sitka spruce, lauan, southern pine and other species. A number of manufacturers provide factory-coated ply-

Before and after views show a typical California stucco exterior resided with textured plywood. The ⅜ inch panels were applied with 1x3 ▶ battens and stained.

A full-width panel with window cutout fits quickly and easily into place. Panels were laid out so the edge nailing penetrated the studs. Each panel butted against the upper soffit or frieze board and the lower edge was approximately 1/4 inch above the brick veneer to prevent moisture absorption.

wood panels. Some firms also offer plywood panels coated with exposed aggregate, high-build textured coatings and metal overlays.

Adding A New Plywood Exterior

Many home improvement projects can add considerably more than their out-of-pocket cost when it comes to increasing the value of a house. For example, the house pictured here was appraised at $31,000 before and $33,000 after application of a new front. Yet the cost of the project, including fence, came to just $800.

Houses with drab stucco fronts can be quickly modernized with the application of textured plywood siding. The material adds warmth through the insulative value of wood, plus extra structural strength to the walls, and requires little maintenance.

Standard textured plywood panels are 4x8 feet, but 9-and 10-foot lengths also are available. For horizontal lines, textured plywood comes in precut lap sidings, in lengths to 16 feet. Or grooved panels may be applied horizontally. For a high-quality smooth or textured paintable surface, medium density overlaid plywood may be used. It comes in ⅜-inch thickness and 8, 9 and 10-foot lengths.

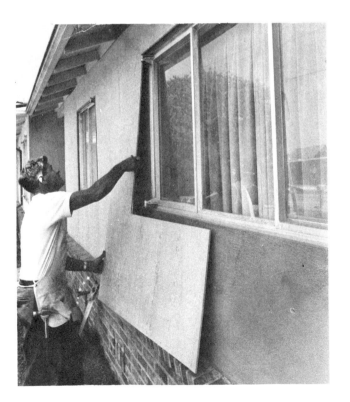

ALUMINUM SIDING

More rigid aluminum alloys are being used today to produce longer-lasting aluminum siding. At the same time, chemical metal pretreatments have greatly improved metal-to-finish bonds so that finishes last longer and require less maintenance.

Aluminum siding now comes in numerous colors, styles and textures for residing purposes and for new construction. Some brands have an insulation backing which absorbs sound and increases rigidity.

Aluminum siding can be used directly over tight sheathing or old siding that can be leveled. Furring strips are required when the material is used over a masonry surface.

Because of its light weight, aluminum siding is quickly installed. The material comes in horizontal double 4-inch, double 5-inch and 8-inch sizes with prepunched nailing slots. Interlocking action of the panels conceals nail heads and insures a firm seal. Each succeeding panel locks securely into the one before, forming a protective shield.

Vertical aluminum siding panels provide a 12 or 16-inch plain, grooved, or ribbed surface and again interlock with one another like lap siding. A 12-inch wide panel also is offered for use as soffit, fascia and siding.

RIGID VINYL SIDING

Developed in the early 1960's, rigid vinyl siding today is being widely used for both new construction and home remodeling. The material is permanently maintenance-free and can be purchased with a 20-year guarantee against peeling, flaking, blistering and denting under ordinary conditions of wear and tear and provided the installation has been made in an approved manner.

Technology calls the material polyvinyl chloride. But most persons have shortened this to "vinyl" in describing the siding material. It comes in both horizontal-lap and vertical v-groove board-and-batten styles and can be installed with optional backing materials — fiberboard, polystyrene foam and honeycomb panel — that slide quickly into place behind the siding.

The two most common types of vinyl horizontal siding are the double 4 inch exposure, and single 6 or 8 inch exposure. Both styles simulate wood clapboard siding in appearance. Embossed and wood grain surfaces are also available. Vertical vinyl siding panels can be used in combination with the horizontal siding (particularly on gable ends) or for total vertical applications. This material is available in various exposures.

Vinyl siding is manufactured in several colors including white, green, yellow and gray, with the color going completely through the material. This eliminates all need for periodic painting; the siding is easy to clean with a sponge and water. Color-matched installation accessories are available.

Rigid vinyl siding can be applied over virtually any nailable surface. The material is quickly cut to desired length with a radial arm saw and fitted with tinsnips. On uneven walls or masonry surfaces furring or strapping may be used to provide an even and nailable base. The furring can be shimmed out at the high and low spots to get an even surface.

Vinyl siding comes prepunched for fast nailing, approximately 16 inches o.c. and the material features a self-aligning lock that speeds installation. End joints are lapped for a weatherproof fit.

Soffit systems offered for use with vinyl siding are similar to the vertical siding. Some panels have a solid surface while others have a perforated surface to allow for ventilation of the overhang and attic. Requirements of the individual house will determine the style to be used. Vinyl gutter systems frequently are used with the new siding.

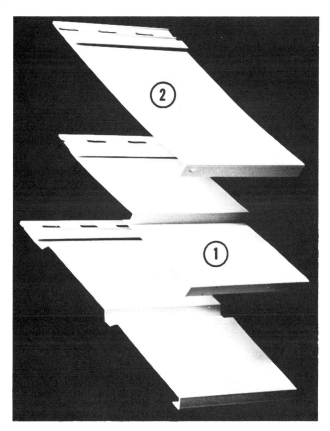

Vinyl siding comes in 6 and 8 inch exposure depths (shown as 1 and 2) and in v-grooved vertical style (unnumbered).

Backing materials for vinyl siding include fiberboard, polystyrene foam and honeycomb panel.

Inside and outside corner posts simplify the installation of vinyl siding. Both are installed before the siding is applied and should be carefully plumbed.

Vinyl siding can be cut to length with a bench or radial arm saw and can be notched with aviation tinsnips. (Photos: Society of the Plastics Industry).

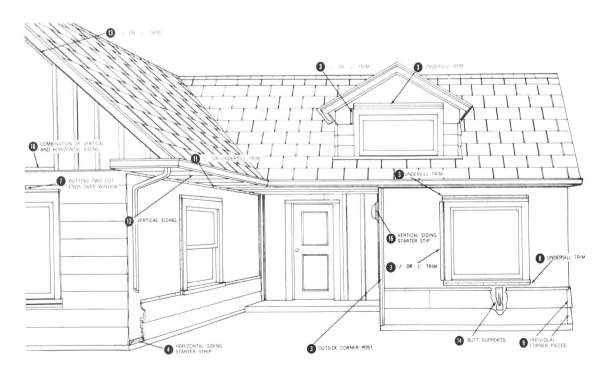

Wood-grain textures and prefinished colors make steel siding an attractive remodeling material. Both clapboard and vertical panel styles are offered, plus a full line of accessories: "J" and "L" trim and undersill trim installed around existing windows and doors (3 & 8), at eaves (11), and at gables (13); starter strip (4) placed at lowest paneling points, with siding panels installed from bottom up; bottom flange of each panel locks into the top flange of panel beneath it and top flanges are secured with galvanized steel nails; panels butt together where necessary (7) using special supports (14); soffit (12) can be covered with vertical siding applied similar to horizontal siding (Art: American Iron and Steel Inst.).

SHINGLE AND SHAKE SIDING

Shingle and shake siding panels eliminate the need to handle many small pieces. The newer 8-foot-long panels are made up at the factory with shingles or shakes applied to exterior sheathing grade plywood and finished in a variety of semi-transparent stains, or solid colors or left natural for job-site finishing.

Western Red Cedar shingle and shake panels are self-aligning and can be applied with matching color, annular threaded nails. The panels have been widely used for both exterior and interior walls in new construction and remodeling.

Where the code permits, 8-foot shingle and shake panels may be nailed directly to studs on 16- or 24-inch centers. Either 7- or 14-inch exposure provides a pleasing horizontal dimension.

STUCCO, BRICK, ASBESTOS-CEMENT, and STONE EXTERIORS

Stucco

Stucco exterior walls are popular in many parts of the country, largely due to their lower cost. Made with Portland cement mortar and applied as a plaster, this material can be colored before it is applied or painted after it has been applied and cured.

Stucco textures range from rough and pebbly to an almost smooth finish. The material can be applied directly to masonry surfaces or with metal lath attached to wood sheathing or composition sheathing boards. Three coats are applied to a total thickness of approximately ¾ inch.

Stucco exterior walls are quick and easy to paint or repaint. Many homeowners first wet the wall area with a garden hose and then apply the paint with a roller while the surface is still wet.

When using stucco in remodeling, the existing wall surfacing materials must first be removed down to the sheathing, metal lath applied, and stucco troweled on.

Brick Siding

Brick siding is common to many sections of the country and the material is widely used in all architectural styles of architecture for one purpose or another. When used above grade, brick masonry walls need no additional treatment if properly constructed. However, surface treatments can be used either to change appearance or make the wall more water-repellent.

Solid, cavity and veneer exterior wall construction offer many design possibilities related to the type of brick selected and the style of bond—running, stacked, Flemish, English—used in laying the fire-baked clay units. Special effects can be obtained by using herring-bone pattern, mosaic styles, etc.

Building brick, called "common," and face brick units measure roughly 2x4x8 inches. Other types and sizes are offered. Almost all bricks made today are some shade of red, buff or cream.

When veneering an existing exterior wall, a concrete support footing (which is also "tied" to the wall framework with metal straps nailed to studs and extended into the bond of the brick) is required. Technically, the veneer wall is a frame wall with masonry used in place of the siding.

Asbestos-Cement Siding

Asbestos-cement sheets and shingles are made of asbestos fiber and Portland cement. The shingles usually are 12x24 inches and the panels 4 feet wide and 4 to 12 feet long in various thicknesses. Plain, woodgrained and grooved types are available for both siding and roofing.

A number of different coloring methods are used to provide homeowners with prefinished material that will go for many years without repainting. Easily cleaned, the man-made material is fire resistant, rot- and vermin-proof. It will shatter from a heavy blow.

This type siding may be used over existing wood and shingle siding if the surface is relatively flat. If it is not, shims may be required. Furring strips are used over masonry surfaces. Shingles come with prepunched holes for fast nailing.

Stone Siding

Natural stone is the highest priced siding material, and not an often used remodeling material because it demands a new foundation. However, when used, highly desirable effects can be achieved.

Stone presents a rugged and rough appearance that requires little maintenance. Periodic pointing of the mortar joints may be required to keep the surface leakproof. Texture and color vary considerably according to the type stone used. Rectangular stones emphasize horizontal lines; rounded or irregular stones provide a random effect.

Stone usually is applied as a veneer material rather than as a solid wall. Pieces are secured to wood sheathing (covered by building paper) with metal ties.

Cultured, or manufactured stone veneer, is becoming more widely used for both exterior and interior wall surfaces as it costs far less than real stone, provides an attractive appearance and requires no foundation, ties or structural changes.

This material installs piece by piece with ordinary mortar over any structurally sound surface. It is available in distinctive stone veneers that rival nature for color, texture and consistent quality. One type is sold in 30x46 inch panels that are then broken at random by dropping or hitting with a hammer. Other types come in preshaped pieces.

Other Siding

Still other types of siding are used occasionally, both for new construction and remodeling. Among these are concrete block, nail-on brick and stone, insulating board, fiberglass, steel, and fiberboard. Local availability can be determined by calling lumber and building materials dealers.

ROOFING

When you are buying or remodeling the older house, give careful consideration to the roof. While its primary function is to shed water and protect against the elements of the weather, it is also one of the most important design elements of the house.

A roof serves many functions. There are numerous building materials available for selection, each with its pros and cons that should be considered before you make a final decision.

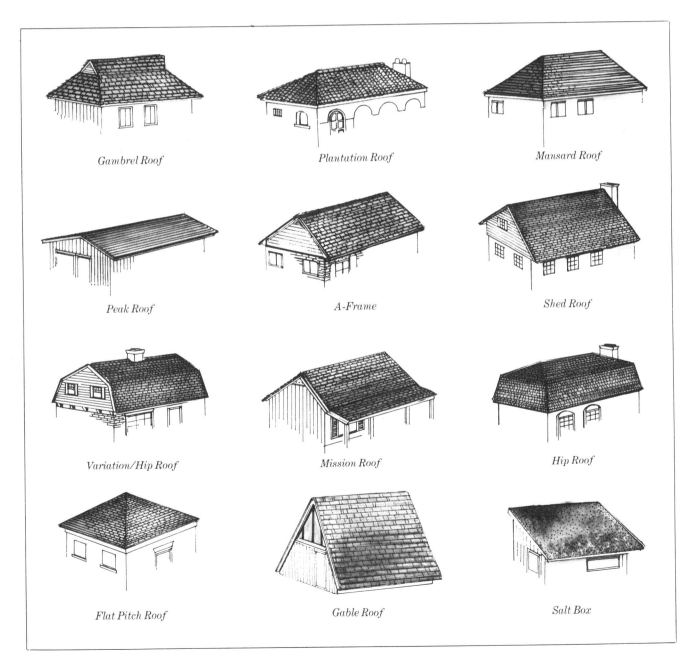

Gambrel Roof   Plantation Roof   Mansard Roof

Peak Roof   A-Frame   Shed Roof

Variation/Hip Roof   Mission Roof   Hip Roof

Flat Pitch Roof   Gable Roof   Salt Box

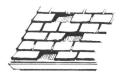  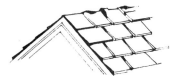 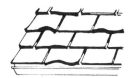

Trouble spots in roofs usually occur in the areas indicated by these drawings, left to right: damaged or missing shingles; flashings around chimney, TV antenna and skylights; torn hip and ridge shingles; popped nails that cause shingles to bulge and crack. Other areas to be inspected periodically include gutters and downspouts which could cause water backup damage.

Here are some basic points to keep in mind:

- The roof should have a long-lasting surface that will need practically no maintenance costs. Some products are designed to last 30 years or longer.

- Roofing materials should be purchased from reputable, nationally known firms. These materials are made to uniform quality standards and the material has been carefully inspected to meet rigid criteria.

- If coloring is a part of the material, it should be impregnated to provide a lasting finish that will withstand weathering with virtually no change for the life of the roof. White or lighter colored roofing reflects solar heat in the summer to reduce air cooling costs and gives more efficient air conditioning. In severe, colder climates the darker colors can absorb winter solar heat.

- Roofing should be water resistant as well as wind resistant. In areas of high wind velocity, roofing materials should be nailed and sealed down with high-strength adhesives. When not done, some roofing materials dislodge and are easily blown off in wind-rain storms.

Roof satisfaction begins with choosing a type and grade roofing completely adequate for the building. Factors include the slope of the roof, local weather conditions, and the roof design, style and size. The roof structure itself should

Gutter and Downspout Components

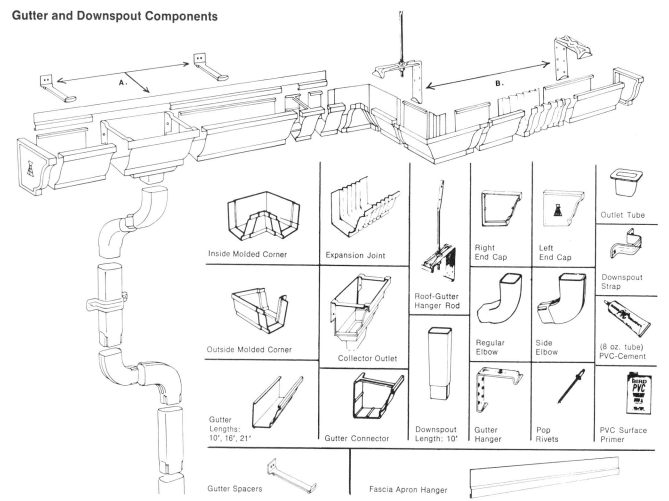

Components of the Bird solid vinyl gutter and downspout system are produced in white and do not require additional painting. They will not corrode, pit, dent or stain. Gutters come in 5 inch width, in 10, 16 and 21-foot lengths. Two methods of hanging are indicated as "A" and "B" in this drawing.

be capable of supporting the finished roofing or reroofing you choose. Rafters should meet the requirements of their span in size and spacing. Decks should be built of good quality materials for the type of roofing selected.

Proper drainage is a must. This involves not only the main surface of the roof, but all the junctions and breaks in the surface area created by wings, gables, dormers, chimneys, vents, etc. Such breaks are protected by flashing and great care must be used to make all flashings watertight and water-shedding. A metal or other suitable drip edge at the rakes and eaves is recommended. Gutters and downspouts must be adequate for maximum drainage loads.

Adequate roof ventilation is another must that requires eave vents, mechanical exhaust units or soffit systems which insure proper air flow in the attic or under-roof area.

Rock ceramic surfaced asphalt shingles are the most widely used residential roofing and reroofing material. Produced by nearly 50 firms across the country, it comes in a wide range of colors, designs, textures and weights for use over any nailable surface with a slope of not less than 4 inches per foot. Double coverage roll roofing may be used with pitch down to 1 inch per foot.

As with all building materials, the manufacturer's installation instructions should be carefully followed to obtain the best performance. Some asphalt shingles are provided with factory-applied adhesive or integral locking tabs. Others have "free" tabs and may require adhesive application, according to manufacturer's instructions.

Wood shingles and shakes usually are made of cedar, redwood or cypress for installation on roofs with a 3 to 6 inch pitch per foot. This type roofing gives an attractive roof and shadow line and can be easily applied over smooth shingle roofs. The wood may be stained or left natural and some shingles and shakes are offered prestained. Double coursing shingles deepens the shadow line.

Clay tile roofing comes in flat, rectangular units as well as special shapes for minimum roof pitches of 4 inches per foot. With integral color, this type roofing has an indefinite life expectancy. Tile is applied over a solid decking covered with felt and may require additional framing.

Built-up roofing (usually flat or maximum 3 inch pitch) is applied over solid wood decking, rigid insulation boards or concrete. This system employs alternate layers of building felt or fiberglass and asphaltic material covered with gravel, slag or stone chips.

Slate roofing is applied over a solid deck covered with felt and shows the grain texture and color of the stone. The high quality material is fairly expensive but has an indefinite life expectancy.

Still other types of roofing to be found on American homes includes aluminum sheet, shingles, galvanized steel, asbestos-cement shingles, terne metal, and copper.

Rock ceramic surfaced roofing can be applied directly over existing roofing to provide a long-lasting surface that requires minimum care.

Thermoplastic adhesive spots factory-applied to shingles are set by the heat of the sun once the shingles have been installed. This gives each shingle an independent gripping power that resists high winds (Photo Bird & Son).

REROOFING WITH SHINGLES AND SHAKES

A reroof or over-roof can work wonders with an older home giving it a dramatic new look. Both wood shingles and shakes can be applied directly over the existing asphalt roof to provide new beauty, insulation and greater structural strength. Shingles are thinner than shakes, which have a bolder appearance and provide a shadow-line effect. While most shingles are finished smooth, the shakes are rough textures with pronounced vertical grain. The reddish-brown color of the wood may be left natural or stained. The accompanying photographs depict a typical over-roof job using shakes.

1. Over-roofing begins with the application of a 36 inch wide strip of 15-pound asphalt felt over the old shingles at the eave line. Then 18 inch strips of felt are applied shingle style, at 10 inch intervals up the roof. Next, a starter course of shingles is applied at the eave line extending approximately 1½ inch over the eave edge.

2. The first course of shakes is then applied directly over the starter course. The tip ends of each course of shakes are tucked under the felt strips. With a 24 inch long shake laid at 10 inch exposure, the top 4 inches of the shake will be covered by felt. The shakes should be spaced about ½ inch apart to allow for possible expansion. These joints or spaces between the shakes should be broken or offset at least 1½ inches in adjacent courses.

3. Felt covers the old shingles, and each felt overlaps the top 4 inches of the shakes. Longer nails are used in over-roofing than in new construction.

146

4. *A metal valley, at least 26 gauge galvanized iron, painted for anti-rust protection, center and edge crimped, is laid in place. When new valley metal may come in contact with old metal, a strip of lumber should be placed in each valley to separate them.*

5. *Shakes are cut parallel with valleys as courses are applied over the metal valley. Valley gutters should approximate 6 inches in width. Metal valley sheets should be at least 20 inches wide with a 4-to-6 inch head lap.*

6. *Shakes are cut parallel to the hip line. The nails visible here will later be covered and concealed.*

7. *Factory-assembled "hip-and-ridge" units finish the hips and ridges. Hip-and-ridge units should be applied at the same exposure as field of roof, and longer nails should be used to ensure approximately ¾ inch sheathing penetration. (Photos courtesy Red Cedar Shingle & Handsplit Shake Bureau).*

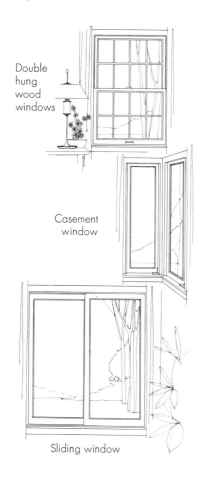

Double hung wood windows

Casement window

Sliding window

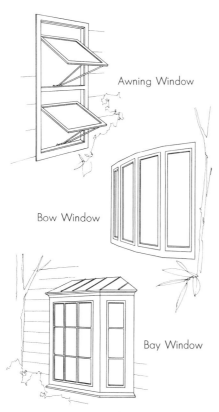

Awning Window

Bow Window

Bay Window

Drawings: Ponderosa Pine Woodwork

WINDOWS

Windows have come a long way. In fact, they account for 30 to 70 percent of your home exterior, and in some houses the "hole" in the wall has become the wall itself, extending from wall to wall, floor to ceiling.

With the trend to larger glass areas has come a greater awareness of windows, of what they can and should do. Original window placement in a home often leaves something lacking and can be overcome in remodeling by orienting the new windows with the sun, taking advantage of the winter sun, and avoiding the intense summer sun.

Closed walls often can be opened to capture natural views, or a wall of glass or sliding glass can open onto a terrace, patio or fenced-in lawn area.

Today's window can be purchased with single or double-pane glass otherwise known as insulating glass. The double-glass unit eliminates condensation in cold climates, provides less heat loss and keeps homes cooler in the summer. The outer glass acts as a buffer against sharp winds and weather to keep the inner glass warm and clear.

Wood, aluminum and vinyl-clad windows manufactured for remodeling and new home construction come in several styles:

- DOUBLE-HUNG — perhaps the most commonly found units in existing homes. Both the top and bottom sash slide up and down past the other.

- SINGLE-HUNG — resemble double-hung units in appearance, but only the bottom sash is freely operable. The top sash is stationary.

- AWNING UNITS — available in two styles, one in which the bottom of the sash swings outward, and another in which the top of the sash swings inward (hopper styles). These units often are combined with one or more nonoperative sash.

- CASEMENT — may be equipped with either stationary or operative sash. The operative casement sash may swing either inward or outward, freely or by means of crank-style hardware.

- HORIZONTAL SLIDING — equipped with sash that slide from side to side and that remove easily for cleaning. These units sometimes have but one sliding sash with the other stationary, and most often are installed three or four feet above the floor.

- JALOUSIE — somewhat resemble venetian blinds with 4- to 6-inch wide louvers opening outward to provide full ventilation. The louvers are fastened into the operating mechanism on each side of the window frame and are operated by a crank from the inside.

Preparation of the Rough Opening.

Installation techniques, materials and building codes vary according to area. Contact your local material supplier for specific recommendations.

The same rough opening preparation procedures are used for Wood and Perma-Shield Windows.

Brick veneer with a frame back-up wall is similar in construction to the frame wall in the following illustrations.

When enlarging the opening is necessary, make certain proper size header is used. (Contact your supplier for proper header size.) For installation of a smaller window—frame the opening as in new installation.

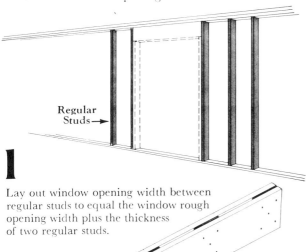

1

Lay out window opening width between regular studs to equal the window rough opening width plus the thickness of two regular studs.

2

Cut two pieces of window header material to equal the rough opening of window plus the thickness of two jack studs. Nail two header members together using adequate spacer so header thickness equals width of jack stud.

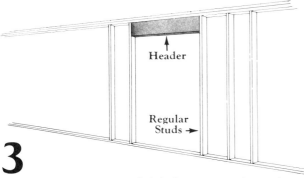

3

Position header at desired height between regular studs. Nail through the regular studs into header with nails to hold in place until completing next step.

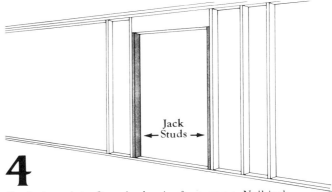

4

Cut jack studs to fit under header for support. Nail jack studs to regular studs.

5

Measure rough opening height from bottom of header to top of rough sill. Cut 2″ x 4″ cripples and rough sill to proper length. Rough sill length is equal to rough opening width of window. Assemble by nailing rough sill into ends of cripples.

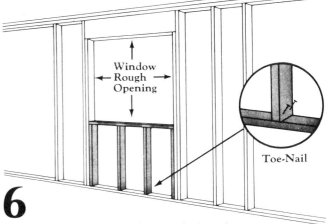

6

Fit rough sill and cripples between jack studs. Toe-nail cripples to bottom plate and rough sill to jack studs at sides.

7

Apply exterior sheathing (fiberboard, plywood, etc.) flush with the rough sill, header and jack stud framing members.

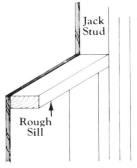

HOW TO FRAME A NEW WINDOW

Old and damaged windows can be replaced with a new unit, even if the wall opening is not the same size for both units. Installation techniques, materials and building codes vary according to the area, but the framing system illustrated here is generally accepted across the country (Drawings: Andersen Corporation).

- FIXED — can be installed in a great variety of sizes, with no possible ventilation. Such installations (picture windows) often are flanked by operable styles.

- BOW AND BAY — these curve out gracefully from the wall — the bay is straight in the center and angled at each end. These units are available in a wide range of preassembled sizes, with or without removable grilles in diamond, divided or horizontal style.

Most window units purchased today are factory weatherstripped to guarantee excellent fitting and operation. Sash cord and sash weight no longer are used (in new units) and modern balancing mechanisms seldom need replacing.

Proper care and treatment will extend the lifetime of a window and insure easier operation. When opening or closing windows, you should use the handle or lift. Keep the channel and weatherstrip clean so that sash may operate freely. Keep with window frame clean without resorting to the use of caustic or abrasive cleaners. When painting, be sure not to paint the windows "closed."

Careful attention should be given to selection of locking devices for both new and existing windows. Lack of same can be an open invitation to a burglar. Many devices on the market offer the convenience of holding a window open for ventilation, but many of these units do not provide the security of a lock. A local locksmith or building materials dealer can show you security devices for various types of windows.*

DOORS

Although they are much taken for granted, doors are a key element of every home — they guard, protect, insure privacy, add beauty and character. They can establish your design theme at the front step, and reinforce it throughout the house.

Among the styles of doors you will find in a house are interior and exterior doors, sliding glass doors, hidden pocket doors, folding doors, mirror-surfaced doors, sliding closet doors and garage doors. You may even encounter the popular Dutch door.

Today there are two kinds of doors to choose from, in a selection of materials, flush doors which are flat and raised panel doors. Flush doors are usually hollow while carved or raised panel doors usually are solid.

Exterior doors are manufactured in 1¾ and and 2¼-inch thicknesses, while the interior door is made in 1⅛, 1⅜ and 1¾-inch thicknesses. Exterior doors should be able to withstand full weather exposure after treatment of both faces and all edges.

*For specifications on window or door locks and other home security items, see *Total Home Protection* by Curt Miller.

Colonial

Modern

Traditional

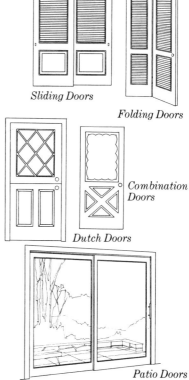

Sliding Doors

Folding Doors

Combination Doors

Dutch Doors

Patio Doors

Drawings: Ponderosa Pine Woodwork

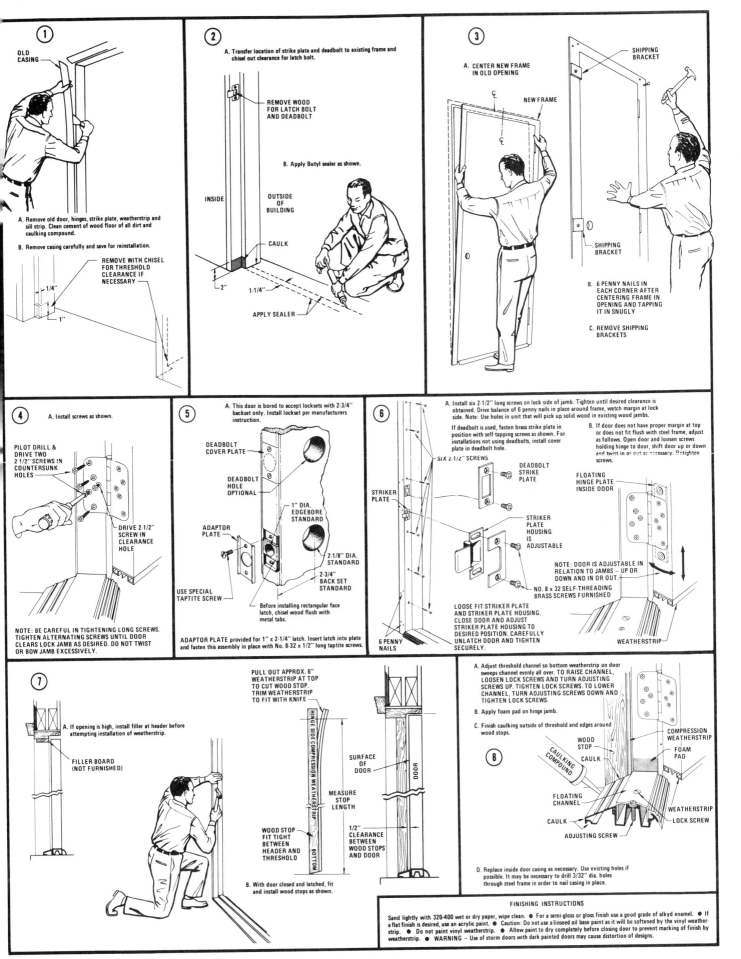

1

A. Remove old door, hinges, strike plate, weatherstrip and sill strip. Clean cement of wood floor of all dirt and caulking compound.

B. Remove casing carefully and save for reinstallation.

OLD CASING

REMOVE WITH CHISEL FOR THRESHOLD CLEARANCE IF NECESSARY

1/4"
1"

2

A. Transfer location of strike plate and deadbolt to existing frame and chisel out clearance for latch bolt.

REMOVE WOOD FOR LATCH BOLT AND DEADBOLT

B. Apply Butyl sealer as shown.

INSIDE
OUTSIDE OF BUILDING
CAULK
2"
1-1/4"
APPLY SEALER

3

A. CENTER NEW FRAME IN OLD OPENING

SHIPPING BRACKET

NEW FRAME

SHIPPING BRACKET

B. 6 PENNY NAILS IN EACH CORNER AFTER CENTERING FRAME IN OPENING AND TAPPING IT IN SNUGLY

C. REMOVE SHIPPING BRACKETS

4

A. Install screws as shown.

PILOT DRILL & DRIVE TWO 2 1/2" SCREWS IN COUNTERSUNK HOLES

DRIVE 2-1/2" SCREW IN CLEARANCE HOLE

NOTE: BE CAREFUL IN TIGHTENING LONG SCREWS. TIGHTEN ALTERNATING SCREWS UNTIL DOOR CLEARS LOCK JAMB AS DESIRED. DO NOT TWIST OR BOW JAMB EXCESSIVELY.

5

A. This door is bored to accept locksets with 2-3/4" backset only. Install lockset per manufacturers instruction.

DEADBOLT COVER PLATE

DEADBOLT HOLE OPTIONAL

1" DIA. EDGEBORE STANDARD

ADAPTOR PLATE

2-1/8" DIA. STANDARD

2-3/4" BACK SET STANDARD

USE SPECIAL TAPTITE SCREW

Before installing rectangular face latch, chisel wood flush with metal tabs.

ADAPTOR PLATE provided for 1" x 2-1/4" latch. Insert latch into plate and fasten this assembly in place with No. 8-32 x 1/2" long taptite screws.

6

A. Install six 2-1/2" long screws on lock side of jamb. Tighten until desired clearance is obtained. Drive balance of 6 penny nails in place around frame, watch margin at lock side. Note: Use holes in unit that will pick up solid wood in existing wood jambs.

If deadbolt is used, fasten brass strike plate in position with self-tapping screws as shown. For installations not using deadbolts, install cover plate in deadbolt hole.

B. If door does not have proper margin at top or does not fit flush with steel frame, adjust as follows. Open door and loosen screws holding hinge to door, shift door up or down and set in or out as necessary. Retighten screws.

SIX 2-1/2" SCREWS

DEADBOLT STRIKE PLATE

STRIKER PLATE

STRIKER PLATE HOUSING IS ADJUSTABLE

FLOATING HINGE PLATE INSIDE DOOR

NOTE: DOOR IS ADJUSTABLE IN RELATION TO JAMBS – UP OR DOWN AND IN OR OUT.

NO. 8 x 32 SELF-THREADING BRASS SCREWS FURNISHED

LOOSE FIT STRIKER PLATE AND STRIKER PLATE HOUSING. CLOSE DOOR AND ADJUST STRIKER PLATE HOUSING TO DESIRED POSITION. CAREFULLY UNLATCH DOOR AND TIGHTEN SECURELY.

6 PENNY NAILS

WEATHERSTRIP

7

A. If opening is high, install filler at header before attempting installation of weatherstrip.

FILLER BOARD (NOT FURNISHED)

PULL OUT APPROX. 6" WEATHERSTRIP AT TOP TO CUT WOOD STOP. TRIM WEATHERSTRIP TO FIT WITH KNIFE

HINGE SIDE COMPRESSION WEATHERSTRIP

SURFACE OF DOOR

DOOR

MEASURE STOP LENGTH

BOTTOM

WOOD STOP FIT TIGHT BETWEEN HEADER AND THRESHOLD

1/2" CLEARANCE BETWEEN WOOD STOPS AND DOOR

B. With door closed and latched, fit and install wood stops as shown.

8

A. Adjust threshold channel so bottom weatherstrip on door sweeps channel evenly all over. TO RAISE CHANNEL, LOOSEN LOCK SCREWS AND TURN ADJUSTING SCREWS UP. TIGHTEN LOCK SCREWS. TO LOWER CHANNEL, TURN ADJUSTING SCREWS DOWN AND TIGHTEN LOCK SCREWS.

B. Apply foam pad on hinge jamb.

C. Finish caulking outside of threshold and edges around wood stops.

WOOD STOP
CAULK
COMPRESSION WEATHERSTRIP
FOAM PAD
CAULKING COMPOUND
FLOATING CHANNEL
CAULK
WEATHERSTRIP LOCK SCREW
ADJUSTING SCREW

D. Replace inside door casing as necessary. Use existing holes if possible. It may be necessary to drill 3/32 dia. holes through steel frame in order to nail casing in place.

FINISHING INSTRUCTIONS

Sand lightly with 320-400 wet or dry paper, wipe clean. ● For a semi-gloss or gloss finish use a good grade of alkyd enamel. ● If a flat finish is desired, use an acrylic paint. ● Caution: Do not use a linseed oil base paint as it will be softened by the vinyl weatherstrip. ● Do not paint vinyl weatherstrip. ● Allow paint to dry completely before closing door to prevent marking of finish by weatherstrip. ● WARNING – Use of storm doors with dark painted doors may cause distortion of designs.

INSTALLING A REPLACEMENT ENTRY DOOR

Replacement entry doors are available in a multitude of styles to harmonize with every architectural design. Units may be obtained completely factory assembled and prehung, or furnished knocked down for job-site assembly. Pictured here are the basic steps to install a steel replacement door (Sketches: Taylor Building Products).

INSTALL A SLIDING GLASS DOOR

1. *Packaged wood gliding doors are relatively easy to install in a plumb opening with level subfloor. The sill is secured to the floor with 8d coated nails spaced approximately 12" apart.*

2. *The jamb must be plumb and square and is temporarily secured in the opening with 10d casing nails through each side. A straight edge checks jambs for bow and shim.*

3. *Following complete nailing of the exterior frame with 10d nails and application of the top flashing, a treated wood sill is fixed under the metal sill with 10d casing nails.*

4. *The stationary door panel is placed in the outer run and forced into the run of the side jamb with a 2x4 wedge. Position is checked by aligning screw holes in door, sill and head jamb.*

5. *The operating door is next placed on the rib of the metal sill facing and tipped into the frame at the top.*

6. *Positioning of the head stop and securing it with 1-9/16"-No. 7 screws secures the moving door in place. The door is then checked for smooth operation and raised or lowered as needed with adjustment screws.*

7. *If it is necessary to adjust "throw" of the latch on two-panel doors, an adjusting screw is turned to move the latch in or out. Photos: Andersen Windowwalls.*

Contemporary standard-style doors can be hinged to function as bifold units in passway areas such as this dining room-family room area. These doors have curved rails, planked panels and three paint tones (Photo: Simpson Timber Co.).

Replacement patio sliding screen doors as well as rescreening kits for doors and windows are available at most building material dealer stores. This unit made by Jim Walter Window Components shows: (top left) the releasing nylon wheels; (top right) placement of the door in existing tracks; (lower left) adjusting the top and bottom plates equally to fit the door opening; (lower right) and custom fitting the bug strip to the door.

Most interior doors are hollow-core flush panel style with the exception that in many older homes you will find beautiful panel-style units, sometimes with highly attractive carvings. Today's interior doors come in a selection of natural veneers in pine, oak, mahogany, birch, walnut and ash.

Where space is a problem, often the answer is use of pocket or slide-by doors. These often are found in dining rooms, bedrooms, family rooms, closets, off entry halls, etc. Folding doors also are used to separate rooms (such as the living from the dining room) without using much space. They also can be used in closets to provide full view of the contents.

LOCKS

The average existing house will have a variety of locks — locks for the entrance doors, garage doors, sliding patio doors, passage way doors, bathroom doors, windows, gates and the like.

Replacing a residential lock can cost anywhere from $10 to $150 or more for a keyed lock, while a passage lockset may be $5 to $40 or more. Manufacturers warn that the "cheapest lock" can prove to be very costly, for the materials may be of inferior quality and have a relatively short life, thereby requiring early replacement or repairs.

CYLINDRICAL LOCK has a large chassis, with strong, precisely designed and assembled parts.

According to Schlage Lock Co., you should never have to replace a good lock. With normal usage and care, it will last 30 to 40 years or more with minimum maintenance. However, changes in the appearance of the metal finish cannot be avoided, and for this reason alone many persons decide to update a door with a new model.

The most practical answer to residential locking is a quality, precision-built cylindrical lock with deadlocking latchbolt. For security with safety, a lock for an entranceway should have the "panicproof" feature for immediate exit — turning the inside knob in either direction to unlock the door. Another lock type in general use is the tubular lock which has a minimum number of springs and working parts. Its vital mechanisms are contained in a small area, sometimes the latch itself. This type of lock often lacks the strength and smooth action of the more sophisticated cylindrical lock. It is not recommended as a keyed lock, but it is acceptable for passageway, bedroom and closet doors. These two locks are generally known as "bored" locks and "key-in-knob" locks and are the most widely used. They are easy to install as door preparation requires only the boring or drilling of two bisecting holes.

Another lock style frequently used in homes is the mortise lock. It costs more, and since the perfection of the cylindrical lock, is less used than twenty years ago. It requires mortising out relatively large sections of the door and jamb.

Still another common style is the rim lock which is usually found installed above existing locks where security is the main requirement. Because of lack of design selection and the problem of installing the strike in the jamb, their use is limited.

Along with the rim lock comes the auxiliary lock which again is used in combination with other keyed locksets. When used with simple latchsets or with push-pull plates, they provide security for swinging doors, Dutch doors, and for doors to storage closets and utility rooms. Deadbolts and deadlocking latches of the auxiliary lock operate only by key and thumbturn; they do not have knobs or handles. They lock automatically when fully thrown and cannot be forced by inserting a shim between the door and frame.

In an interview with the author of this book, Schlage Lock officials made a point that for thousands of years locks were handmade. It has only been during the past 75 years that they have been mass produced and the modern, close-tolerance cylindrical lock, with push-button locking, is less than 50 years old. Accordingly, there are few standard measurements for lock mechanisms so it is impractical to state that particular, newer locks can exactly replace older locks.

However, replacing an existing lock is relatively simple. First, use the accompanying sketch to list the measurements required by your existing lock. With these in hand, your retail building materials dealer or locksmith can help you to select the new lockset which can be installed with the least effort on your part.

A number of lock manufacturers offer replacement-type locksets for both cylindrical and mortise styles. In some instances, the newest security style lockset with "double-locking" deadlocking latch and deadlocking bolt can be used to replace the older mortise style unit.

Most locksets are sold with a mortise template and full installation instructions in the package. You may need a boring jig (which can be rented from dealers), power or hand drill, chisel, rasp, hammer and screwdriver to complete the installation.

In buying an older home, it's well to have the locks rekeyed. This will enable you to rest more easily knowing that another person doesn't have a key to your home. Locksmiths can replace or re-pin your lock cylinders for a modest charge. Another consideration is the possibility of keying all of your locks alike for added convenience.

DEADLOCKING LATCH consists of a latch with adjoining small plunger that is held depressed — or "deadlocks" — when the door is closed, making it impossible to push back the latch with a shim between the latch and door frame.

DOUBLE-LOCKING UNIT offers the ultimate in protection with the double-locking feature, yet it can be unlocked instantly from the inside with a single twist of the knob in either direction (Photos: Schlage Lock Co.).

INSTALLING A NEW LOCK (Photos left to right)

a. *Remove worn out, broken, or low-security lock.*
b. *Lock may also be this type rather than that pictured in (a).*
c. *Remove latch of old lock.*

d. *Use template packed with new lock to mark area to be enlarged.*
e. *If a jig is available (as shown), use hole saw to enlarge area to accept new lock mechanism.*
f. *If hole requires only minor enlargement use a wood rasp or similar tool.*

g. *Cut away excess wood in edge of door, if necessary, to accommodate new latch plate.*
h. *Install latch.*
i. *Insert lock mechanism from outside of door.*

j. *Attach mounting plate on inside of door and snap on trim and knob.*

k. *Installation completed. This lock combines the security of a deadlock latch, with panicproof safety, allowing immediate exit with a twist of the inside knob (Schlage photos).*

ADD-ONS AND CONVERSIONS

GARAGES AND CARPORTS

In most cases, the basic one-car garage is 12x20 feet, and the two-car version 20x20 feet. Although one can live with such limitations, more could certainly be desired. These minimum dimensions provide shelter for the family automobiles, but leave little extra space for storage of tricycles, garden tools, work bench, storm windows, paint cans and the like.

The mere addition of two or more feet along one side or the end of the typical garage dimension will go a long way in meeting day-to-day living needs. If this is not possible, perhaps the addition of a storage shed along one wall or the back end will prove the answer.

Depending upon local building codes and setback requirements, it may also be possible for you to convert your garage to storage and work area and house the cars in a new carport adjacent to the garage.

In remodeling or planning a new structure, be sure that the roof line and style match those of your home. Likewise, the exterior siding should blend with that of the house. Determine in advance exactly what functions you want the new or remodeled structure to provide.

Attaching a garage to an existing house can make the house look larger and provide you with the benefits of walking directly to and from the house interior without facing the elements. Construction and material costs can possibly be lower, too, as one wall of the new structure will already exist.

Minimum size garages have a floor to ceiling height of 7 feet 6 inches, but 8-foot height is preferred. A one-car garage should be a minimum of 5 feet wider than the car to be housed; two-car garages, 5 feet wider than the width of both cars. Dimensions of a 2½ car garage are usually 24x30 feet.

Many local building codes demand a reinforced concrete floor for the garage as opposed to using a combustible material. It's well to use a vapor barrier below the floor to avoid dampness.

Access to and from the garage should include a standard walk-through door as well as overhead doors for car access. If the garage is attached to the house, a solid core door will be required between the two for fire safety. Garage windows are recommended for providing natural lighting, especially if you are going to use the area as a workshop or for other purposes.

Most garages are constructed with exterior walls of wood frame, cinder block or brick. The material selected should be compatible with the existing house construction whether the garage is attached or detached. Roofs, likewise, should harmonize with the house, and the design selected will have an influence on the amount of upper storage area that will be usable.

Gable garage roofs offer the greatest amount of storage space, even permitting the installation of a floored area above the cars which can be made readily accessible by means of a folding stair unit that becomes part of the storage area when not in use. Hip roofs provide less space and capture more heat. Flat roofs eliminate most storage potential, but may provide a sun deck.

Garage interiors can be finished with floor-to-ceiling panels of various type materials including gypsum wallboard, prefinished paneling, plywood, perforated hardboard, etc. Insulation may be desirable in colder climates.

Gable-style garages provide the maximum potential for overhead storage. Sectional-type doors such as this steel unit require little headroom (Photo: Taylor Building Products).

Hip-roof style garages offer minimum overhead storage and usually are built with wider sections on one or both sides of the door to accommodate other storage needs. A service door along the side is desirable (Photo: Taylor Building Products).

Conversion of the garage of this home to a family room sparked the addition of a 20-foot double carport that spans the entire width. The aluminum carport roof has a baked-on enamel finish. Photo: Alcan Building Products.

CONVERSIONS

An attached, two-car garage has about 400 square feet of usable space. Heating systems and water pipes can be extended to it from the house. Open walls and ceilings allow easy installation of electric wiring. A ceiling can be suspended from the existing roof framework. Walls can be insulated and surfaced with prefinished paneling. Floors can be surfaced with resilient flooring, hardwood flooring or carpeting. Built-ins can provide necessary storage. And the existing service door can be maintained as a private entrance if desired.

Space above an attached garage also can be converted to living area. Often times this second-floor space can be made accessible from other second-floor rooms by merely replacing a window with an interior door. And if the interior stairway to the second floor happens to be along the outside wall of the house adjoining the attached garage, you may obtain perfect access to the new area without passing through other rooms.

DOORS

The old-fashioned, hinged-style garage doors (that blew off in winter storms and required snow shoveling before they could be opened) have been replaced in recent years by the convenient overhead style made of wood, steel, aluminum or fiberglass. In addition, bypass sliding doors are used in many residential garages, especially in Western homes.

Overhead garage doors, either sectional or one-piece units, come in a wide range of designs and function with several types of hardware. Some units open totally into the garage, others project primarily outside the garage, and some project about half way in each direction. Headroom required varies according to the style hardware used.

Standard garage doors are 6 feet 6 inches and 7 feet high in widths of 8, 9, 10, 16 and 18 feet. Special size doors may be ordered when the garage opening is made larger to accommodate recreational vehicles, boat storage and the like.

The clean, simple lines of flush sectional or one-piece garage doors will complement any home and may be decorated with a variety of moldings and appliques. Doors also may be obtained with a section-ribbon of glass to provide natural daylighting, or in translucent fiberglass which provides a full wall of soft natural daylighting.

Electric garage door operators are growing in usage each year as more homeowners become aware of the convenience and protection this "appliance" affords. Units can be used with one-piece or sectional doors, to open and close the door from the locked security of an automobile. Units also turn on lights in the garage and lock the garage door, yet will stop instantly and reverse if encountering any obstruction while closing.

Electric door operators for overhead doors can be installed in most garages in a matter of hours, often by the homeowner. Belt/chain, and gear-driven models receive signals from portable transistorized senders the size of a cigarette pack. As the door opens, an overhead light is turned on and remains on for a matter of minutes while the car occupant pushes the button to close and lock the garage door and enter his home safely. A wall-mounted push-button permits operation of the garage door independently of the automobile control.

The automatic garage door operator comes as a packaged appliance and connects to standard household wiring. It operates the door on the original track hardware. Units are factory assembled with all parts, except carrier, completely enclosed.

Accessories for operators include a key switch for convenient operation of the door operator outside of the garage instead of using the car transmitter, and a manual release key lock for quick release of the door operator outside the garage in case of power failure.*

OTHER ADD-ONS

Aside from existing room conversion, attics and basements previously discussed in this book, more living area for specific purposes can be obtained in a number of ways involving room additions or so-called "add-ons". In planning these you again should be aware of local regulations regarding set-backs, lot-lines, total building heights and deed restrictions which may stymie or change your intended plans.

*Step-by-step construction instructions can be found in *How to Build Your Own Home* by Robert C. Reschke, a Successful book.

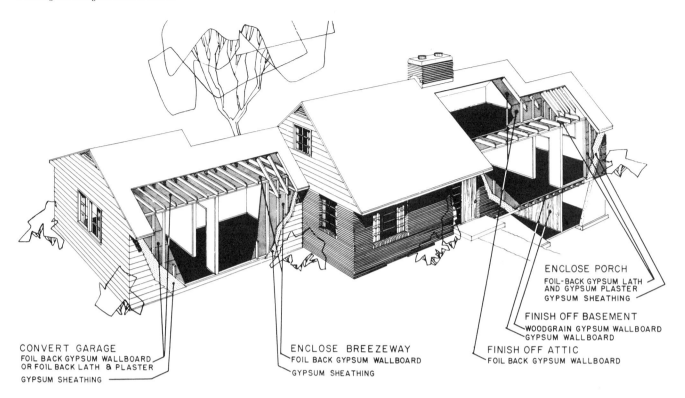

CONVERT GARAGE
FOIL BACK GYPSUM WALLBOARD
OR FOIL BACK LATH & PLASTER
GYPSUM SHEATHING

ENCLOSE BREEZEWAY
FOIL BACK GYPSUM WALLBOARD
GYPSUM SHEATHING

ENCLOSE PORCH
FOIL-BACK GYPSUM LATH
AND GYPSUM PLASTER
GYPSUM SHEATHING

FINISH OFF BASEMENT
WOODGRAIN GYPSUM WALLBOARD
GYPSUM WALLBOARD

FINISH OFF ATTIC
FOIL BACK GYPSUM WALLBOARD

Adding a room can be done in many ways as detailed on this sketch by the Gypsum Association. Ideas suggested are use of garage, breezeway, attic, basement and porch.

Breezeway conversions are possible with many older homes that have such existing space between the house and garage (Sketch: Gypsum Association).

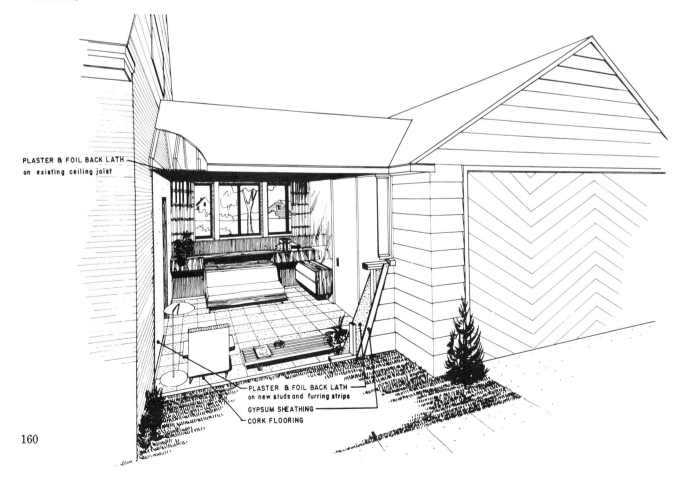

PLASTER & FOIL BACK LATH
on existing ceiling joist

PLASTER & FOIL BACK LATH
on new studs and furring strips
GYPSUM SHEATHING
CORK FLOORING

160

BREEZEWAYS AND PORCHES

Breezeway areas between partially attached or detached garages and homes are areas often enclosed for gaining additional room area. This type of conversion usually is well within setback and lot-line requirements and again you gain the benefits of existing walls and perhaps a partially usable roof and concrete floor.

Many older homes also have large porches, sometimes at both first and second-story levels, which can be enclosed to provide adding living area. Some require only the addition of partial walls to extend the framed and surfaced railing height to the ceiling line. Again, electrical wiring may be present for the existing porch lighting and heating can be easily extended from the house interior.

NEW ADD-ONS

The design of some homes permits removal of a wall and extension of the house by means of a new add-on. Such arrangements frequently are used to create family rooms, a dining-room kitchen combination, or space for other purposes.

Another way of adding on is to remove all or a section of roof and create a second story level. The author and his family did this and gained four bedrooms, a family-size bath and additional storage while enhancing the exterior appearance of the house.

In this particular remodeling, a downstairs bedroom was converted to a laundry with sliding glass door opening into the rear yard. Part of this room was used for the stairway to the second floor and for replacement of the water heater, which previously was located in an attached garage.

The existing framework above the first level of the house was strengthened and most of the shakes removed from the original roof were reused in the new structure. Having the roof off also permitted easy installation of several recessed ceiling lighting fixtures on the first floor which greatly improved the lighting efficiency.

Still another way of adding space is the construction of a separate building on the property if this is permitted. Such rooms can be the focal point of entertaining or a private retreat. And, of course, indoor living areas of the existing home can be extended to the out-of-doors through the use of patios and decks which provide outdoor rooms for warm weather use.

In adding any type of room first determine the space required, room circulation and the changes which the add-on will affect in existing rooms. Plan your layout of furniture so as to best locate windows and doors.

List the structural problems you will encounter: bearing walls and partitions; existing plumbing, wiring and ductwork that may need to be relocated; additional loads on heating and electrical systems.

Determine the appearance of the finished structure by using sketches to show the suitability of materials, roof lines, scale and other details. Walls should match or harmonize with existing materials. Roofing should be compatible with existing roofing and will require flashing to the existing structure, plus additional gutter and downspouts.

And after you know what you want, prepare a careful estimate of the costs involved. Be sure to include fees, permits, landscaping and furnishings.

As a last word of advice, don't hesitate to consider the use of an architect in making such major changes in your home. His fee may run to 10 percent of the cost of the improvement, but this investment may bring back many times that amount in the future resale of your home.

A traditional Cape Cod house was expanded by adding an 18x20 foot room and attached garage. Materials and design correspond to original house design.

MANUFACTURERS LIST

American Bankers Association, 1120 Connecticut Ave. N.W., Washington, D.C. 20036

American Iron & Steel Institute, 150 E. 42nd St., New York, N.Y. 10017

American Olean Tile Co., Lansdale, Pa. 19446

American Plywood Association, 1119 A. St., Tacoma, Wa. 98401

American-Standard, Box 2003, New Brunswick, N.J. 08903

American Title Insurance Co., 150 S.E. Third Ave., Miami, Fla. 33131

Andersen Corporation, Bayport, Minn. 55003

Armstrong Cork Company, Lancaster, Pa. 17604

Automatic Doorman, Inc., 166 Gould Ave., Paterson, N.J. 07503

Black & Decker Mfg. Co., Towson, Md. 21204

Bilco Company, 37 Water St., New Haven, Conn. 06505

Bird & Son, East Walpole, Mass.

California Redwood Association, 617 Montgomery St., San Francisco, Ca. 94111

Celotex Corp., Tampa, Fla. 33622

Certain-teed Products Corporation, Ardmore, Pa. 19003

Closet Maid Corporation, 720 S.W. 17th St., Ocala, Fla. 32670

Conwed Corp., 332 Minnesota St., St. Paul, Minn. 55101

Crown Aluminum Industries Corp., 100 Delta Dr., Pittsburgh, Pa. 15238

Flintkote Co., 201 E. 42nd St., New York, N.Y. 10017

Fluidmaster, Inc., 1800 Via Burton, Box 4264, Anaheim, Ca. 92803

Formica Corp., Formica Building, 120 E. 4th St., Cincinnati, Oh. 45202

Frigidaire, 3555 S. Kettering Blvd., Dayton, Oh. 45439

GAF Corp., 140 W. 51st St., New York, N.Y. 10020

General Electric, Appliance Division, Louisville, Ky. 40205

Georgia-Pacific Corporation, Portland, Ore. 97204

Gerber Plumbing Fixtures, 4656 W. Touhy Ave., Chicago, Ill. 60648

Grand Pulley & Hardware Corporation, High Street, W. Nyack, N.Y. 10994

Gypsum Association, 1603 Orrington Ave., Evanston, Ill. 60201

Imperial Wallcoverings, A Collins & Aikman Co., 3645 Warrensville Center Rd., Cleveland, Oh. 44122

IXL Furniture Co., Rt. 1, Elizabeth City, N.C. 27909

Jenn-Air Corp., 3025 Shadeland Ave., Indianapolis, In. 46226

Jim Walter Company, 1500 N. Dale Mabry, Tampa, Fla. 33607

Johns-Manville Corp., Greenwood Plaza, Denver, Colo. 80217

Kentile Floors, Inc., 58 Second Ave., Brooklyn, N.Y. 11215

Kinkead Industries, Inc., 5860 N. Pulaski Rd., Chicago, Ill. 60646

Kitchen-Aid Div., Hobart Corp., Troy, Oh. 45374

Knape & Vogt Manufacturing Co., Grand Rapids, Mi. 49505

Kohler Co., Kohler, Wi. 53044

Kwikset Sales & Service Corp., Anaheim, Ca. 92803

Lawyers Title Insurance Corporation, Box 27567, Richmond, Va. 23261

Leviton Mfg. Co., 59-25 Little Neck Pkwy., Little Neck, NY 11362

Magnavox Company, 345 Park Ave., New York, N.Y. 10022

Majestic Co., Inc., Huntington, Ind. 46750

Marlite Div., Masonite Corp., Dover, Oh. 44622

Masonite Corp., 29 N. Wacker Dr., Chicago, Ill. 60606

Maytag Company, Newton, Ia. 50208

National Association of Realtors, 155 E. Superior St., Chicago, Ill. 60611

National Fire Protection Association, 60 Batterymarch St., Boston, Mass. 02111

National Forest Products Association, 1619 Massachusetts Ave., N.W., Washington, D.C. 20036

National Oak Flooring Manufacturers Association, 814 Sterick Building, Memphis, Tenn. 38103

National Paint, Varnish & Lacquer Association, 1500 Rhode Island Ave., Washington, D.C. 20005

NuTone Div., Scoxvill Manufacturing, Madison & Red Bank Rds., Cincinnati, Oh. 45227

Ondine Div., Interbath, Inc., 3231 N. Durfee, El Monte, Ca. 91732

PPG Industries, Inc., One Gateway Center, Pittsburgh, Pa. 15222

Phone-Mate, Inc., 325 Maple Ave., Torrance, Ca. 90503

Plumbing-Heating-Cooling Information Bureau, 35 E. Wacker Dr., Chicago, Ill. 60601

Ponderosa Pine Woodwork, 1500 Yeon Building, Portland, Ore. 97204

Red Cedar Shingle & Handsplit Shake Bureau, 5510 White-Henry-Stuart Building, Seattle, Wa. 98101

Roto International, Essex, Conn. 06426

Schlage Lock Co., 2201 Bayshore Blvd., San Francisco, Ca. 94119

Simpson Timber Co., Washington Building, Seattle, Wa. 98101

Society of the Plastics Industry, Inc., 355 Lexington Ave., New York, N.Y. 10017

Suba Mfg., Inc., Building 116, Benicia Industrial Park, Benicia, Ca. 94510

Tappan Co., Tappan Park, Mansfield, Oh. 44901

Taylor Building Products Co., 19800 Fitzpatrick Ave., Detroit, Mi. 48228

United States Gypsum Co., 101 S. Wacker Dr., Chicago, Ill. 60606

United States Plywood Corp., 777 3rd Ave., New York, N.Y. 10017

Universal-Rundle Corp., Box 960, New Castle, Pa. 16103

Western Wood Products Association, Yeon Building, Portland, Ore. 97204

Westinghouse Electric Corp., Westinghouse Building, Pittsburgh, Pa. 15222

Whirlpool Corp., Benton Harbor, Mi. 49022

Wilson Plastics Co., 600 General Bruce Dr., Temple, Tex. 76501

Z-Brick Co., 2834 N.W. Market St., Seattle, Wa. 98107

INDEX